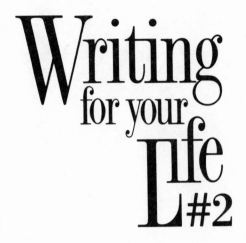

Writing for your Life #2

Writing
for your
Life
#2

edited by
Sybil Steinberg

**with an introduction by
John F. Baker**

PUSHCART

ISBN 0–916366–94–4 (cl)
ISBN 0–916366–87–1 (pb)

For information address Pushcart Press,
PO Box 380, Wainscott, NY 11975

Distributed by W. W. Norton & Co., New York, N.Y.

CONTENTS

INTRODUCTION

A *Publishers Weekly* author interview is like no other author interview you will ever read. It is not merely a character sketch, an account of difficulties overcome, an opportunity to plug a book or one's beliefs, or a description of working methods—though it may, and often does, include elements of all of these. It is above all a study of the writer as a working person in a serious cultural and commercial context, and therefore of enormous value to anyone living—or even contemplating living—the writer's life.

All our interviewers are sent about their task with the same brief: to bring back an account not only of the writer's work as he or she sees it, but also to describe how the author first experienced the call or broke into print, to talk about relations with agents and publishers, how the books performed—or failed to perform—commercially, how they created a *career* as a writer. Some of our subjects don't always respond to all these questions, of course, but we do make the try; and the results, more often than not, offer a remarkable range of salutary snapshots.

You'll read of highly successful authors dissatisfied with their work; world-famous ones resentful of early neglect; seasoned writers who discover that their ideas come ever more easily; equally seasoned ones who experience intense torture every time they sit down at their worktable; perhaps a majority who experience the writing life as a roller-coaster of depressing lows and occasional ecstatic highs; and certainly a majority who find life in the current hit-or-miss publishing climate to be more fraught with anxiety than it needs to be—and often used to be.

Because we interview more writers than any other publication—we figure we have talked to something like 1,200 in the 25 or so years we've been running the feature—those who star in the *PW* Interviews represent a much wider variety than you're likely to find anywhere else. They include novelists both highly popular and highly literary, poets, biographers, celebrities, memoirists, reporters, children's authors, foreign authors, even the occasional romance writer. Our only criteria are that they not be neophytes (they must have at least a small body of work on show) and that they have something interesting to say, about themselves or their profession.

Editor Sybil Steinberg has a terrific eye for a good potential subject, and is merciless about dropping the interviewees who don't come across on the page. Still, inevitably some get by that are less interesting than others. A great advantage you have as the reader of this book is that you get the cream. The 50 that follow are, along with those in the previous volume (still in print from Pushcart Press), the best interviews available with many of the most significant, if not always best-known, writers of the present and immediate past. Good reading.

—JOHN F. BAKER
EDITORIAL DIRECTOR
Publishers Weekly

Editor's Note

Do writers' lives fascinate their readers? I thought so when I compiled the first volume in this series. Response to that book confirmed my conviction that readers want to know why authors write as they do, and how they go about the publishing process. Fifty new interviews are collected here. The format remains the same as in the earlier edition, with one difference in chronology. While the profiles in the first volume were drawn from a decades' issues of *Publishers Weekly*, the interviews in this book all were conducted over a period of three years, from January 1991 through July 1994.

SYBIL STEINBERG
INTERVIEWS EDITOR
Publishers Weekly

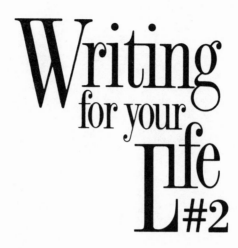

Writing for your Life L#2

MARY CATHERINE BATESON

"MARY CATHERINE BATESON was born on December 8, 1939, and looked very much herself," wrote her mother, Margaret Mead, in her 1972 memoir, *Blackberry Winter*. But today Bateson seems to look more and more like her mother—the same cheekbones, the same broad, open face, the same purposeful eyes, the same self-possession. She is Clarence Robinson Professor of Anthropology and English at George Mason University in Virginia, but she is in Cambridge the weekend she meets with *PW*, to speak at a Radcliffe College conference on women over 50, and to talk about her new book, *Peripheral Visions: Learning Along the Way*, published by HarperCollins.

It owes its genesis in part, she writes, to reactions to her last book (*Composing a Life*, Atlantic Monthly Press, 1989), a collection of narratives about improvisation and creative possibility in the varied, individual lives of five women, as well as to the realization that its message about life and learning was not just for women. *Peripheral Visions*, she says, "is for both men and women in a world of cultural diversity. Here I'm talking more systematically about using encounters with other cultures to open up understanding" and to get beyond the individual focus of *Composing a Life* to ask "If we are all improvising, and we are all different, how are we going to develop community and empathy?"

Bateson's first book, *With a Daughter's Eye*, was a memoir of her exceptional parents, the anthropologists Gregory Bateson and Margaret Mead. It was published 10 years ago by William Morrow—"my mother's primary publisher all her life," Bateson says. "I would have happily stayed at Morrow, but they wanted a full book proposal for *Composing a Life*. I decided if I had to do that, I was going to let my agent, John Brockman, shop it around. He was also my father's agent. After Gregory died, I finished his book, *Angels Fear: Towards an Epistemology of the Sacred* (Macmillan, 1987), and John was already the agent, so I met him in that context. He told me there was only one way I could answer the people who wanted to interview me about my mother after she died—[and that was] by saying that I was going to write my own book. He's been marvelous."

Her mother's editor at Morrow had been Thayer Hobson, and Bateson recalls that "he made the suggestion that she add the last two chapters of *Coming of Age in Samoa*—the dreamy, impressionistic description of a day, and the discussion of the relevance of her Samoan work to this country. I'm sure his suggestion was critical to the shape that her career took.

"She always had her own line-editor working for her—it was an old friend who edited her first several books, and later she had a staff and a professional bibliographer—and she didn't do a lot of polishing. I am a compulsive polisher, so when a manuscript of mine goes in, it tends to be an extremely clean manuscript that I believe in. I don't want somebody else taking it and putting it into a different kind of style."

Bateson finds that many of the same themes she confronts in her books—change, continuity, discontinuity, ambiguity—pervade the book publishing business. "My experience has been that editors at a particular publisher are so evanescent that the old model of an author with an ongoing relationship to a particular editor at a particular house does not work. With every one of my books, there has been some issue of discontinuity with relation to the publishing house, or changes in policy—they're no longer doing books of that sort—or what have you. When I put together my next book proposal, I'll try to figure out whether it makes sense to take it to Susan Moldow, my editor at HarperCollins. But I don't feel any confidence that she will still be there, because people move around so much." (Perhaps Bateson is prescient: Moldow's appointment as publisher of Scribners has just been announced.)

Bateson says she's been told that her books themselves might have something to do with that discontinuity. Her clear call to readers of *Composing a Life* to reassess their lifetime goals often had immediate ramifications. "When Plume/Penguin bought the paperback rights to *Composing a Life*, and it was being passed around the company, two or three people quit. They read the book and thought, 'I can do something else!'—you know [they were responding to] a subversive point of view."

Although *Composing a Life* did not really take off until the paperback edition was published, Ann Godoff, Bateson's editor at Atlantic (she is now at Random House), says she knew immediately that the book was special. "I absolutely saw a unique thesis on Catherine's part. She was saying something that had not been said before: that women's lives were composed differently than men's. Men's lives go in a straight trajectory, while women's lives are a crazy quilt of experiences. Catherine has a tremendous ability to articulate the complicated in an approachable way; she was on to something new. It was a wonderful experience," Godoff says.

Bateson does admit to being "rather eccentric" when it comes to putting together a book proposal. "I write a description of the kind of relationship I wish to have with the editor," she confesses. "In the case of *Peripheral Visions*, Susan Moldow has observed it to the letter. I've never missed a deadline, and she's never not come through. It's useful to spell it all out."

This includes asking for a copy editor who will "leave my prose alone," Bateson says. "I had a terrible copy editor for *Composing a Life*," she laments, "somebody who broke up every sentence to make it simple and obvious. I went through [the galleys] with an eraser in a rage, a total fury. So you learn. A good working relationship is one in which each person knows what to expect. With each new project I have more clarity about the relationship that will allow me to be productive."

Peripheral Visions is a book about learning in adulthood, Bateson writes, and its intellectual roots, like her own, are in "the habits of thought and observation of cultural anthropology." As she said in *With a Daughter's Eye*, "In my family we never simply live, we are always reflecting on our lives."

Her latest narrative travels to and from four countries: Iran, where she lived in the early '70s with her Armenian husband and young daughter; the Philippines, where she was teaching and doing field work when she lost her first baby at birth; Israel, where she was a high school student, and, 30 years later, a researcher; and the U.S. Bateson uses her own experiences to show us that the world has become a place in which we all need to possess "a consciousness ready to be schooled by complexity." We all must "learn how to share enough with strangers to make learning possible," and to "accept ambiguity and allow for learning along the way." If only we can find constancy in the change that is inevitable in modern life, "then we don't have to be frightened of change," she explains. "Lots of social problems come about from people frightened of what they are going to lose if they go through a certain change."

The book is shot through with paradoxes ("That's almost a mode of argument for me," Bateson admits, "turning something all the way over and looking at it from the other side"), as well as parables, metaphors and stories "strung together to suggest a style of learning from experience" because, she writes, "our species thinks in metaphors and learns through stories." At the Radcliffe conference she has just attended, she says she was struck by a metaphor to express making new beginnings at mid-life and all the way through old age. ("It didn't make it into this book, but it'll probably make it into the next one," she notes.) "Biblical texts speak of building on firm foundations, and educators always talk of foundations. But skyscrapers are not built on stone. They have a floating foundation, and conceptually, that's what we need—to float."

How did Bateson learn to float? "In many ways I learned it from my parents. The difference between them was very important in my development. I wasn't taught to think there was one model I had to follow. That allows me to make my own synthesis from two very different kinds of minds. I learned from listening to their conversations. That's part of the notion of peripheral visions— the things you hear adults saying and doing while you are a child— not saying them to you, perhaps, but to each other. A lot of the most important learning in life is from things you are not paying 100% attention to going on around you, allowing you to see the same thing in different moods and tones, allowing you to accumulate understanding."

One early intellectual collaboration with her father on a conference about human adaptation and the environment resulted in her interpretation of the proceedings in *Our Own Metaphor*, originally published by Knopf in 1972 and reissued by the Smithsonian Institution Press in 1991. She also joined with Richard Goldsby, a colleague at Amherst College, where she was dean of the faculty for three years, to write *Thinking AIDS* (Addison-

Wesley, 1988), an examination of the questions that pandemic poses for all social sciences.

Bateson writes freely about spirituality and religion, and she draws deeply from religious vocabularies, texts and rituals for her insights into learning. "That was a flaw in *Composing a Life*," she admits. "The women I had chosen were either less interested in religion than I am or reticent about it. I have been interested in spiritual questions all my life and full of curiosity about the odd human behaviors that arise in relation to religion. In the final essay in *Angels Fear*, I argue that there may be truths we can't talk about or pass on to the next generation except in metaphorical form, and that's what religious language offers.

"Any metaphor offers the possibility of distortion as well as insight. I must say I do believe the worst religious idea the human species has ever come up with is the idea that there is a single religious truth. My suspicion is that our religious language is a way of talking about profound truths that we don't have an alternative way of talking about, but we need to be tolerant of other people's efforts to zero in on the same kinds of truth. But persecution and enforcing literal fundamentalism—that itself is the most profound untruth."

Bateson makes allusions in her prose to lines of poetry with the same ease with which she waves in and comments on passages from the Bible. She attributes this facility to the poetry her mother knew by heart and in turn had her memorize as a child: Frost, Millay, Eliot, Spender, cummings, the Sitwells. "It's so important if you are going to write. Very often a sentence that rings true for people, that makes them say 'Yes, that's how I feel, too,' echoes something they have heard before. That is the role that biblical texts and Shakespeare and the Gettysburg Address play in our unconscious. We respond to echoes of the same cadences."

When she's at George Mason, Bateson teaches a course on ecology and culture, and another on women's life histories. "My own reading usually has to do with what I teach," she says, "and I am constantly reading autobiographies. That's a big industry at the moment. They keep coming out." She notes that there are two women at work on biographies of her mother—the historian Virginia McLaughlin, who is also making a documentary on Mead, and Margaret Caffrey, who wrote a biography of anthropologist Ruth Benedict.

5

In a phrase that echoes Bateson's own preoccupations in her new book, one early biographer of Margaret Mead described her as "a patron saint of the peripheral." Mead wrote masses of field notes and diaries; that's the anthropologist's way "to keep track of your own state of mind as a filter for what you are observing," explains Bateson. Does life itself become field work? "Of course," Bateson says, "of course. Participant observation is a critical idea. It is a stance in the world to say, 'I am a participant, and I am an observer.' I also use the phrase disciplined subjectivity. Be subjective, but be disciplined in your subjectivity. Be self-aware. If you can't understand yourself, you're not going to be able to understand anything else."

MISSY DANIEL
May 30, 1994

LOUIS BEGLEY

LOUIS BEGLEY has just returned from business in Japan, but he brushes off the notion of jet lag. "I never have it," he says. Looking at the man in the unimpeachable gray suit, in his beautifully ordered corner office on the 25th floor of a building in midtown Manhattan, it's easy to believe him. It would take a lot more than crossing the international dateline to discomfit Mr. Begley, an internationally acclaimed novelist whose literary career is no less astonishing than the rest of his remarkable history.

His is a story worthy of Hollywood: Guided by a preternaturally quick-witted mother, a young Jewish boy survives World War II in Poland, living among Christians under a series of false identities. After the war, the boy's father finds his wife and son, takes them to Paris and, in 1947, to the United States. After attending high school in Brooklyn, the boy wins a scholarship to Harvard, where he earns a *summa cum laude* degree in English literature. He marries a woman of means; he attends Harvard Law School and enters one of the whitest of Manhattan's white-shoe law firms. He sets up high-stakes international deals of fiendish complexity, is made a partner. His first marriage ends in divorce, and he eventually marries a French intellectual, a published historian; they have five gifted children. He is at home in Paris; he is at home in New York. At age 55, he takes a brief sabbatical from law and starts to write a novel about a child who survives the Holocaust. Three months later, the book is completed, and when it is published it wins literary prizes throughout the world.

His second novel, written during weekends, appears the following year, and critics call his prose Jamesian and Whartonian (others invoke Balzac and Proust, while a few express reservations about the main character, an international financier who in childhood survived the Holocaust). That same year *Vanity Fair* certifies his mainstream appeal with a flattering profile, while the literary community decrees its approval by tapping him for the presidency of the PEN American Center.

Begley's success with his first two novels, *Wartime Lies* (Knopf, 1991) and *The Man Who Was Late* (Knopf, 1992), entitle the reader to great expectations of *As Max Saw It*, out from Knopf.

And while the author is modest, his pleasure in his work—legal and literary—is evident in the very care he takes in choosing his words. He answers questions in what sound like polished paragraphs, thoughtful arguments reasoned in measured, deliberate phrasings. He apologizes that he mumbles, but his voice, while soft, is clear and his language elegantly articulated. Only his aristocratic, not quite definable European accent would indicate that English is not his native tongue.

There is "nothing mysterious," he says, about his command of language. "You see, obviously, I like language. I like words. I dislike sloppiness in language. I love the English language, and I think I did from the very moment I began to learn it.

"In Central Europe, learning another language is not an unusual undertaking," he continues, pausing to confirm that Polish is his first language. "For a brief period when I was a boy, I spoke Russian, which is a language I've completely forgotten; I can't speak it anymore but I still understand it when it's spoken distinctly and I have a notion of what the conversation is essentially about, so that I get my bearings. I spoke nearly perfect German, I learned French and I learned English. I began to learn English in Cracow when I was in my first year of high school, the gymnasium or *lycée*, whatever you want to call it. There was an interval [after the war] during which my parents and I lived in Paris, and I went, I think, to Berlitz, and that was it."

By the late '40s, when Begley was a student at Erasmus Hall High School in Brooklyn, his English was sufficiently fluent that the school magazine was publishing his stories; he continued to write during his first years at Harvard, where his work appeared in the Harvard *Advocate*. He did not, however, entertain thoughts of a writing career: "I did not think that I had any talent, particularly. More important, I did not think I had anything to say. I did not think I understood this country at all. And I was tired of writing sad-little-boy stories."

On the other hand, he thought he might like to earn a graduate degree and become "some kind of professor of literature."

8

But after graduating, he volunteered for the draft and served in Germany, and the urge to devote himself to literary theory "passed."

He applied to Harvard Law School, although becoming a lawyer "was not something I had ever wanted to do," he says. "I needed to do something that would put me in the way of making some money. It was done out of pure ignorance. I knew nothing about the law, and I knew nothing of what being a lawyer implied. It was as if someone had said, You know, there's a coffee plantation, do you want to run a coffee plantation? And I had said yes. It would be just as plausible."

As Begley discusses his legal career, his enthusiasm—and his ironic wit—become even clearer. Describing his first years in practice, then as now with the firm Debevoise & Plimpton, he mentions unnamed but complicated-sounding projects: issue of debt in Scandinavian countries; a "rather ambitious" program of financings of installations in Holland and Belgium; "some obscure subventions" in English ship construction.

Begley went to Paris when Debevoise & Plimpton opened an office there in 1956. "That gave me—like a private detective's license—my international-lawyer license. I became a partner when I was in our Paris office, and when I came back," he says gleefully, "I was a towering authority on international matters."

International law, says Begley, "is the most amusing form of practice: there is the most variety, in terms of the problems and the people with whom one works, the cross-cultural—to use a pompous word—aspects and the reconciling of seemingly impossible-to-reconcile points of view."

At this stage the lawyer and the writer converge: "I like the elegant solution to a difficult problem. I like bringing some sort of order out of chaos. I like the process of negotiation, because it's sort of a demonstration, usually, of the proposition that right reason prevails."

This passion for order can be seen in his approach to his fiction, much of which has very visible autobiographical roots. But do not mistake his work for memoir. "As soon as you begin to tell a story you begin to organize reality in a way that life is not organized.

"Of course, everything in a serious novel comes out of a writer's life, inevitably. Where else would it come from? At least in my

9

case, it comes out as a very changed production. If I wanted to, I could take particular scenes and say, This is something that happened, not here but in some other place, in the following, different ways.

"But I'm not sure that I would get it completely right," he adds, "because there is a process of idealization, there is a process of parody at work, there is the desire to pull somebody's leg—I'm not quite sure whose—so all these things are there, and then there is the strange power of words. Words lead one on. A word will come into one's head, and one wants to do something with that word, and pretty soon there is a sentence. And all the things that are inside you go into that sentence."

Begley can't say just what prompted him to write his first book at the age of 55. "People had always asked me, Why aren't you writing a novel? And I would say, I have no novel to write, and besides, I have no time—both of which were completely true. And then I had this short sabbatical, and I began to write—on the first day of it. I did not stop until I finished. Why then? I cannot tell you. There must be some things that one cannot explain."

In fact, a few years before, Begley had written approximately 30 pages that would find their way into *Wartime Lies*. He had kept the pages and, after rereading them, took up where he'd left off. "Why did I not continue earlier? I do not know. Those 30 pages are the introduction, and they could have led in many directions."

Three months later, he was finished. He showed his work to his friend Gregor von Rezzori, the author of *Memoirs of an Anti-Semite*. "I wanted to know Grisha's views," he says. Meanwhile, Von Rezzori was so impressed that he showed the manuscript to his own editor, Elisabeth Sifton, then at Knopf. ("I had an agent, Georges Borchardt," Begley explains. "This was quite out of the normal or authorized course of events.")

"I've always been in love with the little borzois, so I was just thrilled," he continues. He remained with Knopf following Sifton's departure: "I am a very loyal type. I always buy my vegetables at the same grocer's stand, I always go to the same restaurants. I like Knopf, and I like George Andreou, with whom I principally deal now. I'm very happy."

He wrote the second novel, he says, "just to make sure that I could." As for *Max*, "I think I also wrote it to be sure I could write Number Three."

The source of *As Max Saw It* is less seemingly obvious than the sources for *Wartime Lies* and *The Man Who Was Late*. Begley, who, prior to completing *Max*, had told interviewers simply that it was about "death," amends his description: "I suppose that it sounds pretentious, but it's a story about the ripening of the narrator's heart. That's one story, and the other story is a love story. And to me that's the most important. It's a book about human solidarity."

Max, the narrator, has lovers and wives, but the principal love story in the book revolves around Max's Harvard classmate, Charlie, and the much younger Toby. Charlie, says Begley, is a kind of demiurge, a man of extraordinary vitality, while Toby, described in the book as "Eros himself," is destroyed by AIDS. Charlie's response to Toby's illness "ripens" Max's heart.

Toby's disease is not named in the book. "AIDS as such is not the point of book," explains Begley. "The point of the book is the sharing in the act of dying, the willingness to share, knowing that the action itself is absurd.

"A number of very, very close friends have died of AIDS. I was very deeply affected by their deaths and I was very deeply affected by the position of their lovers who survived.

"The sorrow of the dying, and the sorrow of surviving, meant a great deal to me. There is also a great question, in the case of AIDS, for the survivor. Is he going to survive, is it just a suspended death sentence? To me we're all in the process of dying, anyway, which is something I think about all the time—and so AIDS, on a certain level, for me, is just a more horrible way of dying than some. In the inventory of horrors that everyone has in store for her or for him, there is a lot to choose from," he says with a grim laugh. "We don't have the choice. I have the health of a horse, but none of us know what is going on inside our little cells, just what nasty surprises are being prepared for us.

"So I was very much affected. I've always been obsessed—although I do not want to use that word—by dying. What is it like to die? What is it like to be with someone who is dying? How does one maintain the flow of love and sympathy in the face of suffering? How does one not yield to the very human—for me, anyway—instinct to turn one's face away, because, after all, it's a horrible spectacle. In relation to one such death, I happened to be taking a long walk, and I imagined an ending to such a process of dying exactly like the ending of that book. And so, having imagined that ending, I then constructed the rest of the book.

"Paradoxically, I claim that I hate sick people. I have a stock story that I did not become a doctor, which is what my father wanted me to do, because I hate sick people. That is not entirely true. I am very good with sick people myself. But I know that for me it is almost unnatural. Because I think I know the face of sickness very well. It is as though it is the face that I see in the mirror, although I have never been sick. I have a passion for life, and I also have complete certainty of my own death.

"You could say that I'm a person of some contradictions."

ELIZABETH DEVEREAUX
May 2, 1994

MAEVE BINCHY

"Maeve's already here," says the desk clerk at Arbutus Lodge in Cork City, where we are meeting Ireland's best-selling and most beloved living author. Maeve Binchy has driven down from Dublin this morning, and as we introduce ourselves she explains with an infectious laugh that she's early since she allowed extra time, "because I'm a terrible driver. I only got my license four years ago, if you can imagine that. Most people won't admit to being bad drivers—they would sooner tell you they're bad in bed!"

Binchy in the flesh (of which there is an ample amount on her six-foot frame) is a beguiling and irrepressible storyteller. Her focus is acute and her smile is genuine. Conversation is an enthusiastic, generous flow of anecdotes and observations, punctuated by quips, queries and conspiratorial asides. Not only is Binchy one to suffer fools gladly—she would do so graciously.

Binchy's fifth novel, *The Copper Beech*, was published in Great Britain and Ireland by Orion, and a month later in the U.S. by Delacorte. This more or less simultaneous publication on both sides of the Atlantic is a first for Binchy, who calls it "a huge vote of confidence" on the part of Delacorte. The success of her best-selling previous novel, *Circle of Friends* (Delacorte, 1991), was undoubtedly a factor. Last year's invitation to lunch at the White House with Barbara Bush, who has called Binchy her favorite author, probably didn't hurt sales either.

Additionally, the Dell paperback of *The Lilac Bus* (also a 1991 Delacorte hardcover), a collection of stories which was made into a British TV film last year, hit the paperback bestsellers list after its publication this past July.

The Copper Beech is a series of linked stories about the lives of characters who have shared years in a small schoolhouse in the Irish village of Shancarrig. Their romances, secrets, betrayals and

13

triumphs are told with a vivid charm; the result is a lively portrait of the entire village.

With a whopping first printing of 160,000 copies, *The Copper Beech* is a BOMC main selection and a Time-Life Book Digest Condensed Book. First serial rights have gone to *Good Housekeeping*. Meanwhile, Binchy remains notably modest and easy to work with. Jackie Farber, her editor at Delacorte, calls their relationship "a joyful experience."

Binchy, now 52, has developed a style that has made her four previous novels, three collections of stories, and three plays extraordinarily successful. Her audience, she has discovered, "is grateful for the absence of sex and violence. They're people who like being able to buy a book that will suit their mothers and their children."

This distinction is inadvertent on Binchy's part. "It's just that I would be embarrassed to write about sex, and I wouldn't get it right. I try to write the way people talk, and I can't imagine talking with my friends about our sex lives the way we talk about our feelings, and wishes, and disappointments."

Binchy recalls a British editor's observation that in her books everybody is obsessed with sex but nobody ever actually has any. "I was thrilled, because I knew that I had got the '50s right!"

What Binchy does write about is life in Ireland and England, and she does it in a way that has universal appeal. Her books have been translated into six languages; she loves the story about the French translator who kept calling the Irish consulate in Paris with questions like "Is *eejit* stronger or less strong than *idiot?*"

She writes about romance, but her characters are realistic. "I don't have ugly ducklings turning into swans in my stories. I have ugly ducklings turning into confident ducks." Her characters tend to be her own vintage, she admits, because she knows all the details will be right. ("Having lived it, I've already done the research.") Other themes common to her fiction include the contrast of small village to big city, the differences between England and Ireland, the hypocrisy of the powerful, and the constant issues of friendship and betrayal.

Literary success hasn't distanced Binchy from her sources. Patsy Ryan, one of the lodge's proprietors, comes over to remind her that she taught school with Patsy's sister in Cork years ago. "Oh yes!" Binchy exclaims. "I remember that we used to huddle together in a tiny lounge at the school—the room was so small one person had to breathe in if the other breathed out—united in our loathing of that frightful headmistress!"

It sounds like the beginning of a Maeve Binchy novel. Schools and schoolteachers often figure in her fiction; Binchy, born in 1940 in the village of Dalkey, outside Dublin, became a teacher after graduating from University College Dublin, and thought for several years that she had found her calling. But at 23, on a visit to Jerusalem that was a gift from the parents at a Jewish school in Dublin where she had taught, she lost what Christian faith she had had (and now calls herself "a collapsed Catholic") when she visited the site of the Last Supper, and realized that "none of it was true." This revelation made her question other assumptions about her life.

Her letters home to her father—she had now joined a kibbutz— were so fascinatingly full of her observations about kibbutz life and the threat of war that he submitted one to the *Irish Independent*, which printed it. Binchy thought she "had arrived," as the article paid £18 and she had been earning a weekly £16 teaching. But it was four years before she was able to break into the *Irish Times* with some freelance articles, and finally a job, in 1969. Today, she is a fixture there, and writes a twice-weekly column and occasional celebrity interviews.

Two collections of her *Irish Times* pieces were published in the early '70s, *My First Book* and *Maeve's Diary* (which Binchy recalls was humiliatingly remaindered for five pence), but thoughts of writing fiction didn't surface until Binchy's husband, former BBC commentator and writer Gordon Snell, encouraged her to give it a try. (They've lived together, in London and Dublin, since 1973, and were married in 1975.)

Her first fiction consisted of interlocking short stories. Two collections, *Victoria Line* and *Central Line*, were moderately successful, selling 5000 and 4000 copies respectively. (Dell issued them here in 1986 in a single volume, entitled *London Transports*.)

Binchy's agent, Christine Green, urged her to produce her first novel, suggesting that she write about what she knew best. That, she realized, was "the differences between the Irish and the English." She was living in London at the time, and she wrote for the *Irish Times* during the week while working on what was to become *Light a Penny Candle* on weekends.

Green, who Binchy says "typed the manuscript herself, she believed in it so much," first sold it for £5000 to a fiction editor at MacDonalds, Rosemary Cheetham. (Cheetham also discovered Colleen McCullough, who has since become a good friend of Binchy's.) When Cheetham moved to a fledgling publishing venture, Century, Binchy agreed to repay the MacDonalds advance and follow her. *Light a Penny Candle* was the first book Century published.

Binchy has stayed loyal to Cheetham through Century/Hutchison and Random/Century permutations, and now that Cheetham has moved to the new British house Orion, it seems a good omen that *The Copper Beech* is Orion's first title.

The prepublication paperback auction for *Light a Penny Candle* set a British record for a first novel at £52,000 from Coronet, the paperback arm of Hodder & Stoughton. (In the U.S., *Light a Penny Candle* was published by Viking in 1982, and in Dell paperback in 1989.) Binchy was stunned by the news, as she had hoped for "the amazing sum of £10,000 at most." For a long while afterward she wondered "if it was all a mistake and I would have to give it back."

A steady series of successes followed: *Echoes* (Viking, 1985; Dell, 1989); *Firefly Summer* (Delacorte, 1988; Dell, 1989); *Silver Wedding* (Delacorte, 1989; Dell, 1990) and *Circle of Friends*, in 1991, her first American bestseller. On the other side of the ocean, Binchy has long been both a household name and a regular on bestseller lists. (In Ireland, the tiniest, barest shop stocked with little more than biscuits and tinned beans is likely to carry paperbacks by Jeffrey Archer and Maeve Binchy.)

Binchy was apprehensive about her first author tour, for *Light a Penny Candle*. "A book signing is a masochist's dream," she says with a chuckle. "There are so many potential humiliations. When I go into a bookshop for a signing, I still wonder, are all these people the relatives of the owner?"

She recalls arriving in Manchester, sympathetic about the sales rep's dilemma ("He probably thought, 'God help us, some book by an Irishwoman with no sex and no violence!' "). The rep, expecting her at the airport, had brought a carton of *Penny Candle* copies and spread them around the airport bookstall, promising the clerk to collect them after Binchy had come and gone. When he discovered that Binchy's plan was to arrive by train, he took another carton of *Penny Candle* and spread *those* books around the

16

bookstall at the train station, explaining to that clerk as well that he would be back later to collect them.

What happened next, says Binchy, was his hysterical call to the head office to tell them they had a runaway bestseller on their hands. By the time Binchy's book signing was over and he had returned to both places to retrieve his books, they had *all* sold out.

Binchy's daily life hasn't changed much since her success, except that "obviously, we don't worry about money anymore." The Snells maintain a habit from earlier days: they discuss money matters only on Saturdays. "Bills, checks, whatever, it all goes into a drawer until then," she says.

Binchy and Snell are now making a trip around the world, with a stop to visit Colleen McCullough on Norfolk Island. "Your readers can imagine us together, two large, cheerful, bestselling authors in the South Pacific!" she says with glee. In January they return to their daily routine in Dalkey, the town from which Binchy couldn't wait to escape and to which she now escapes. (She and Snell have no children, but do have two very important cats who reside there, which makes Ireland their main residence.)

In Dalkey, they sit side by side at a large desk, sometimes for more than six hours daily, with two word processors "like twin pianos." (Snell has become a successful writer of children's books.) "Anyone who sees this thinks we're mad," says Binchy. "But the discipline of another writer sitting beside you *makes* you work."

Binchy feels she has been blessed by enormous good fortune, despite crippling and painful arthritis, though she regrets that her parents didn't live to see her success. "I had a happy childhood, and they told me how marvelous I was all the time," she says. She also recalls the way she would interrupt her father when he would start to tell her a bedtime story.

"He would say, 'Hansel and Gretel were in the woods,' and I would ask, 'Where was I?' And he would say, 'You were right there behind the tree.' I always wanted to be part of the story."

Wishes like this one have abetted the creation of various characters who may seem all the more real because they have some basis in Binchy's own desires. "I would like to have been a really good teacher like Maddy in *The Copper Beech.* I would like to be Aisling in *Penny Candle.* I rewrote history when I had Benny in *Circle of Friends* have great success at the dance—I was an absolute failure at a similar dance! I was the most awful-looking person there, even though my parents had told me I looked great. I wore a terrible borrowed dress that had to be let out, and I had painted-on earrings, and blue ink ran down my neck, and no one danced with me."

Perhaps that was the night a fiction writer was born; when the miserable, blue-inked, un-danced-with Maeve came home, and her parents inquired eagerly how it had gone, she recalls, "I told them it had all been absolutely marvelous. I couldn't bear to disappoint them, you see. So I made it all up, and described everything in glorious detail!"

KATHARINE WEBER
October 26, 1992

ROBERT BOSWELL

IN THE TAWNY DESERT of southern New Mexico, only 40 miles or so from the Mexican border, the city of Las Cruces rises beside the Rio Grande, flanked on the east by the jagged spine of the Organ Mountains, on the west by the Mesilla Valley, an oasis of farms renowned for growing fiery chilis.

Las Cruces is an agricultural center and an utterly unpretentious town, which is precisely why Robert Boswell—who teaches here at New Mexico State University and whose third novel, *Mystery Ride*, is recently issued by Knopf—finds it congenial. It is, like Boswell himself, quiet and unassuming, a good place to raise a family, as Boswell does, in a spacious, comfortable old house, built in the classic Southwestern adobe style and painted a pristine white, set behind a high, mudbrick wall in a yard dominated by an elaborate jungle gym.

Boswell seems very much a family man, devoted to his young son and daughter and to his wife, the writer Antonya Nelson. By his own description, his family is the center of his life, just as the idea of family has long been at the heart of his fiction. It is the subject of his new book, though Boswell's own happy situation contrasts sharply with *Mystery Ride*'s broken home, whose members are split between a suburban Southern California town and a farm in Iowa.

Mystery Ride is, like much of Boswell's work, about love and loss, about the ways in which ordinary people endure the pain of their lives, about the histories—the stories—that forever connect even a sundered family. Deploying his widely praised technical gifts— a lucid, deceptively simple prose style, the ability to orchestrate time and point of view, to create characters with unforgettable voices—in this novel Boswell set out "to explore the idea of whether it's possible any more to engage the world and live a life that embodies decency."

Boswell's previous novel, *The Geography of Desire* (Knopf, 1989), also raised that question as part of an investigation into the nature of love, but did so in a vastly different setting—a magic realist sort of town in an imaginary Central American country, a place where natives, expatriates, and exiles, though bound together by isolation rather than blood, constitute a kind of extended family.

In *Crooked Hearts* (Knopf, 1987), his acclaimed first novel, Boswell created one of the most memorable families in recent American literature—an eccentric clan in Yuma, Ariz., that throws parties to celebrate its failures, that both nurtures and suffocates its members, whose interactions define the term "dysfunctional" but nevertheless have a haunting universal resonance. This tour de force grew, in turn, from a story in *Dancing in the Movies* (Univ. of Iowa Press, 1986), the collection of short fiction that established Boswell as a writer and launched what seems a model career.

Now 39 years old, with curly, light-brown hair and a close-cropped beard, Boswell is a lean and fit-looking six-footer with a passion for basketball, which he plays twice a week. He was born in Sikeston, Miss., and spent his early childhood on a farm in southwestern Kentucky, near the confluence of the Mississippi and Ohio rivers, "where Huck and Jim missed their turn," Boswell notes, making the first of what will be several references to *The Adventures of Huckleberry Finn*, a book that he says influenced him enormously.

While he was still in elementary school, Boswell's family moved to Yuma, where he grew up. He earned a bachelor's degree at the University of Arizona in Tucson in 1977, with a double major in creative writing and psychology, and then made the only real detour of his career. In 1979 Boswell completed a master's degree in rehabilitation counseling and moved to California to work as a psychological counselor.

"My friends thought I was crazy to give up that job and my house on the beach in San Diego," he says, flashing a boyish grin. But two years later Boswell finally succumbed to his longest-held desire—"I can't remember a time when I didn't want to be a writer," he says—and entered the University of Arizona's master of fine arts program in creative writing. He began by producing "very bad poetry," he recalls, but, after a teacher pointed out that his poems were narrative and that he really seemed most interested in telling stories, he returned to fiction with a vengeance.

"I'd always felt that I had some sense of story, but I didn't know how to read as a writer," Boswell says. "The close, bitter scrutiny that you have to give every word, every sentence, was very important for me to learn, and now as a teacher it's one of the things I emphasize—that a lot of the discoveries you make as a writer happen when you're trying to find the right word.

"I knew I needed to work hard on matters of craft," Boswell recalls, and so, as a graduate student, he immersed himself in the art of fiction, working 16 to 18 hours a day, writing "an enormous number of pages" and absorbing the influences of Twain, Melville, Faulkner, Chekhov, Flannery O'Connor and such contemporary writers as Toni Morrison and Alice Munro. That hard work paid a rapid dividend.

At the University of Arizona, Boswell met visiting writer Larry McMurtry. Impressed with Boswell's early efforts, McMurtry introduced him to his own agent, Dorothea Oppenheimer, who took Boswell under her wing and placed his first published work, a story titled "The Right Thing," in the *Antioch Review* in 1983. That story was part of Boswell's 1984 MFA thesis, a collection that won the Iowa School of Letters Award for Short Fiction in 1985 and, with one story switch, was published the next year by the University of Iowa Press as *Dancing in the Movies.*

By the time that first book appeared, Boswell was at work on *Crooked Hearts*, which Oppenheimer placed with Knopf and editor Ashbel Green—Boswell's publishing team until Oppenheimer's death in 1987. Boswell then signed with Jane Cushman, who handled *The Geography of Desire* and *Mystery Ride.* Feeling, he says simply, that it was time for a change, Boswell switched a few months ago to his current agent, Kim Witherspoon of Witherspoon and Chernoff, but his relations with Knopf have remained constant. "I know there are a lot of good houses, but I'm happy to be there," he says, "and especially happy to be working with Ash—a great editor and a wonderful man."

Boswell's fiction has sparked interest in many quarters. *Crooked Hearts* was produced as a film—a 1991 MGM release, now in video. His stories, appearing steadily in literary journals and such magazines as the *New Yorker* and *Esquire,* have been widely anthologized, included in such collections as *Best American Short Stories*

21

and *O. Henry Prize Stories*, and he's won a string of awards, including fellowships from the Guggenheim Foundation and the NEA.

Throughout his career, Boswell has also taught writing—first at the University of Arizona, then moving to Northwestern University in 1986, the same year that he accepted his ongoing position with the Warren Wilson Master of Fine Arts Program for Writers, a group that meets twice annually in brief, intensive sessions. He left Northwestern in 1989, when New Mexico State offered precisely what Boswell and his wife were seeking—the opportunity to share a teaching position, which would, at a stroke, give them equal academic status and allow Boswell more time to write. Boswell and Nelson, who met as students in the Arizona MFA program and for whom literature seems very much a family affair, have indeed managed to achieve a remarkable parity. Boswell's literary success is paralleled by that of Nelson, a recipient of the Flannery O'Connor Award for Short Fiction who has two story collections to her credit (*The Expendables*, Univ. Georgia, 1990; *In the Land of Men*, Morrow, 1992). Boswell says she is "my most valued critic."

Boswell continues to teach, and likely always will, he says, "because I want to help students as I was helped, and because I think their enthusiasm helps my work. It's an ideal situation for a writer to teach half-time—part of the job is to write and publish, and where else does a fiction writer find quite that kind of encouragement? One of the reasons I like teaching is that it places me in a community of writers—graduate students, colleagues here and at Warren Wilson, talented people who really care about their work, people you can talk to about particular writing problems."

Because he takes his role as a father quite seriously—he works a day each week as a teacher's assistant in his daughter's kindergarten class—Boswell has altered his writing habits. "Before the kids, I'd write two to six hours every day, but that's gone now," he says, with a wry chuckle that carries no bitterness. "Some people need the same hours, the same desk, but I'm pretty flexible—with two kids under six, to try to have a schedule is foolish—and it doesn't really matter that much to me. There's less time, but I make better use of it; I'm fairly happy just stealing time when I can." Summer, however, brings more freedom, and Boswell retreats with his family to an old mining shack in Telluride, Colo., to spend three months, he says with obvious relish, "just writing and playing with the kids."

Boswell prefers to compose directly on his computer, a laptop that's easy to carry back and forth between the dining room table in his house, where, often listening to jazz or classical music, he works while he cares for his children, and the nearby, more private studio/guest house, remodeled from an old adobe structure once used to dry chili peppers. Even with juggling his schedule and his workspace, he remains as productive as ever.

During the four years he spent writing *Mystery Ride,* Boswell also finished a new collection of stories and drafted a play. He's currently completing the dramatic piece—his first—and is deeply enmeshed in a new novel. "It's a real departure," he says of that work-in-progress, "more comic, though there's darkness too. That's a family in it, and the second half is turning into a road trip.

Partly from superstition, but mainly because he does not yet have a full draft, Boswell is reluctant to say more. "I tend to write fast. I scramble, mess around, follow whatever thread seems to be there, until I have this big, messy first draft, and then I revise endlessly," he says, noting that he distilled a thousand pages of *Mystery Ride* manuscript into half that number.

"It's different every time," Boswell says of the genesis of his stories, "but often there's an image or event, a line of dialogue, that won't let me alone, that I can't let go of, so I start writing about it and try to discover why it's powerful for me, letting it take me wherever it takes me. Then I step back and see what I have.

"It's a matter of excavating the raw material of the story," he says. "In early drafts [there will be from 10 to 30 of them] something is usually missing, buried in the story, and my way of bringing it to the surface is, typically, by paying close attention to the language, to see if every sentence is honest or if I'm avoiding something, dancing around something that should be addressed. I keep revising, shaping, determining—this is the difficult part— what's essential and what's not.

"It's always a mystery to me where the material is going to take me and whether it will be worth the ride," Boswell says with a shrug, a smile that evokes both bemusement and good-humored acceptance. "Eventually I get to the point where, intuitively, it sounds right, feels right—though it's never quite the brilliant thing I thought it would be.

"But the writer's job is to embrace the next impossible task," Boswell says, "and here, in Las Cruces, this life in the slow lane allows plenty of time for that. I'm just trying to be honest and decent, to be true to the people I love and the things I hold dear, which includes literature—*the story*. Because I believe that storytelling is crucial to humans for existence, that in very complex ways, it helps us to see our own lives with more clarity."

WILLIAM CLARK
January 25, 1993

ROSELLEN BROWN

Rosellen brown says she knew from the age of nine that she would be a writer and a mother. Her work is not autobiographical per se, but her experience as a mother and her reflections on that experience clearly influence her fiction. Though conditioned by maternal empathy, however, hers is not a sentimental approach; Brown's novels deal with the deeper, darker sides of family life. She writes about the nightmares that haunt anyone who has ever feared that something terrible might happen to a loved one. Her novels explore how ordinary people are transformed by the freak accidents and sudden violence of fate.

Before and After, Brown's fourth novel (Farrar, Straus & Giroux), continues that theme, portraying the emotional devastation and social isolation that engulf a New Hampshire family whose 17-year-old son has murdered his girlfriend.

One of the catalysts for the book, Brown explains, was a newspaper account of a teenage murder case, in which she discovered that the court can require parents to be cross-examined by the prosecution.

The parents in Brown's novel, however, react in different ways to the state's power to compel their testimony in their son's trial. Gender, personality and family history are factors in their opposing decisions: Ben is willing to break the law rather than offer evidence that will help send their son to prison, while Carolyn, a physician who saw the victim's body, decides that someone has to tell the truth for the sake of the dead teenage girl.

Before and After is not so much a study of murder, Brown says, as about "how you cease to know your children very well after a certain point, or as well as you think you know them, anyway. It's about the terror that perhaps you don't know what your children really are like."

As the mother of two daughters, ages 22 and 25, Brown sees

the subject in a personal way. She says the novel springs from "reflecting on the painfulness of watching your children grow beyond your ken" and questioning the extent to which parents are responsible for the kind of people their children become.

"So there's a case where having children and thinking about motherhood and fatherhood has totally informed the work as it's informed my life. And I've written the book out of that total experience of parenthood over time," she says.

A main selection of the Literary Guild, *Before and After* has also been optioned by TriStar Pictures for a movie to star Meryl Streep. The script will be written by Ted Tally, Academy Award-winning screenwriter for the movie *The Silence of the Lambs*. "Although you're usually very hesitant to imagine what they will do to your work in Hollywood, in this case the people are so wonderful that I'm intrigued," Brown says, noting, however, that her third novel, *Civil Wars*, was sold to Columbia Pictures but never produced.

Kate Nelligan and Dennis Boutsikaris will read a condensed *Before and After* on a Simon & Schuster audiocasette; an unabridged version will be released later "for purists like me," Brown says.

The author of eight books, she has won many honors for her work, including an award from the American Academy and Institute of Arts and Letters; fellowships from the MacDowell Colony, the Radcliffe Institute and the Guggenheim, Ingram Merrill and Howard foundations; and two National Endowment for the Arts grants. *Civil Wars* received the Janet Kafka award in 1984 for the best novel by an American woman. In 1985, Brown was honored as one of *Ms.* magazine's Women of the Year. Since 1982, she has been a professor in the creative writing department at the University of Houston.

PW first encounters Brown at a reading at Boston University, and speaks with her again at her summer home in Peterborough, N.H. She has a round, expressive face, an open, friendly manner and a rich, compelling voice.

Born in Philadelphia in 1939, Brown began writing full time in 1962, after earning a B.A. from Barnard College and an M.A. from Brandeis University. In 1965, in the midst of the civil rights struggle, the Woodrow Wilson Foundation asked her to go to Mississippi to teach at the predominantly black Tougaloo College. Brown and her husband, Marvin Hoffman, lived for two years on campus, immersed in their students' lives. She drew on her observations of the South for her first book of poetry, *Some Deaths in the Delta* (1970), and later for *Civil Wars* (1984).

Brown's daughter Adina was born during the couple's third and final year in Mississippi, and Brown produced most of the poems in her first book during Adina's infancy. "It's a good thing I was writing poetry, because that is something you can do in a more fragmented way than fiction. I'm not sure it would have gone so well if I had been trying to write a novel, which is so labor-intensive that 24 hours a day is hardly time enough," she observes.

The family moved to Brooklyn, N.Y., where their second daughter, Elana, was born in 1970, and where Brown began writing fiction. She set the stories in *Street Games* (1974) in an ethnically mixed Brooklyn neighborhood not unlike her own; several of them won O. Henry prizes and were included in the annual *Best American Short Stories* volume.

"The reason that again I didn't miss a beat when the baby was born was that I already knew myself as a writer. It was my job and I got up every day to do it just as surely as my husband went off to his job," she says.

"Just as I can't imagine my life without children, I can't imagine what my writing would be without having had them. Now, obviously, I would have written about something if it hadn't been kids, or maybe I would have been one of those people who can write well about kids without having had them. But I feel that so much of what I know about the world has come from having had children. The idea that I might not have had them in order to preserve myself for my work seems like the most absurd, self-defeating protection imaginable."

The child characters she conceived in *Civil Wars* were "crucial to the whole idea of how one is educated morally." When their segregationist parents are killed in an accident, Helen and O'Neill move in with their aunt and uncle, both civil rights activists. "The idea for that book came to me from contemplating how it is that children get their moral underpinnings and their sense of the world, both politically and morally, not to mention emotionally," Brown observes.

The theme of exile also runs through *Civil Wars*, as it does through Brown's other novels. The orphaned children in *Civil Wars* not only lose their parents; they are forced to leave behind their home, friends, possessions, indeed their whole way of life.

In *Before and After*, New York natives Ben and Carolyn realize that they are still outsiders despite having lived for a decade in their small New Hampshire town. Her characters' experience of uprooting is familiar to Brown, who as a child moved often, from one side of the continent to the other. The effect of this has been to enrich her fiction with a fine awareness of place.

In her publishing career, too, Brown has moved from one house to another, "for an assortment of reasons." She is full of praise for her new editor, John Glusman, at FSG. "Actually, I've had lovely relationships with all of my editors; I've never been given a hard time by anybody," she says.

Doubleday released her first short story collection, *Street Games*, and her first novel, *The Autobiography of My Mother* (1976). But the house wasn't interested in her third book, *Cora Fry* (1977), a novel in poetic form, so Brown moved to Norton. Knopf won the auction for her second novel, *Tender Mercies* (1978), and also issued *Civil Wars*. Brown has also worked with smaller houses: Penmaen Press published *Banquet: Five Short Stories* (1978); Milkweed Editions reprinted *Street Games* in paperback last year; and the University Press of New England released *The Rosellen Brown Reader* this spring. Brown is hoping that if the new novel does well, she will be able to get her first two novels back into print. "Every writer dreams of a set of their stuff all coming out at the same time," she says.

Brown dedicated *Civil Wars* to her agent, Virginia Barber, with whom she has enjoyed a close relationship for nearly 20 years. She describes Barber as "a serious, good reader" of her work and "a very effective agent."

Teaching only occasionally while establishing herself as a writer, Brown was dependent for many years on her husband's income as an English professor. The couple collaborated with Martin Kushner, Phillip Lopate and Sheila Murphy on *The Whole Word Catalog: Creative Writing Ideas for Elementary and Secondary Schools* (1972). Brown's only nonfiction book, it has sold far better than her much more labored-over novels.

"When I got married in 1963 it was not shameful—or even something that you thought much about—to marry somebody who was going to support you," she recalls. "Early on, we had very little money, but we always made sure we had enough for day care or the baby-sitter." The financial payoff was a long time coming:

Brown received a total of $5000 for her first short story collection and her first novel.

Brown acknowledges that it is psychologically, as well as practically, more difficult for a young writer today to be supported by a spouse. But she believes that writers and their partners must make financial decisions that will enable them to support the writing.

She is particularly scornful of graduate students who claim they can't write the way they were trained because of the need to earn money. "A lot of young writers have a huge sense of entitlement these days. What they consider the absolute minimum they need to get along on is one hell of a lot higher than it has to be. I think a lot of writers need to redefine what they mean by need" says Brown, who buys most of her clothes at thrift shops, and whose unpretentious hairstyle and lack of cosmetic artifice signal a woman more interested in her inner life than in a compulsion to be chic.

Her husband has supported her writing not only financially but in other ways as well. Brown recalls one December when he took their daughters to visit relatives for a week while she stayed home working on the final revisions of a novel. Having met her deadline, Brown started *Cora Fry*. "I never would have been able to begin it without that perfect concentration. I felt as if I'd been given a gift. Again, that goes back to having a husband who understands that from time to time I need some kind of silence."

For many years, Brown wrote only during the hours her daughters were in school. Although she was often reluctant to stop working when the schoolbus arrived, she feels there was a hidden benefit. "I really do believe that you tend to have an easier time starting up the next day if you stop before you're finished than if you actually come to the end of something. If you're writing continually it's a little bit like a marriage in that you know—or hope, anyway—that it is ongoing. You figure you're going to be back at the notebook tomorrow," she says, suggesting that a short hiatus can enrich the germinating thoughts.

Disciplining herself has never been difficult, Brown says, "because what I always wanted to do was to write. The problem was disciplining everybody else to stay out of my way. But you have to take yourself so damn seriously in order to get other people to take you seriously! I've been lucky because I started publishing

29

fairly early and I've won prizes. And all of those things, aside from the fact that they were good for my ego, brought me some community respect."

Yet she continues to find the process of writing somewhat daunting. "It's still easier to be in the world than it is to be home alone with a piece of paper. Every demand that's made of me, to serve on a committee at school, to do any public thing—whether I like doing it or not, whether I find it easy or difficult—every bit of it is easier than the one thing I have to do: which is sit down in front of a blank piece of paper every day."

JUDITH PIERCE ROSENBERG
August 31, 1992

JAMES LEE BURKE

ANNETTE'S IS A COFFEE SHOP located on Dauphine Street near a quiet edge of the French Quarter in New Orleans. Vinyl-covered tables and the hand-lettered sign in the window declaring "The Best Po-boys in Town" proclaim it as a place where locals gather. It's just the kind of spot you'd imagine meeting Dave Robicheaux, the Cajun sometime-cop whose dilemmas and adventures are the subject of James Lee Burke's series of crime novels, the fifth of which, *A Stained White Radiance,* is just out from Hyperion.

Chatting with Burke over cup after cup of strong New Orleans coffee, it's obvious to us that there are plenty of reasons to confuse him with his series hero. Like Robicheaux, Burke is in his 50s. He's big-boned and beefy, with a wide face, large features and speech modulated to a soft Gulf Coast drawl. His brown hair and pale blue-green eyes, set under eyebrows canted like a raised drawbridge, are a muted version of the black curly hair and turquoise eyes that declare Robicheaux's Cajun ancestry. Author and character share fierce moral concerns for such values as integrity, loyalty and the responsible use of power.

But Burke's exuberant, outgoing nature distinguishes him from his sometimes withdrawn, often tormented Cajun creation. Despite the peaks and valleys of his writing career, Burke wears his current success with the same unstudied ease as he does his low-slung jeans and scuffed Nikes.

"I wanted to be a writer since I was a little boy. In the fourth grade my cousin Lynn and I started writing stories for the *Saturday Evening Post* in Big Chief notebooks. I published my first story when I was 19 in the college magazine at Southwestern Louisiana Institute, saw my first published novel in print when I was 23 and by 34 had published three novels in New York. [*Half of Paradise,* Houghton Mifflin, 1965; *To the Bright and Shining Sun,* Scribners, 1970; *Lay Down My Sword and Shield,* T. Y. Crowell, 1971.] I thought the early success was there to stay. But that was a vanity. It was 13 years before I was in hardback again."

From the early 1970s to the mid-'80s Burke wrote unceasingly, publishing his stories in magazines but getting nowhere with the novels he produced. He and his Beijing-born wife Pearl, whom he met in graduate school at the University of Missouri, raised four children in that period, covering the country as Burke took up a blistering variety of work.

"I did all kinds of things over the years," he recalls. "I was a social worker on skid row in Los Angeles and a land surveyor in Colorado. I worked on the pipeline in Texas and in the oil field. I was a newspaper reporter, an over-the-road truck driver, worked for the U.S. Forest Service and the Job Corps. I taught in five colleges and universities." Although Pocket brought out *Two for Texas* in paperback in 1982, the author felt that he'd never sell a novel in New York again. "The book I thought I'd publish after the third novel was *The Lost Get-Back Boogie*, a long novel about a country singer I worked on very hard. It was under submission for nine years and drew around 100 rejections, many of which were condemning. That book wasn't just rejected, it was flung back at me with a catapult.

"Then in 1985 Louisiana State University put me back into print. I'll never be able to repay the debt," Burke acknowledges, citing the publication of a collection of short stories called *The Convict*. The following year LSU Press published a revised version of *The Lost Get-Back Boogie*, which was nominated for a Pulitzer.

Even before his rescue, Burke insists that his belief in himself and his writing never flagged. "I thought that my talent was there for a reason and honestly believed that these guys were all wet. Theodore Roosevelt wrote an essay about the nature of the contest, in which he said there are two kinds of people basically, participants and spectators. Using a boxing metaphor, he pointed out that inside the ring, all that counts is the contest and you know the mentality of those that hoot and cheer—they're inconsequential. To me those editors were just dumbheads."

He got some help shoring up this faith in 1978 when his cousin Andre Dubus introduced him to agent Philip Spitzer, who still represents him. "Philip has a romantic heart and the stance of a gladiator when it comes to principle," Burke characterizes with the kind of hyperbole that marks his appreciation of all his supporters. Among these is the writer Rick DeMarinis, a kind of macho midwife to the Dave Robicheaux stories.

"Rick and I were fishing one day during the time I couldn't publish anything in New York and he said, 'Try a crime novel, Jim. You've written everything else. Just write one good chapter and you'll get an advance. That's all it takes.'

"I sent two chapters of *The Neon Rain* to Charles Willeford, who wrote the Hoke Mosley series: *Miami Blues* and *New Hope for the Dead.* He told me some things I was doing wrong but encouraged me by saying I had a terrific character.

"So I wrote the book and sent it to Philip, thinking it might be just another book I couldn't publish. Philip sent it out to three publishers and all three bid on it. I was stunned."

Rob Cowley, an editor at Henry Holt, bought *The Neon Rain* and also the next Dave story, *Heaven's Prisoners,* which came out the following year, 1987. "Rob, who's a real gentleman, left Holt, and Philip and I, somewhat disappointed with their promotion efforts, decided to put the next book, *Black Cherry Blues,* up for auction."

Lasting two days and involving six houses, that well-publicized auction brought Burke together with his current editor, Patricia Mulcahy, then at Little, Brown. Burke is rhapsodic about her: "Pat will take a book from the minute it hits her desk and walk it all the way through to the retailer's shop. She oversees the marketing, the production, the jacket design, the blurbs. She makes the contact with the sales force. She has tremendous integrity and her instincts are uncanny, they're so accurate."

Black Cherry Blues won an Edgar from Mystery Writers of America in 1987, increasing Burke's already burgeoning group of fans. That book draws Robicheaux from the bayous of New Iberia, 120 miles west of New Orleans, to Montana where he takes on organized crime and a psychotic who threatens the life of his adopted daughter, Alafair, a young Central American girl whose rescue was part of *Heaven's Prisoners.*

Burke has lived in Missoula, Mont., since a 1989 Guggenheim fellowship allowed him to give up teaching and write without interruption. Around this same time Dave Robicheaux was being noticed in Hollywood.

"I had been turned down by all the top agencies out there. Then Robert Olen Butler, a Louisiana writer, introduced me to

Patricia Karlin, who also handles Dean Koontz and Judith Guest. She took me on when no one else would touch the material, predicting 'Jim, this is going to be major-league big, I guarantee it.' She took *The Neon Rain* and *The Lost Get-Back Boogie* and placed them both."

The actor who will bring Dave Robicheaux onto the silver screen is Alec Baldwin, one of the hottest names in Hollywood. His playing Dave Robicheaux is a satisfying turn of events for an author who'd been cold-shouldered for years.

Baldwin and a partner, Hildy Gottlieb, have acquired four Robicheaux novels for a series of films. Burke himself wrote the screenplay for *A Morning for Flamingos*, the fourth Robicheaux book, issued by Little, Brown in 1990. "Hollywood was different from anything I had anticipated," Burke observes. "I was told that world was contemptuous of writers. But the people I've dealt with have been courteous, thoughtful, educated and bright. They're New Yorkers with Southern manners."

The Hollywood connection confirms the appeal of his hero and stories that is borne out by his reception during his 22-city promotional tour for *A Stained White Radiance*. His readings draw standing-room-only crowds to bookstores. Burke believes the series is his best writing, but when asked where Robicheaux and the plots for the novels come from, only shakes his head and repeats, "I don't know. I just don't know."

Robicheaux is a Vietnam vet whose experiences in that war, often revisiting him in dreams, figure large in his reactions to the evil he encounters in Louisiana. In the earlier books, Robicheaux is a cop, first in New Orleans and then in New Iberia. In *A Stained White Radiance*, he runs a boat and bait shop in the bayous of New Iberia, is married to his third wife, the first having divorced him prior to the series' time span, his second a murder victim in *Heaven's Prisoners*. Burke, married to Pearl for 31 years, had neither been in the armed services nor belonged to a police department.

"I don't think up the stories," he says. "I'm convinced they're already written in the unconscious. My work is simply a day-to-day discovery. I never see more than two scenes around the corner and I don't know a book's ending until the last pages. The best metaphor I know for how it happens comes from Michelangelo, who said he didn't carve his sculptures, he released them from the marble.

"I see my characters as living people inside me, almost whole populations that live in my unconscious. They come out of my dreams too. I wake up in the middle of the night and see them clearly.

"I believe this is a gift. If a writer convinces himself that he generated his talent out of his own willpower, he'll lose it. Such a person may be visible on TV or panels for a while, but not for long. He's living yesterday's box score."

That last phrase, with its implication that each day brings another challenge and a fresh chance, is pure Robicheaux and points directly to the greatest similarity between author and character: their struggle with alcoholism. As does Matt Scudder in Lawrence Block's Manhattan detective series, Dave Robicheaux offers a recovering alcoholic's take on life in the genre.

"Dave has no illusions about the nature of alcohol," says Burke. "In effect, whiskey for him is like putting his head in a blast furnace. I reached a point myself where I didn't care whether I lived or died.

"After I bottomed out, I was a white-knuckle alcoholic, dry for five and half years and more miserable than I'd ever been before. It was far worse than when I was drinking. After a buddy of mine pointed out that I still had all the problems of an alcoholic, I went with him to a 12-step program. At that first meeting I knew that I was home.

"I used to think that alcohol somehow enhanced a person's writing. It took me years to realize that I had written in spite of alcohol, not because of it. If a writer is drinking, it gets onto the paper. One way or another, it's on every page. The 12-step fellowship gave me back my life, literally. Then I began to write about it in *The Neon Rain*. Dave and the 12-step recovery program came together.

"I'd say there are two very large influences in my success. One, the biggest, is sobriety. The second is the investment of other people in my career, people whose names will never appear on a book jacket: Martha Hall, the senior fiction editor at LSU Press, and Michael Pinkston, the publicist there. Spitzer and Mulcahy and Karlin. Rob Cowley and Sara McFall, my editor and publicist at

Holt. Shannon Ravenel, who included my short story "The Convict" in *New Stories from the South* and then sent it to Raymond Carver who put it in *Best American Short Stories* in 1986. Bruce Carrick, who published my second novel at Scribners."

Like Robicheaux, but without his smoldering rage, Burke is ready to condemn all those—whether editors, academics, cops or politicians—who wield power with disregard for the welfare of others. But at this point in his career, with 11 books in print (and a strong memory of being entirely out of print only seven years ago), his dominant impulse is to focus on those who merit gratitude and respect. This benevolent, generous view seems as authentically a part of Burke as his Southern good manners and his rolling, uninhibited laugh.

DULCY BRAINARD
April 20, 1992

ROBERT OLEN BUTLER

CALL HIM BRAVE, call him foolhardy, but admire his perhaps quixotic courage. With his literary reputation finally achieved courtesy of a Pulitzer last year, Robert Olen Butler has moved into new territory with *They Whisper*, a novel in which a man's erotic musings are interwoven with the voices of all the women to whom he has made love. Butler calls *They Whisper* "my best book." He is anxious to establish that it is "a serious literary novel that concerns heterosexual love between men and women. The most difficult challenge was to deal explicitly with sexuality without losing control of the language so it would retain its artistic resonance."

Indeed, *They Whisper* (Henry Holt) is far more than a litany of sexual couplings. The 35-year-old protagonist is not a womanizer in the classic, derogatory sense of the term; he is a man who worships women's bodies and femininity. The book's celebratory tone comes from Butler's vision of the world, he says. "*They Whisper* conveys my deepest feeling about sexuality, the relationships of men and women, the nature of intimacy—in the sense of secular sacrament. The writing was an act of self-exploration as well as expression."

Ironically, Butler's protagonist is caught in a nightmarish marriage in which his wife, obsessed by guilt and religious fervor, constantly demands physical evidence of his sexual desire for her, so that he must make love to her every night or risk the onset of her jealous frenzy.

Butler himself understands the ironies of life all too well. During the 1980s he published six novels that were highly praised by critics but sold in only modest numbers. His first, *Alleys of Eden*, the story of a Vietnam deserter and a prostitute, endured 21 rejections before finding its way into print. A succession of agents, editors and publishers failed to produce a breakthrough book until editor Allen Peacock at Holt brought out *A Good Scent From a Strange Mountain* in 1992. In addition to winning the Pulitzer, that collection of stories, featuring Vietnamese émigrés living in cultural exile in two Louisiana communities, also received the Richard and Hinda Rosenthal Prize given by the American Academy of Arts and Letters; it was a PEN/Faulkner finalist and earned Butler a Guggenheim. For a man who had tasted the bitter gall of obscurity, 1992 was a sweet year indeed. Now that his work has come to prominence, his so-called "Vietnam novels," *Alleys of Eden* (1981), *On Distant Ground* (1985) and *The Deuce* (1989) will be reissued in Holt's Owl paperback line next spring. *Wabash* (1987), *Countrymen of Bones* (1983) and *Sun Dogs* (1982) will follow in the fall.

Throughout the lean years, Butler never had any intention of abandoning his craft. "I decided that the only way to avoid madness was to take out my lapboard and legal pad, or in recent years, to sit down at my computer, every day—and just to do the work, to articulate the vision I have of the world. Not to think of critics or sales—and certainly not prizes."

In conversation, Butler has the bright, unwavering gaze of a curious bird; he leans forward earnestly and speaks volubly, his careful enunciation the legacy of a brief career in the theater. He has an actor's presence and nervous energy; on the day he meets *PW*, he is attired in clothes Robert De Niro might comfortably wear: purple shirt, floral jacket and black tie. Though at 49 he is balding, luxuriant brown curls graze his collar.

Butler grew up in Granite City, Ill., a steel town near St. Louis which he describes as a "place of cultural collision," and he majored in theater at Northwestern University (his father chaired the theater department at St. Louis University). But the event that turned him into a writer was the Vietnam war. After earning an M.A. in playwrighting from the University of Iowa in 1969, Butler enlisted in the army and was sent to language school in Washington, D.C., where he studied Vietnamese for a full year. His fluency with the language sets him apart from other Americans who have written about that time and place.

When Butler arrived in Vietnam in January 1971, he immediately found that his linguistic skill gave him entrée to a fascinating culture. "I made it a central part of my life to become deeply engaged with the Vietnamese," he says. The steamy back alleys of

Saigon beckoned each night; he would leave his hotel at 2 a.m. to wander the streets, often "crouching down in doorways with the warmest, most gentle and welcoming people I have ever known. This ravishingly sensual experience illuminated my future as an artist. I understood that what I knew about the world was demanding expression in a fully sensual, moment-to-moment way. I saw that fiction was the medium that would permit me to do this."

In light of Butler's post-Vietnam life, it was a heroic decision. Trapped in a destructive marriage but afraid to lose his young son in a divorce (a situation not unlike that of the protagonist in *They Whisper*), Butler spent the next eight years writing four novels as he commuted from his home in Long Island to Manhattan, where he was editor of a business newspaper. *The Alleys of Eden* endured 12 rejections before it was accepted by Methuen in 1981. While it was still in the galley stage, however, the book was cancelled when Methuen cut its trade division. Butler peddled the galleys to seven more publishers before Ben Raeburn at Horizon Press took the book. He speaks fondly of Raeburn, whom he calls "a remnant of a former time, a gentlemanly publisher."

Alleys won a rave review in the *New York Times* from Anatole Broyard, who became Butler's mentor. "I miss him terribly," he says of the late literary critic. "He kept me going. I called his widow when I won the Pulitzer." The book had "isolated, wonderful reviews," but negligible sales. "I was toiling in obscurity in spite of the fact that my books were intensely admired," Butler says.

Horizon published his next two novels, but when Raeburn was bought out and left the firm, the atmosphere changed radically. Butler took his next two books and half of the manuscript of *On Distant Ground* to agent Candida Donadio. "A week later I was her client, and three days later I was a Knopf author and Lee Goerner was my editor," he recalls. After Knopf issued *Wabash*, however, Butler felt it was time to make a change.

"I have the greatest respect for both Candida and Goerner," Butler says, "but I *amicably*—stress that word—moved to Bob Tabian at ICM." Butler urged Tabian to send the proposal for *Deuce* to Allen Peacock, then at Simon & Schuster. Peacock snapped it up. When he left S & S, Butler followed him; *Scent* became Peacock's first book at Holt. When Tabian himself exited ICM last year, however, Butler signed with Kim Witherspoon of Witherspoon and Chernoff. "Kim is sensational," he says. "She aggressively followed up on the Pulitzer," selling foreign rights for "satisfying" sums. Witherspoon and West Coast agent Michael Siegel recently sold the movie rights to Wayne Wang.

During the time he moved between publishing houses, Butler also moved physically from the northeast to Lake Charles, La., where he is the sole professor of fiction writing ("I teach it like method acting") in McNeese State University's Master of Fine Arts program. He calls it "just extraordinary and providential" that he ended up at McNeese, because it was only when he flew down for an interview that he saw from the plane window what looked like the landscape of the Mekong Delta. "There was the same calligraphy of waterways, the rice paddies, the subtropical climate, the French influence." In this area so geographically similar to Vietnam, with the two nearby villages of Gretna and Versailles both havens for Vietnamese immigrants, *Scent* was born.

If Butler has been peripatetic in some respects, he feels his publishing roaming days are over, since he has found his "lifetime editor" in Allen Peacock. He calls Peacock "the best literary editor in New York, an extraordinarily receptive and perceptive reader. He has the ability to get inside his writer's vision of the world." Butler cites as evidence of Peacock's dedication the editor's insistence that the Vietnamese names in *Deuce* and *Scent* be provided with appropriate accent marks.

"A good relationship with an editor should be like lovemaking: 'that feels good, no, a little higher, a little over to the left . . .' In lovemaking there is the inevitable mutual adjusting of the experience, which is absolutely necessary to the process. Allen is good at that." Butler is obviously delighted with this analogy because it allows him to segue to *They Whisper*.

"I've been loving women for 48 years but I didn't have access to the voices of women until I wrote *Scent*," he says. "Half those stories are written in women's voices. In fact it was only when I found the woman in myself that I was able to write about what it is to be a male heterosexual."

Ira Holloway, Butler's protagonist in *They Whisper*, is "gloriously heterosexual and comprehensively in love with women. He is trying to figure out the nature of his inner landscape, which is populated by all the women he has ever loved. These women are always alive in him. As he meditates on them, he moves into their first-person voices."

Butler claims that it's taken him many years—and perhaps the felicity of a successful marriage (he and his third wife, Maureen, were married in 1987)—to be comfortable writing this book. "It requires a kind of a lyrical gift to be able to write explicitly about sex without falling into the worn-out rhetoric of sexual parts. I could not have written this novel until every woman I have known had been deeply composted in my imagination. But the women characters have no true counterparts. Fuentes defined the novel as a pack of lies hounding the truth. This is a book full of the truest lies I can tell."

On the verge of a 15-city reading tour, Butler's enthusiasm for reaching the public is as fervent as his praise of his publisher. "Before I came to Holt, I had never spent a single night at a hotel at a publisher's expense. I had never been sent around the corner to do a reading. As soon as I got to Holt, I had a three-week coast-to-coast tour—for a book of short stories! My loyalty to Holt was won with that. And it could be that the Pulitzer was won with that."

Butler explains that teaser with his flair for the dramatic. Only 10 people turned up when he read at Elliott Bay Bookshop in Seattle, he recalls. "By some cynical objective standards, that's a terrible turnout. But because I was there, the book got a little flurry of publicity. Several days later, Charles Johnson came into the store and said he was sorry that he had missed my reading. He bought a copy of *Scent*. Some months later, Johnson was one of the members of the Pulitzer jury."

He goes into verbal overdrive when he discusses the value of a book tour. "In other areas of business, a certain amount of money is put aside for research and development. In the book industry, long-term development should consist of getting the writer on the road to meet his audience. No other industry would *think* of neglecting its future by omitting that step." Writers who insist on "vanity things" like space ads that drain their publishers' limited resources are as much to blame, he says. "Instead of one ad, there should be a sequence of ads to fund reading appearances. The cost of one ad in the *New York Times* could be used to fund readings where the grassroots seed work is done."

Musing over the effect of the Pulitzer, he says, "I'm the same writer with the same vision and the same voices in me. The blessed difference is that people are listening to me now." He claims that his routine will remain unchanged. "I expect to write a book every 18 months for the rest of my life. My next two books are already conceived and four more are nearly in final shape in my head," he announces.

"Wonderful literary careers are sometimes made out of two or three books. But I always knew that I had a lot of books in me. I've had so many experiences in my life, so many places I can write about: Louisiana, New York, St. Louis, Vietnam, the steel mill towns . . ." Butler takes a dramatic pause. "I'm life-drunk!" he announces, a perfect exit line for a raconteur with an actor's feel for his audience's emotions.

SYBIL S. STEINBERG
January 3, 1994

FRANK CONROY

LEGIONS OF AUTHORS have produced a shelf-ful of books without coming close to the literary reputation that Frank Conroy earned with his first effort, his now-classic memoir of a miserable youth, *Stop-Time*, published when he was 37. Seventeen years elapsed before the appearance of a highly praised short story collection, *Midair*. Conroy is 57 now, and he seems surprised that his first novel, *Body & Soul*, has been so eagerly awaited. He's somewhat stunned, he says, that it has thrust him into the limelight. In fact, commercial success, in the form of celebrity status, boffo rights sales and a perch on the bestseller ladder, appears imminent for this book, out from Houghton Mifflin/Seymour Lawrence.

A second major career is surely one reason why Conroy's literary output has been limited. He has a distinguished reputation as a teacher and administrator, notably as the director of the renowned Writers Workshop at the University of Iowa. Another reason is that he is a slow writer and a careful one. "I have pretty high standards for myself," he observes, a statement borne out by his precise and resonant prose.

This time out, however, his ingrained caution may be blown away by fair-weather winds. Word of mouth preceded *Body & Soul* to the ABA and escalated there. With a 125,000-copy first printing, foreign rights sold in 10 countries, film rights picked up by Spring Creek Productions, and a tap by the BOMC, the novel is making beautiful music for its author, much as its protagonist finds transcendent joy in the music he plays and creates.

Body & Soul is a novel about a musical prodigy, a story that carries its young hero from his first exposure to music—fiddling with keys on an out-of-tune piano—through stages of increasing mastery of technique, concert performance and composition.

The boy, Claude Rawlings, is to some extent Conroy's alter ego, a fantasy of what his life might have been had he been rescued from his neglected childhood by a loving father figure. Conroy acknowledges that the key to the book is Claude's mentor, Aaron Weisfeld. The owner of a music store in Claude's 1940s Upper East Side New York neighborhood (a time and place evoked with fidelity and affection), Weisfeld makes himself responsible for Claude's welfare and his musical education. "He is the father I did not have," Conroy says simply.

More than wish-fulfillment, the novel satisfied another need. "The plot emerged from the two great preoccupations of my life, books and music," Conroy says. The idea came to him about five years ago as he was driving from Iowa to his summer home on Nantucket. Conroy confesses that he felt "a little leery—because music is very difficult to write about." Besides, he had given himself a difficult task, namely, "to recapitulate the history of piano pedagogy in Claude's teachers." Cognoscenti may recognize that Claude's professors represent Clementi, Beethoven and Chopin. But musical knowledge is hardly a requisite for appreciating the book.

For as Conroy himself says, "*Body & Soul* is a real old-fashioned novel—a big fat book with a lot of people and a lot of plot." He was inspired by the romantic writers he read as a boy: Dickens, Tolstoy, Stendhal. "Those books kept me from going crazy. I *like* that old stuff." He gives a deep, chesty laugh. "I'm sorry, but I just *do*."

The laugh is genuine, and frequent, but not simply mirthful. The effects of the childhood he described in *Stop-Time* could not have rendered Conroy carefree. He is the son of an emotionally unbalanced man who spent most of his life in institutions, and a cold and irresponsible woman who withheld tenderness and love. The world of books was his solace and salvation, jazz improvisation his emotional therapy. His first wife, whom he met at Haverford College, took him into the milieu of New York's social register.

At 35, divorced after 12 years of marriage and "in bad shape emotionally," Conroy reluctantly left his two sons and Manhattan, and came to Nantucket. He supported himself (none too successfully) with freelance journalism and, during the summer months, by playing with jazz combos at island clubs. For a small price, he bought the five acres on which his house now stands, acquired the genuine barn beams from a farmer in Pennsylvania, and rounded up "eight hippies" to build it. Today, the gray-shingled house is weathered and snug, virtually one large open, high-ceilinged room with a view of woods and a pond. Comfortable and unpretentious, it is dominated by a beat-up piano that also serves as a haphazard bookshelf. Toys belonging to Tim, Conroy's six-year-old son from his second marriage, are scattered on the Oriental carpet.

Conroy fits his lanky six-foot frame into a canvas chair facing a well-used kitchen. A long lock of his once-blond hair, now faded to the color of coffee cream, falls across his forehead, and he brushes it back with an absentminded gesture. In a nearly two-hour conversation he uses a mild profanity twice, both times prefacing the vernacular expression with a courtly "excuse my French."

Though his name brings instant recognition in literary circles, Conroy considers himself primarily a teacher. He entered the profession when he was 40, a "late age" he regards as an advantage in preserving his enthusiasm. Even during the years (1981–1987) when he served as Director of the Literature Program at the National Endowment for the Arts, he insisted on teaching at least one class. And he finds working with students the most gratifying part of his job as head of the Writers Workshop. Houghton Mifflin has arranged his tour for *Body & Soul* so that he'll be back in Iowa for his classes each week.

To Conroy himself, it's quite logical that he has written only three books to date. "I really never thought of writing as a career. Although *Stop-Time* was a critical success (and has never been out of print in paperback), I never got any signals that I could make a living as a writer. So I had to look elsewhere to figure out how I was going to support myself."

Stop-Time sold only 7000 copies when it first appeared from Viking in 1967, despite a "terrific editor," Aaron Asher, who "did what he could," but could not surmount the '60s atmosphere. "Everybody was taking drugs and making love, and here was this sort of neoclassical memoir. It was just the wrong time for it to come out." In the wake of the excitement attending *Body & Soul*, Viking Penguin is now issuing new editions of *Stop-Time* and *Midair*. New translations are in the works, too.

Much credit for the upsurge in his fortunes, Conroy claims,

should go to his agent, Candida Donadio, and to Seymour Lawrence, his editor for *Midair* (published under his imprint at Dutton) and *Body & Soul.* Donadio "found" Conroy more than three decades ago, when a few chapters of *Stop-Time* appeared in the *New Yorker.* "She's the smartest person I know, both as a reader and as an agent," Conroy says. "What's nice is that now, finally, she will make a lot of money. She deserves it; she hung in with me for 30 years, when other people probably thought I was dead."

Sam Lawrence, whom Conroy calls "an impresario, the Sol Hurok of the publishing world," has been the guiding angel of *Body & Soul.* "Bob Stone and I were speaking at a conference in Key West," Conroy recalls, "and during lunch at Sam's house there, he gave me a tip about buying some stock. I told him I didn't have any stock, or money to buy any, either.

"Sam is loyal to his writers. It's his hallmark virtue," Conroy continues. Determined to improve Conroy's fortunes, Lawrence and Donadio decided to show the first 200 pages of *Body & Soul* to a few people in Hollywood. "Then everything went crazy. It leaked from those four people to all the studios, from Hollywood to Europe. At Frankfurt, everyone came to Sam about it. He wasn't even planning to offer it; it was a long way from finished." After the feedback at ABA, Houghton Mifflin raised the initial printing of the book. Conroy still seems astonished by the hubbub. "I'm very heartened," he says.

Perhaps his cautious elation comes from his sense that he has pulled off a risky undertaking: into the form of a bildungsroman he has managed to pack a great deal of musical background. This entailed night courses at Juilliard and "a tremendous amount of reading and research. I wanted to go back and learn everything over again—and learn it right," he says.

As indicated in the Author's Note, he is "deeply indebted" to Peter Serkin, who served as the book's unofficial vetter. The two met a decade ago when Conroy did a profile of the pianist for *Esquire.* "Once I was launched on the book, I thought of him," he says. "He's a very generous man, and very cultured. He looked at the manuscript, 100–150 pages at a time over the course of five years, made marginalia and sent it back to me. That allowed me to take chances that I otherwise would have been afraid to do."

Because of Serkin's enthusiasm, Conroy feels sanguine about readers' responses to the explanations of musical theory and descriptions of concertos, symphonies and jazz arrangements. "I think readers are interested in process," he says, "if it is *conveyed* as a process: the natural development of a child who's being taught by people who really care about music. As the child learns it, so can the reader."

While the title may suggest the familiar song, Conroy had other reasons for choosing it. "The concept of the body and the concept of the soul seemed to me to be what the book was really about. I knew that most people would immediately think of that song, but I also hoped that they would examine the phrase both in terms of the novel's musical component and in terms of the love story," he says.

What remains mysterious to Conroy is the manner in which the characters became so vividly alive to him. "Maggie [his wife] talks about last summer as the summer I wasn't here. I was so involved with the characters I walked around in a daze. That's every writer's dream, a situation when you don't have to push the story or flog it: you just have to follow it."

Another mystery is his choice of his protagonist's surname. Tobey Rawlings was the name Conroy gave to his boyhood friend in *Stop-Time.* He had originally used the boy's real name, Conroy recalls, "but the lawyers made me change every name in the book except my own." He says he has no idea why he elected to bestow it again on Claude in *Body & Soul.*

Though the resemblance between Conroy's youth and that of Claude Rawlings is hardly coincidental, Conroy's use of his boyhood memories was a far different emotional experience this time. The memoir resulted from an "almost therapeutic" need to exorcise his childhood. "Ted Solotaroff said the engine behind *Stop-Time* was anger. If *Stop-Time* was anger, *Body & Soul* is love, largely because of the relationship between Claude and Weisfeld."

In granting Claude an incredible string of good luck, Conroy concedes that he has made the novel "in many respects a fairy tale." That was part of his pleasure. "The material was exhilarating. It was like being in a sailboat on a perfect day. The wind is going, the sun is shining, the ropes are tight. The boat is just *tearing* through the water."

Describing the serendipity of discovering the book's epigram— "That which thy fathers have bequeathed to thee, earn it anew if thou wouldst possess it"—Conroy bolts from his chair into the

47

kitchen and takes down a well-worn copy of *The Joy of Cooking*. "I get sort of manic at the end of the day when I'm writing," he says, in what at first seems like a non sequitur. "My head is bouncing all over the place. I have a couple of beers, then I cook dinner. It helps me reenter." One day he happened to flip to the front of the cookbook and the epigram from Goethe's *Faust* leaped out at him.

"I felt a thrill go through me. I said: 'That's it, that's what I'm writing about!' " The loving protection of fathers, the ineluctable blessing of love, the empowerment of knowledge, the joy of music, that indeed is what *Body & Soul* is all about.

SYBIL S. STEINBERG
August 23, 1993

DENNIS COOPER

IN THE TRADITION OF the best grass-roots art, Dennis Cooper has been publishing his poetry and fiction at the margins of the cultural marketplace, in fanzines, chapbooks and obscure literary journals, since graduating from high school in the early 1970s. Yet many of Cooper's readers know only his more recent work, a series of slim and startling books from Grove Press—the novels *Closer* and *Frisk* and the short-story collection *Wrong*—each an ice-cold glimpse of gay teenage sexual turmoil, drug abuse and obsessive violence rendered in his signature spare and meticulous narrative style.

At once clinical and creepily meditative, Cooper's fiction has been championed by some as a bold, dystopian vision of sexual desire and moral laxity in contemporary life, but it has also proven too unsavory for others. Even Cooper's books with Grove have until now remained cultish and marginal: his emotionally drained, gay teen and 20-something characters are hustlers, punk rockers, artists and loners who fill their time with anonymous sex, horror films, amateurish artistic ventures and random acts of self-mutilation.

With the publication of *Try* by Grove/Atlantic, Cooper may finally win over a much wider audience. *Try* is a wrenching portrait of a manic teenager named Ziggy who is sexually brutalized, in excruciating detail, by his two gay foster fathers. Spaced out, deeply confused and magnetically sexy, Ziggy ditches high school, struggles to articulate his own emotional turmoil by publishing a fanzine about his sexual abuse and devotes himself to his best friend, a hopelessly strung-out writer. *Try* presents a broader spectrum of male, female, gay and straight characters, and a far more compassionate view of the complexities of human relationships than any of Cooper's previous books, broadening the horizons of his fictional world while retaining its stylistic tautness and its power.

Cooper receives us in his modest East Hollywood apartment on a sunny Saturday a few days after the Los Angeles earthquake. Compared to the malevolent look of his publicity photos, the 41-year-old author, dressed casually in a T-shirt, black jeans and white Converse sneakers, is genial, with pale, angular features that give him a lanky and ascetic appearance. Asked how he's weathered the earthquake and its aftershocks, Cooper admits, "I'm really enjoying it. I know it's terrible, but I grew up with it."

Like the disaffected teens of his fiction, Cooper came of age, in his own estranged and unhappy fashion, in Arcadia, Calif., an improbably named affluent Los Angeles suburb. "I was raised very badly," he points out. "I was a mess and miserable and did a lot of drugs." Cooper attended a private boys' school and began writing obsessively after discovering Baudelaire and the Marquis de Sade at the age of 15. At that stage, he explains, "I was writing these weird parodies. I wrote this whole novel that was based on *The 120 Days of Sodom,* and I took all the guys in high school that I wanted to sleep with and I cast them in it and just killed them off."

Cooper was expelled from private school in 11th grade, which raises the question of whether his subsequent fixation with high school reflects a desire to come to grips with whatever trauma he experienced at that age. "There's no literal event it's about," he shrugs. "I set them in high school because I like young people, and because I just resist the adult world." Cooper's voyeuristic fascination with adolescent runaways, punks and social castoffs has led some to view him as the Jean Genet of the American suburbs. Indeed, the glory that Cooper, like Genet, finds in social abjection reflects a relentless revolt against authority, and adults appear in Cooper's fiction in the most reprehensible roles—as serial killers, cold-blooded fetishists or drunk and neglectful parents. "I always hated adults, and I still do," he observes nonchalantly. "Most of my heroes were rock stars or writers, so I had imaginary adult mentors more than real mentors."

But, according to Cooper, the conflicted desires and hang-ups of adolescence make the strongest grist for his fiction. "It's a point at which your childhood's eating at you and adulthood's eating at you and you're just in chaos. I feel like that's the *truth* or something. People in that state are in touch with what the world's really about."

Cooper's work is also about the ephemeral, awkward beauty of teenaged boys, and throughout his fiction, there is one recurrent physical type, a thin, pale, sleepy-eyed figure with smooth skin and untidy dark hair who tends to subsume all others. Cooper acknowledges that many of his friends are much younger than he is and that the cadences of adolescent slang and the linguistic turmoil of teenagers attempting to give weight to authentic emotions without sounding clichéd remain a powerful source of inspiration. "What I love about living in L.A. is that type of inarticulate grasping for clarity. The way those kids talk, it's very poetic. I find them incredibly sympathetic."

Choosing to emulate literary rebels like Rimbaud and Genet, Cooper dropped out of school after a year at Pitzer College in Claremont, Calif. A prolific period of writing and publishing followed, and in 1976, Cooper launched *Little Caesar*, a literary journal which he sought to infuse with the anarchic spirit and do-it-yourself ethic of the nascent punk scene. He also began publishing volumes of his own poetry, including *Tiger Beat* (Little Caesar Press, 1978), *Idols* (Seahorse Press, 1979) and *The Tenderness of Wolves* (Crossing Press, 1981). In 1983, he composed a prose poem called "My Mark," a gritty, Petrarchan reverie for an estranged lover that was incorporated into *Safe*, a novella published a year later by Seahorse Press. Shortly thereafter, he stopped writing poetry altogether.

Cooper reflects with some dismay on his early writing and is not eager to see much of it reprinted. *Safe* was reissued by Grove/Atlantic last year in the short-story collection *Wrong*, a hodgepodge of older sketches and stories which Cooper now wishes had never been assembled. "*Wrong* has a bunch of horrible old stuff in it," he says. "I wish it hadn't happened. My agent did *Wrong* as a two-book deal to get me a little extra money. I like about five things in it and the rest just embarrasses me."

When *Safe* was first published, however, in 1984, Cooper suddenly gained the attention of mainstream New York publishers. Jonathan Galassi, then an editor at Random House, expressed interest in his next project, so Cooper moved to Amsterdam and confidently began work on *Closer*. "I was so naïve, I thought, wow, this is pretty much a guarantee he's going to publish it, so I wrote it for him. And I sent it to him as soon as it was finished and he didn't like it at all." Agentless and still living in Amsterdam, Cooper persuaded his friend, the late Chris Cox, then an editor at Ballantine, to pitch the manuscript to Michael Denneny and other major editors of gay fiction. "Nobody wanted it," he explains. "And I was pretty despairing." Eventually Ira Silverberg, then publicity director of Grove, showed it to Walt Bode, Grove's editor-in-chief, who bought the manuscript for $2000 on the condition that Cooper rewrite the first chapter. Silverberg has been Cooper's agent ever since.

Closer is an ingenious conceptual study of a circle of solipsistic high school boys centering around the angelic, drugged-out George Miles, who is seduced by an older man whose fetish is to inject his lovers with novocaine and dissect them. Cooper claims to have derived the pitiless, uninflected style of *Closer* from the French filmmaker Robert Bresson. "No one's seen his work but he's like my god. There's a kind of monotony to it and a kind of hermeticism. In *Closer*, what I was trying to do was to flatten everything out into these equal paragraphs so it's almost like you're watching a train track, so it would numb everything out."

Closer also relates the serial iconography of the mass media to the repetition-compulsion of serial murder, a theme Cooper explored fully in his next novel, *Frisk*, published by Grove two years later. "By the time I was finishing *Closer*, I knew what I didn't like about it anymore," Cooper explains. "I wanted to work on the violence more. That's what *Frisk* came out of." *Frisk* depicts the fantasy life of a character named Dennis, who at age 13 encounters some snuff photos of a disemboweled teenager. Obsessed with the notion of killing the boys he picks up for casual sex, Dennis later moves to Amsterdam and pens a letter home describing a series of ritualistic murders he claims to have committed, but which prove to be imaginary.

More thoroughly than his previous work, *Frisk* evinces Cooper's fascination with human flesh and with the sexually laden pathological desire to open the body up to explore its secret interior. "I believe Sade," Cooper states bluntly. "The information about life was there, the horror and power abuse. The idea that the body is this package, there's no spirit or anything, it's just this machine and if you take apart the machine then you'll understand it, but you'll never understand it even then. Life's so hopeless. *Frisk* was a confrontation," he adds. "*Frisk* seduced you into believing something was true, and then left you with your own pleasure or whatever you got out of that experience."

Although Cooper has avoided the denunciation one might expect from the political right (as Edmund White observed, "This is the very stuff of Jesse Helms' worst nightmares"), he has been the target of much criticism from gay-rights activists. During the book tour for *Frisk*, says Cooper, "People would come up to me and say: you have no right to do this." The most shattering attack followed a reading at A Different Light in San Francisco, where Cooper was approached by two men who handed him a pamphlet headlined "Dennis Cooper must die." It consisted of drawings and quotes from the savage reviews in area gay papers. "I freaked out," Cooper recalls. The pamphlet had been produced by a faction of Queer Nation, which had conducted a literal-minded reading of his work and deemed it politically dangerous. "The idea was that fiction was real, and that by killing them in my fiction I had really tried to kill them. It didn't make a lot of sense." Cooper eventually found a mutual friend who put him in touch with the director of the group, and the death threat was officially lifted.

Nevertheless, he is still dogged by criticism that his work is sadistic and politically irresponsible. "My response is that for better or worse, gay identity doesn't interest me. It never has. Everybody in my work, until the new book, has been gay. It's a hermetic world, it's a closed system. And they're not interested in their sexual identity. It's one of the few things that isn't a problem for them. They're totally happy about being gay. *I'm* totally happy with being gay. If anything, being gay should allow a massive amount of freedom in terms of the imagination. So I feel like that's just pure policing."

Cooper contends that such literal interpretations often fail to grasp the experimental ideas and complex aesthetic effects he seeks to achieve in his books. "I always want them to come from a place that's not conventional and then only get conventional when they absolutely have to make a point or to keep the eye moving down the page." In *Try*, however, Cooper avails himself of more traditional narrative techniques, and as a result, Ziggy is one of the most nuanced and sympathetic case studies in child abuse in recent fiction. Cooper acknowledges that when he wrote the novel, he was breaking off a long-term relationship and, like

Ziggy, was trying to care for a friend who was addicted to heroin. "It was a really deep fucked-up period in my life. The book was kind of to ground myself in the real world." He adds, "Ziggy's the first character I've ever done who is trying to understand what's happening to him. And he hasn't gotten very far, but he's trying, and that's like a big step."

Although pleased with the security he's found at Grove, Cooper is wary of attracting too much attention with his new book. "It's tricky. I like the margins. I've always admired artists who've made an incredibly narrow, obsessive body of work. I feel like I'm mining this stuff that's really like a psychosis for me. It's really personal, and I'm gonna keep doing it until I'm bored with it."

JONATHAN BING
March 21, 1994

LEN DEIGHTON

THOUGH MOST AUTHORS would give their eyeteeth for publicity, Len Deighton, best known for his British espionage thrillers beginning with *The Ipcress File*, hasn't granted an interview in at least 10 years. The publicist at HarperCollins, who is trying to promote Deighton's new book, *Violent Ward*, has never spoken to the author, doesn't know where he lives, doesn't know if he's married or if he has children. To set up an interview during Deighton's visit to Los Angeles, we call the publicist, who faxes the agent, Jonathan Clowes, in London, who, one assumes, contacts the author. After a time and place are agreed upon—a hotel coffee shop, with the reservation under our name—the whole communication process works in reverse. Two days before the interview, as Los Angeles waits nervously for a verdict on the Rodney King beating, Deighton's wife (so he has a wife!) calls to verify. She leaves a number—not her own, mind you, but that of a go-between—and an alternate plan is formulated in case the verdict comes in and the city erupts once again in violence. Either Len Deighton *is* a spy—which book jacket photos of him in a trenchcoat certainly suggest—or he's doing a superb job imitating the suspicion, intrigue and mystery of a clandestine agent.

Contrary to every expectation, Deighton turns out to be an affable, outgoing man. Within minutes, he's describing his home— a 250-year-old house perched on rocks above the sea in Portugal; his wife, a Dutch woman who's fluent in eight languages; and his two sons, who have lived and attended school in 10 countries in the last 15 years. A clever disguise for a clever espionage agent? Hardly. Just consider the man's work habits. There simply couldn't be enough time in the day to write as prolifically as he does and still do his bit for the British Empire.

Since 1962, Deighton has published 36 or so books: 23 novels, guidebooks to London, three cookbooks (including *French Cook-*

ing in 50 Lessons—which grew out of his cooking comic strip for the London *Observer*—and *The Action Cookbook*), nonfiction works (*Fighter: The True Story of the Battle of Britain, Airshipwreck* and *Blitzkrieg: From the Rise of Hitler to the Fall of Dunkirk*), and technical treatises on the postal system of Germany in 1928 and the flying post office of the Graf Zeppelin. He's been published in this country by a veritable smorgasbord of houses: Simon & Schuster, Putnam, Harper & Row, Mysterious Press, Atheneum, Holt, Rinehart & Winston, Harcourt Brace Jovanovich and Knopf.

In 1989, after *Spy Line* was issued, and after his editor Bob Gottlieb left Knopf for the *New Yorker*, Deighton moved to HarperCollins, where he received what was described at the time as a $10 million deal for four books: *Spy Sinker* (the last in the Bernard Samson series), *MAMista* (a tale of revolution and espionage set in a South American jungle), *City of Gold* (set in WW II Egypt), and now *Violent Ward* (which takes place during last year's Los Angeles riots). To support Deighton's latest effort, HarperCollins has planned a $100,000 marketing campaign and is sending Deighton on a five-city tour.

The author's daily routine is anything but suspenseful. By 9:00 a.m. every day he is at work on his word processor. At 1:00, his wife serves his lunch and he listens to the news on the radio or TV. At 2:30, he goes back to his office and works until 7:00, when he and wife have dinner, after which he attends to the mail and looks at the newspaper. Just before bedtime, at 10:30, he reads through what he has written during the day. He follows this routine six days a week, and works on Sundays until lunchtime. He doesn't smoke. He doesn't drink. He's simply a working machine who says he never gets tired, just "optical tired."

Deighton took a circuitous route to the career that has brought him fame and fortune. A native of London, he was raised in a house that epitomized the highest strata of society. He often tells people, "I was born in a house with 15 servants," then adds that his mother was the cook and his father the chauffeur. His first ambition was to be an artist. At the age of 18, he was drafted into the RAF, where he became a photographer, shooting operations in a service hospital and dashing to crime and accident scenes with investigative units. Two years later, he took advantage of the British equivalent of the GI Bill and entered St. Martin's School of Arts; then he attended the Royal College of Art. After graduation, he moved to New York where he worked as a magazine illustrator for *Esquire* and *Good Housekeeping*, and occasionally got a chance to design a book jacket.

In 1960, while on a three-month working vacation in the Dordogne, Deighton began writing *The Ipcress File*—purely "for fun. I had the book around for a long time," he notes. "I'd work on it, put it aside, go on vacation again, work some more. I thought I'd go on that way for the next 20 years."

A series of fortuitous events changed all that. At a party in London, he met agent Jonathan Clowes, who soon afterward sold Deighton's manuscript to Hodder & Stoughton in London and to Bob Gottlieb, then at Simon & Schuster. The book was optioned by producer Harry Saltzman, who had just finished his first James Bond film, *Dr. No*, which, according to Deighton, was bruited in advanced as a sure flop. The surprising success of that movie sparked an interest in the espionage genre, and *The Ipcress File* did very well. Later, the film would make a star of Michael Caine—whose first hardcover book purchase had been *The Ipcress File*—and the producer would ask Deighton to consider writing a sequel.

"I didn't know what a serial character was," says Deighton. "It had taken me several years to write *The Ipcress File*, but I was so caught up in the exciting milieu that had come to me I said I'd do two a year." Eventually Deighton was to produce another half-dozen books featuring the character of Harry Palmer. Not coincidentally, he became a magnet for people who claimed either that they were spies or the friends of spies. Most of the information he learned in this way was anecdotal; he incorporated much of it into his books, giving them the ring of authenticity.

As his readership continued to grow, Deighton began to explore the difference between English and American literary tastes. "I think Somerset Maugham said that it's a characteristic of English literature that no one knows how to plot anything. English writers care about atmosphere, character and motivation. But in America, plot is very important. In this country, all you have to do is go into a restaurant, order a ham sandwich and a martini, and you'll see a whole story unfold. Do you want rye or wheat, mayo or butter, the martini up or on the rocks? Americans are very immersed in the precision of the language. Americans read a work of fiction like a menu—what kind of ham sandwich will it be? If you bring the British demands for atmosphere and character together with the American demands for precision and plot, then you can have a very good book."

To meet these demands, Deighton works five years in advance, planning several books at a time. Once he decides to go ahead with a particular concept, he spends six months on plot and research. "One of the richest things in a writer's life is that people will cooperate with you," he says. That cooperation has put him in the back of an F-4, the cockpit of a Concorde, the kitchen of the Savoy and the backseat of an LAPD squad car.

Perhaps his books are compulsively over-researched, Deighton muses, but his reasons run deep. "All you need is a profound inferiority complex: no training as a writer and growing up a victim of the English class system." He thinks his persistence pays off. "Americans want all the loose ends tied up. If I forget something, I can always put it in the next book," he says.

For a man who professes not to "mix with writers much," preferring the company of cops, private investigators and artists, he is quite forthcoming with thoughts about writing and the business of publishing: "Plot is always the product of the scene in which it's set." "I always tell illustrators that book jackets are to prevent people who won't like the book from buying it and badmouthing it." "I tell young writers to write a blurb, pin it up and write to it." In a more expansive moment, he says: "For simplicity, I say there's no such thing as art. There's only entertainment. Once you say that, a lot of things become clarified. It's the difference between Renoir and Andy Warhol. The first needs no assistance from anyone to be entertaining. The second has a terrible need to be explained. When you think in terms of entertainment, the work can be so much broader.

The Bernard Samson series is probably Deighton's most successful "entertainment." The seed was planted when a philandering friend asked Deighton to cover for him if his wife called. "I didn't like that, so I suppose I thought about it more than I would have otherwise," Deighton remembers. The writer part of him began to muse: "If you have a man, a spy, who's married to another spy, then their marriage becomes a matter of life and death." Deighton hung a chart on his office wall and began to plot the first six Sampson novels, which would tell the story of how English agents helped to bring down the Berlin Wall.

The first three—*Berlin Game* (1984), *Mexico Set* (1985) and *London Match* (1986)—end up with Fiona Samson defecting to the east, the next two—*Spy Hook* (1988) and *Spy Line* (1989)—bring her back, and the final one—*Spy Sinker* (1990)—ties together all the "loose ends." In 1987, between the two trilogies, Deighton wrote *Winter*, which covered the story of Bernard Samson's family as well as 50 years of German history. "When I started writing the series, I had no idea the Wall would actually come down. But I think that even if that hadn't happened, the story still would have been valid. There were signs in the German economy that it *might* happen, but it could have taken another 10 years."

His prescient writer's instinct again came into play with *Violent Ward*. Four years ago, he thought up the title and created the characters. When he finally sat down to write the book, he already suspected that Mickey Murphy—a criminal lawyer with a house in the San Fernando Valley and an office in the low-rent district of downtown L.A.—would become another serial character. "Here I was writing a book called *Violent Ward* and all of a sudden the first Rodney King verdict came in and pop, pop. The riots certainly weren't part of the planning, but there they were."

The book owes much to the tradition of Raymond Chandler. "I grew up reading Chandler. I think he was able to produce a wonderful effect by combining the serious and the funny," Deighton observes. *Violent Ward* also presented the author with the opportunity to write about Southern California, where he has taken to spending several months a year, avoiding the rainy seasons of whatever country he is living in at the time.

Deighton is currently putting the finishing touches on a 15-year project, a 700-page nonfiction book titled *Blood, Tears and Folly*. He calls it "a hobby. The book asks the question, 'If we won the war, why are the Japanese and the Germans so rich?' " Deighton elucidates. "It's a history of World War II that attempts to show that some things are inevitable."

Once *Blood, Tears and Folly* is behind him, Deighton will go back to his five-year plan. He's working on notes for his next novel and putting together some ideas for another cookbook. Bernard Samson fans will be pleased to know that Deighton has hung a chart on his office wall and is plotting another three-book series tentatively called *Faith, Hope* and *Charity*. (So far, no publisher has been announced for these four books.)

Finally, Len Deighton has come in from the cold, as it were, leaving the solitude of his word processor to display his considerable charm to a long-ignored public. "I advise writers to do publicity," he says. Realizing the irony of this statement, he laughs, then adds, "I always have good advice, but I don't always follow it myself. Interviews are very stressful for me. The greatest thing you can tell a writer is, 'You don't have an interview appointment for 10 years.'"

LISA SEE
July 12, 1993

E. L. DOCTOROW

THE AUSTRALIAN NOVELIST Peter Carey, a very visible public figure in his native land, once told E. L. Doctorow, who is one of America's supreme novelists but hardly a public figure at all, how amazed he was by Doctorow's ability to fade into the woodwork. He's right. Meeting the great American writer on a sparkling spring afternoon in a Greenwich Village cafe much frequented by writers, we enjoyed an almost two-hour conversation with him without a head being turned in his direction.

Doctorow is a slight, bearded figure with a broad forehead and an alert but brooding gaze, who seems younger than his 63 years. He speaks quietly, thinking carefully before he utters a word. He seems to wonder, much as an interviewer does, how he achieves his stirring effects, where his dramatic visions come from. In the case of *The Waterworks*, the highly praised novel about New York City in the 1870s just out from Random House, its predecessor is in plain view: a short story with the same title in his 1984 collection, *Lives of the Poets*. But that is much less than half the tale—for where did *that* waterworks come from?

"I don't know," says Doctorow. "Perhaps it was an embellished dream. But it was very haunting. It wouldn't go away, and two novels later [*World's Fair* and *Billy Bathgate*] I found I was still thinking about it. It seemed, judging by the people's clothes, to be in the 19th century, and so were the buildings of the waterworks. I'd seen pictures of the old reservoir with its towers, on 42nd Street in New York, where Bryant Park and the Public Library are now, and became aware that was still in my mind."

Born of that fleeting vision, the observer in the short story became McIlvaine, the elderly newspaperman who narrates the novel, and the shadowy stranger he follows becomes Sartorius, the novel's mad-genius doctor who creates a form of eternal life for elderly millionaires by preying on children. Once the images

61

are in his mind, Doctorow says, "I try to tease out of them what it is I find so evocative. Sometimes it's a struggle, but the extent of the struggle never seems to have any bearing on how it comes out." He laughs. "When someone asked Dickens what was his own favorite among his books, he said *David Copperfield*, because it was the easiest."

In the case of *The Waterworks*, a number of themes gathered. "One was of generational betrayal and reversal, a reversal of the normal succession, a questioning of previous generations, like Clinton in the postwar era with Bush and his World War II generation—that occurred to me, as I was writing, during the elections. Then, too, I had the strong sense of New York at that time, as a period of furious energies—my New York is not at all Edith Wharton's—and I was much attracted to the idea of a kind of culture that begins as enlightenment and turns into a kind of prison. I also had the idea that the villains of the time were all elusive, and I liked that. So although Boss Tweed is a presence in the book, I don't bring him in; and Sartorius himself is more a philosophical concept than a person. I have this kind of attraction to figures who achieve great things and then continue on to the point where they pass beyond the pale of acceptability, from glory to absurdity. Look at Wilhelm Reich at the end, with his orgone box!" he exclaims, referring to the great behavioral scientist who ended his life as an apparent confidence trickster.

Finding a narrative voice is an important endeavor for Doctorow: "Somehow all my books are deductions from the first sentence, and the tone has to be just right." In the case of *Waterworks*, he wanted a voice that was struggling with its own perceptions. "McIlvaine is very much a man trying to communicate a dark, complex story, and there are a lot of pauses while he gropes for a word, as a man to whom language is important, so I put in a lot of ellipses." Too many? He is scrupulously fair. "I can imagine it might be an irritation to some readers. The copy editor and I discussed it, and we even took some of them out."

Doctorow shares technical problems with a rare freedom. "Who is the narrator talking to? In Conrad you have him settling down in the club, with the chaps, lighting his pipe, then of course that all gets abandoned. I thought I might have McIlvaine dictating his account, but then the person he is dictating to becomes the audience, and that in turn affects what he says. In the end I wanted it to be a *tale,* to participate in the telling of a tale as it was known in the 19th century: *The Rime of the Ancient Mariner,* for instance."

Research, for the meticulously visualized mise-en-scène of New York six years after the Civil War? Not much, really: "There was a Dover book of photographic street scenes, and a wonderful book of steel engravings of machinery of the time." He is certainly aware that each of his half-dozen books of the last two decades has focused on aspects of New York, touching down just after the turn of the century (*Ragtime*), in the '20s and '30s (*Loon Lake, World's Fair, Billy Bathgate*) and in the present (*Lives of the Poets*). "Presenting New York at different times and from different angles isn't what I set out to do, but it's definitely the field I work," he acknowledges with a smile. As to a current minor spate of prominent novels set in the *Waterworks* period, notably Peter Quinn's *Banished Children of Eve* and Caleb Carr's *The Alienist,* he hasn't read them, but "if it shows there's an appetite for the time, that's all to the good." He continues: "There's been a lot of recycling of cultural materials in the last 25 years or so. Things keep popping up in different forms, and achieving their final reduction as rides in Disneyland!"

Does he think of himself as a historical novelist? "All fiction is historical fiction—if it isn't now, it will be later, if it lasts. The historical novel is one that endures."

As is apparent to any careful reader of Doctorow's supple, leaping, always surprising prose, he has a meticulous ear, and it comes as no surprise that he is a lover of poetry. "I read a lot of it, more probably than of fiction. I love the *sounds* that words make, the rhythm of sentences. Verbal music is very apparent to me, but I don't want it to control things. I would never force a line for the sake of a visual or musical effect, which is what a poet does." He advises students in his creative writing class at New York University to read plenty of poetry.

Uniquely among major American writers, Doctorow had a significant publishing career before settling down to become a supplier of material. During the 1960s, after a stint as a reader for Columbia Pictures, he became in turn an associate then senior editor at New American Library, and from 1964 to 1969 was editor-in-chief and later publisher at the Dial Press, during one of its most venturesome periods, which he remembers fondly as being infinitely more freewheeling than the publishing world of today. About the future of the trade in the hands of "conglomerate enterprises," he is not very optimistic: "I have always maintained that as long as a generation of classic book people was in charge of editorial questions, the line would be held. Good editors today form a kind of Sierra Club of literary ecology. What this will mean 20 years from now, when they're all gone or retired, I simply don't know."

He himself, however, has enjoyed a very long relationship with Random House, where he has been under contract since 1969 ("longer than most marriages," he comments wryly). His books there began in 1971 with *The Book of Daniel*, which, he says, "got me on the map critically and introduced me to a wider audience." *Ragtime* was a runaway success in 1975 and then a hit movie (though he has scant regard for the movies made so far from his books: "I regard them as mostly promotional devices"). On the departure from Random in 1978 of his then editor Jim Silberman, he was inherited by Jason Epstein, with whom he has worked happily ever since. Only once was the harmony ruffled, when Doctorow spoke out publicly at the time of the Pantheon affair, declaring that Random had "disfigured itself." "But nobody said anything to me about it, and it went away."

Doctorow speaks out on public and political issues more than most of his contemporaries and feels strongly this is something writers should do. "Writers have always shot their mouths off— look at Hemingway, Mark Twain—though people conducting the lit courses tend to forget it. There's a play by Yeats in which a poet demands a place in the nation's brain trust—though of course he's a dying poet, Yeats being Yeats!" The only problem he has with speaking out is a writerly one. "It's a question of diction. Using the terminology of political discourse can be a terrible danger for a writer. It was Auden who said that 'a writer's politics can be more of a danger than his cupidity.' So quite often I find that I don't say something when I think I should because I'm so wary of language that isn't my own, so it's a constant conflict. As a result I often have to disappoint people who think I'll sign something or say something, and I don't."

One reason he would *not* hold back is from any sense of timidity. "After one speech, someone came up to me and said how brave I'd been. Brave? What's so brave? What country did he think he was living in?"

Impressive samples of Doctorow the political thinker, including pieces he has written for the *Nation* and a combative 1989 commencement address at Brandeis University, can be found in a book of political and literary essays, *Jack London, Hemingway and the Constitution*, published late last year. "A book like that makes its way much more slowly than fiction," he says. "The reviews just trickle in, but, much to my astonishment, they've been 98% favorable. Everything's on a different scale with such a book. I don't even know how many Random printed."

For his next outing, Doctorow says, "There's lots in my head, but nothing has stepped forward yet to say, 'This is it.' I've always wanted to be at work on my next book when I publish the present one, but so far I've never managed it. I seem to need a certain period of recovery. But I believe by the summer I'll be at work again."

One of the major items on his horizon, of course, is Booknet, the 24-hours-a-day, books-only cable TV series he and two business and legal colleagues announced last year, and which inspired huge interest in the book community. Doctorow remains deeply involved in the notion, though progress on implementing it has slowed since the euphoric early days. "Young people now define themselves through music and film, they live in an electronic world; so much so that what we do has acquired a name, Print Culture, with scholars debating its historical meaning and its possible end. As we approach the millennium, everyone gets nervous about being seen to be living in the past. So Booknet is an essential way to combine *our* culture and the other one. It could do marvelous things for the whole book industry, including booksellers."

There have been some problems, Doctorow acknowledges. "There's developed a bit of a bottleneck in cable channels, which haven't expanded as fast as we expected. And many companies have been made nervous by the new regulatory tone coming out of the FCC, and the Supreme Court ruling on relations between the networks and the cable companies. All these things have paralyzed investment and expansion, so things are on hold at the moment. But it's clear that when the logjam begins to move we'll be moving too. We were offered three hours a day on a multicultural network, but we turned that down, and someone else offered to buy us out entirely. We get inquiries every day. But we're sticking to our original idea. We have a detailed business plan, and I have reason to believe something good can be announced in three or four months."

What role is there for him in Booknet, beyond his present one as public spokesperson? "None," he laughs. "I just want to see it happen, and as soon as it does I'm out of there. You know, the more I see of business, the more I realize how lucky I am to be in something that requires just one person in a room with the door closed."

JOHN F. BAKER
June 27, 1994

HARRIET DOERR

THERE ARE A LOT of things that Harriet Doerr, author of *Stones for Ibarra* and her new novel *Consider This, Senora*, from Harcourt Brace, won't discuss. "I don't talk about the olden days," she responds when asked about her youth. "I don't talk about my family history. I don't talk about my antecedents, just about me," she answers when asked what brought her family to Pasadena just after the turn of the century. "Don't put that in," she commands, after telling a story about her stint at Stanford as a writing student. "Don't put in anything about my health. I'll sue you if you do," she adds.

Doerr lives in a grand old house in Pasadena surrounded by hedge-rimmed gardens designed years ago as individual "rooms" for citrus trees, roses and an English garden. She lives alone. A Guatemalan woman comes in for day work; another woman drops by to help with accounting and such. At 83, Doerr is small and birdlike. Her hair is white. Her eyes, a watery blue, deliver a piercing stare when a reporter brings up any of several forbidden topics.

If pressed, Doerr will speak—fleetingly—about her childhood. She remembers orange groves, fields of poppies, picnics in arroyos and "mustard everywhere, instead of building projects." She will admit that her family came to Pasadena "via the East," but little else. They lived in a brown shingle house. The mailman drove a pony cart. Her mother played the piano, had six children and never worked. Her father (occupation not disclosed) died when Doerr was 11.

Why so few details after a long and rich life? "There's something about old age," Doerr ventures. "It's nature's anesthetic. You gradually forget the very worst things unless you consciously remember the bad things—like the little punishments you wish you hadn't given your children." She concludes, "Memory and imagination are so closely intertwined."

She does reveal a few more facts of her youth: in 1927 Doerr joined friends in applying to Vassar, Wellesley and Smith. "I just witlessly went where my friends went." She attended Smith for a year but didn't care much for the Massachusetts winter. Besides, she had already met the Stanford man she was going to marry. In her sophomore year, she transferred to Stanford, where she continued to work on her history major. In 1930 she wed Albert Edward Doerr and, over the next 40 years, had two children and did "good works": helping at the dispensary and raising money for the Community Chest—activities that, Doerr now says, "sound absolutely useless but took up all my time."

During their life together, the Doerrs traveled frequently to Mexico. Albert, an engineer, had been born there, but his family—the owners of extensive land holdings, including a mine in central Mexico—had fled north during the revolution. Although raised in the U.S., he and his siblings considered themselves "from" Mexico, and Harriet too was soon swept up in a love of that country. In 1950, after Albert's father died, they moved to Mexico City for a year to take charge of the land he had accumulated, including the mine and an isolated strip along the Michoacan coast where the indigenous population spoke no Spanish.

"Here we were, in this really fancy place," Doerr reminisces, "but people would come by and throw their cars and dead animals down in the *barranca* [ravine]. That's one of the reasons I love Mexico. Not because of the dead animals, but because everything is mixed—funny, hopelessly sad, everything together."

Ten years later, the Doerrs began traveling between Pasadena and the mining town which she admits is the model for the community in *Stones for Ibarra.* "I can't tell you where it is exactly, except that it's on the central plateau," she says elliptically. "Chihuahua is north by a stretch; San Miguel de Allende and Guanajuato are to the south."

As for writing, she came to it late in life. Her high school's class poet, she wrote "terribly sentimental" poems heavily influenced by Edna St. Vincent Millay. Once married, she joined a "little housewives' group where we wrote little things and criticized them." Moreover, "it never would have occurred to me to write as a career, what with going back and forth to Mexico, having a husband and children. I certainly never thought I'd do it professionally. I didn't even keep a diary in Mexico—which I regret very much."

All that changed after her husband's death in 1972. ("Don't say passed away," she pleads. "I can't bear euphemisms. I just say he died.") Three years later, at age 65, and on a bit of a dare from her son and daughter, she enrolled at Scripps College, where she resumed work on her history major and took writing courses from Clive Miller.

The age difference between herself and other students was considerable, but not overwhelming. "You only know you're over the hurdle when they ask you to have a beer or invite you over to their house and you go, or you invite them to a party and they come." In 1975, after a 45-year hiatus, she transferred back to Stanford, where she enrolled in the classes of John L'Heureux, the guiding light of the university's writing program.

Upon graduating in 1978, she was accepted into the Stanford graduate fiction program. Under pressure to produce for class, she wrote a short story, 12 to 15 pages long, every five weeks. "I was absolutely by myself, and staying in this little apartment," she recalls. "It never would have occurred to me before to closet myself away from my husband like that, although he did at times [from me]."

Her love of Mexico kept Doerr's clear-sighted, graceful prose focused on the people and the life of the fictional village of Ibarra. Despite similarities between her own life and the life described in her first novel, Doerr insists that the book is not autobiographical. "I glamorized the place and changed the people."

After *Stones for Ibarra* was published, however, she gave copies to the people of the town. "They were happy to have it, even though they couldn't read it," she says. "Most of the people only have a second- or third-grade education. It's just as well, because they wouldn't recognize anything, not even the two Americans, and would find it frustrating."

In L'Heureux's class, students were encouraged to submit pieces to magazines and publishing houses. Six of Doerr's stories appeared in the *Art River Review,* one in the *Southern Review* and yet another in *Quarterly West.* In 1982, she won the *Transatlantic Review*'s Henfield Foundation Prize for her work. At the urging of one of her classmates, Ron Hansen (author of *Mariette in Ecstasy*), Doerr signed with agent Liz Darhansoff.

"The first couple of years, Liz didn't make enough money off me to pay for stamps," Doerr quips. Darhansoff sent out the work, but publishers didn't seem interested. "They would write rejections saying they liked the writing but they didn't understand what it was exactly—a reminiscence, short stories, a dreaming or what," Doerr recalls. "I called them linked stories." Then Viking's London scout suggested that Doerr submit her work to Cork Smith.

After having a look at several of the "linked stories," Smith suggested they be turned into a novel. If it hadn't been for Smith, Doerr says, the book never would have been published: "He's a man of few words and he's very patient." Doerr's loyalty is strong. When Smith moved to Ticknor & Fields, she followed. When he left there, he took the new book with him to Harcourt Brace.

And so, with help from L'Heureux, Doerr began to conceptualize the novel. Together they spread out the stories on her dining-room table and put them in order while L'Heureux made suggestions of where introductions and "a few joining things" might be added. Before leaving Stanford, L'Heureux suggested that she start on her next book. "He said, 'You've got to start now,' which I did. Then there was a long pause while all this other stuff intervened," she says modestly.

Stones for Ibarra was published in 1984, when Doerr was 73, and immediately took off, both in terms of book sales and critical acclaim. According to the *New York Times*, it was "a very good novel with echoes of Gabriel García Márquez, Katherine Anne Porter and even Graham Greene." In the *Washington Post*, Jonathan Yardley opined that Doerr had "mastered the art of fiction to a degree that would be remarkable in almost any writer of any age."

In addition to critical accolades and an NEA grant, she picked up an American Book Award for the novel, as well as fiction awards from the Bay Area Book Reviewer's Association, PEN Center USA West, the American Academy and Institute of Arts and Letters, and the Commonwealth Club of California. In 1988, Hallmark Hall of Fame produced a two-hour TV movie based on the book and starring Glenn Close.

Consider This, Senora has taken Doerr almost a decade to write, at an average of six months a chapter. During that time, two stories taken from it appeared in the *New Yorker*, while another ran in *Epoch*. "It was much slower going," Doerr explains. "Partly that was because of age, but partly because I had no fellow students to pounce on me. In class we would hand out copies of our work, and it would come back with all these comments like 'horrible word,' 'ugh' or 'fine' written in the margins. But at this age, you don't delay. You simply don't get more and more energy as time passes. That doesn't mean you're going out of your mind, but that finding the words you're looking for doesn't happen as quickly."

In addition, she also felt the pressure of trying to come up with a substantial encore to *Stones for Ibarra*. She grudgingly accepts that reviewers may be more critical of the new book after the huge success of her first. But what really seems to bother her is the possibility of appearing, in her words, "like a publishing freak." She adds, "I don't want critics to say, 'She's 83, what else do you expect?' You know, blaming any little flaws on the passage of time."

In *Consider This, Senora*, Doerr examines the lives of four North American expatriates living in a small Mexican village set on a barren mesa. Each of the characters—an artist, an ambitious investor fleeing tax-evasion charges, a lovelorn woman seeking true love and a 79-year-old widow, who was born in Mexico and has now returned to pass her remaining days and, if possible, make sense of life and love—encounter the Mexicans with sometimes tragic, sometimes confused, sometimes loving results.

As with *Stones for Ibarra*, random tragedy is always waiting to strike. "That happens," Doerr insists. "In a village you see it right before your very eyes. Here in the U.S., you see it on TV. In Mexico, calamity, contentment and joy seem to go hand-in-hand. The people are disposed to accept tragedy, and yet never feel it less. It's just part of the life they've been given." In portraying the people of Mexico, she tries not to come across as an ugly American. Her wish is that a reader will learn through her books to regard unfamiliar places and people with an open mind.

And again, as with *Stones for Ibarra*, Doerr claims that her characters are not "necessarily" autobiographical, not even Ursula Bowles, who is a widow. "All I have in common with Ursula is her age," she declares.

Is she sure? Consider this, written by Doerr from Ursula's perspective as she lies dying: "Our lives are brief beyond our comprehension or desire, she told herself. We drop like cottonwood leaves from trees after a single frost. The interval between birth and death is scarcely more than a breathing space. . . . She could see now that an individual life is, in the end, nothing more than a stirring of air, a shifting of light."

When asked if Ursula's view of life resembles her own, Doerr hesitates, then advises, "That's how she sees life, and I invented her." A moment later, she adds, "I'm trying to think up an elusive answer. How about, 'Up to a point?' "

LISA SEE
August 9, 1993

ERNEST J. GAINES

O<small>N THE PUBLICATION DAY</small> of *A Lesson Before Dying*, (Knopf) Ernest Gaines's sixth novel and his first in 10 years, the Louisiana-born author best known for *The Autobiography of Miss Jane Pittman* is in Chattanooga for the Conference on Southern Literature and an adjoining convocation of the Fellowship of Southern Writers.

Founded in 1987 to recognize outstanding writers from the region, the organization had inducted Gaines as one of 26 charter members. The weekend, then, is for him a combination of a book launching and a reunion with his literary peers.

A large, amiable man whose reticence easily yields to an animation belying his 60 years, Gaines is constantly stopped by well-wishers in the headquarters hotel lobby and between conference sessions as well. Many of those who greet him have a copy of the new novel for him to sign.

"*A Lesson* seems to be getting off to a good start," he comments to *PW* when the demand for his attention momentarily slackens. Indeed it is. In addition to the warm Chattanooga welcome, BOMC chose his eighth book as a May selection. The previous Sunday he was featured in a long profile in the *Atlanta Journal-Constitution*. Earlier this year, Gaines, who teaches creative writing at the University of Southwestern Louisiana in Lafayette and divides his calendar between there and San Francisco, was gratified by a TV documentary on his life that premiered on the Louisiana Public Broadcasting network and has since been shown on PBS. And now he is looking forward to another milestone—marriage (his first).

Gaines's formal role at the conference is to participate in a panel discussion titled "Fiction to Stage and Screen." *The Autobiography of Miss Jane Pittman*, *A Gathering of Old Men* and his much anthologized "The Sky Is Gray" from the *Bloodline* story collection have been adapted for TV, so he's well qualified to address the subject. But he bristles when another panelist, a well-known playwright and screenwriter, comments on the "sacrifice" made by a famous actress when she was paid "only $60,000" for a few months' work on a movie. Many writers, Gaines exclaims, support themselves for a year on much less.

Perhaps he was recalling his long apprenticeship at writing in San Francisco. "I know what it's like to live in one room and sleep on a Murphy bed, because I've done it," he says emphatically. In fact, his life as a writer represents a triumph of talent and determination over daunting odds.

Gaines first achieved publication in 1956, when a short story appeared in the *San Francisco State* magazine. (It caught the eye of agent Dorothea Oppenheimer, who thereafter represented him until shortly before her death in 1987, at which time she had placed her devoted client with the JCA agency.) Though in 1959 he earned acceptance to Stanford on a Wallace Stegner creative writing fellowship on the basis of his short fiction, he shifted his literary sights after listening to a visiting critic from New York. "He told us that no collections of stories by unknown writers were likely to be published; the novel had to come first. So I quit writing stories, but the only novel I could think to write was the one I had tried when I was in high school and had burned."

The oldest of six children, Gaines was brought up on the River Lake plantation in Point Coupee Parish, where black sharecroppers had lived in the "quarter" behind the big house since the slavery era. A bright, active child, he was a favorite in the quarter, but his education in Louisiana was limited to the five or six months between the plantation's harvesting and planting seasons. Classes were taught in a church that doubled as a one-room schoolhouse. Gaines later attended a small Catholic school in New Roads, a nearby town upon which he would later model his fictional Bayonne. "Had I remained in Louisiana two more years," Gaines surmises, "I would have been broken and become bitter," which is how the area's tenacious racism affected many of his male contemporaries from the quarter.

In 1948, when Gaines was 15, he left Point Coupee for California. His mother and stepfather, a sailor in the merchant marine, had moved to Vallejo across the bay from San Francisco during WW II, and he joined them, in part because the educational opportunities in California were much greater than those in his home state. The move opened the door to new horizons. As a teenager he was active in sports, and he joined the track team at the integrated high school he attended. But he found the door that opened widest at the Vallejo public library. In New Roads, the public library did not admit blacks.

At first he sampled the shelves indiscriminately. "I just pulled out books to see what they were about, but eventually I found I liked fiction the best. I suppose I was searching for myself, the South, or my people. When I couldn't find that—at the time, of course, there were few books published by or about blacks—I began reading books about peasantry."

He worked through Steinbeck and Willa Cather before moving on to the great Russian writers of the 19th century. Inspired by Turgenev's depictions of Russia's serfs, with whom he found parallels to the plantation slaves, he also began to write. "I was 17 when I thought I could write a novel and send it to New York and get it published. But I didn't know a damn thing about doing it; I didn't even know how to type. I started in longhand, but my mother rented me a typewriter, which I typed on with one finger. I must have used the cheapest paper I could find, because we couldn't afford anything else. I cut the paper in half, the size of a book, and typed on both sides, single space. I thought it was pretty good. I wrapped it in brown paper, tied a string around it, and sent the thing off. It came back, of course."

Gaines used $1,000 saved from a stint in the army to attend San Francisco State College. Later, a $2,500 Stegner Fellowship enabled him to enter the creative writing program at Stanford, where he studied under the master teacher and writer. He used a small amount remaining in his fellowship fund to support himself while he tried to produce a saleable book. "After that ran out, I got a job in the Post Office," he says, adding, with a deep, rolling chuckle, "all artists get a job in the Post Office; even Faulkner did at one point."

The plot outline from his first amateurish effort—a young black man returns from California to his native South and falls in love with a woman in his old community—remained stubbornly alive, and Gaines determined to do it justice this time around. It took him five years. "I tried every point of view I could think of, but nothing worked. I knew I *had* to write a novel, but the truth is I didn't know how," he admits. Turgenev's *Fathers and Sons* provided the answer. "It's about a young man who goes back home to visit his people. He's changed since he left and plans a short stay. Then he falls in love with a beautiful woman. That's what I was writing about, so all the moves Turgenev made I followed. *Fathers and Sons* was my Bible when I was writing *Catherine Carmier*."

The title of Gaines's first novel came from legendary editor Hiram Haydn at Atheneum, where the book was published in 1964. It met a cool response, however, and most of the 3500-copy first printing was remaindered. (Reprinted by North Point in the early '80s, it has been reissued as a Vintage trade paperback.) Nevertheless, Gaines had found the place and voices that would continue to engage him as sources for his fiction.

His next three books—the novel *Of Love and Dust*, a collection of short fiction called *Bloodline*, and the children's book *A Long Day in November*—were published by Dial when E. L. Doctorow was editor-in-chief. Each is set in the region of his boyhood, a place of sugarcane and cotton fields where the people who work them say "mon" for mother, "gallery" (or "garry") for porch, and "fair" for a house party. While he did not base any of his characters directly on the people he knew in the quarter, he freely used the sounds of their voices and concentrated on capturing the rhythm of their speech.

His beloved Aunt Augusteen was the inspiration for the 110-year-old former slave who is the title character in *The Autobiography of Miss Jane Pittman*, which has sold over a million copies worldwide since its 1971 publication. Miss Jane, he points out, "was never my aunt physically. Miss Jane goes everywhere and does everything, and my aunt, who was crippled and could only crawl, could not. I never saw Aunt Augusteen in front of me when I was writing, but I felt her spirit." He dedicated the book to Augusteen, "who did not walk a day in her life but who taught me the importance of standing."

Miss Jane Pittman, which he researched in Baton Rouge libraries, took him two and a half years to write, but he feels that it had germinated for 38 years, his age when it was published. "Probably I couldn't have written it had I not come from Louisiana. I grew up listening to the old people in the quarter, and all that I heard, in some way, I buried in my subconsciousness. I just didn't begin putting it down on paper until I was 35. I wrote letters for those folks, too, as young Jimmy—my middle name is James—does in the novel. As I said on the [LPB] documentary, I don't think I'm finished with those letters yet, although the people for whom I wrote them have been dead for 40 years or more. Maybe that's what I'm still trying to do as a writer."

Gaines says he has no particular audience in mind when he writes, just as he's certain that Turgenev, Joyce and Gertrude Stein—in whose *The Autobiography of Alice B. Toklas* he found the method he used to tell Miss Jane Pittman's life story—did not have him in mind either, although he's learned much from each.

"Wallace Stegner once asked me for whom I write, and I told him: no one. He said if he put a gun to me and forced an answer, what would I say? If he did that, I told him, I'd probably say I write for the black youth of the South, to make them aware of who they are. Who else? he asked. I said the white youth of the South, to make them aware that unless they understand their black neighbors they cannot understand themselves. But, in fact, I have no intention of addressing any group over another. It's dangerous for writers to think of their audience. I try to write as well as I can, and that's tough enough."

In his last three novels from Knopf, where his editor is Ashbel Green, Gaines has focused on men, and in *A Lesson Before Dying*, as well as *In My Father's House*, he confronts the separation of black men from each other and their loss of mutual support. "My thesis is that black fathers and sons were separated in Africa in the 17th century and have not come back together since. They can eat across the table, but that is not the same as coming together."

In *A Lesson Before Dying*, a black schoolteacher and a young black fieldworker sentenced to be electrocuted for a crime at which he was a bystander are forced to do just that. "I've written a lot about men going to jail, and there are schoolteachers throughout my books—it was about the only thing an educated black in the South in the '40s, the time of the novel, could do for a living. I wanted to bring them together and see what a schoolteacher would say to someone in jail."

The novel is authenticated by what he learned from two lawyers in Louisiana who had defended young black men sentenced to death (one was mildly retarded and another went through the ordeal twice, because the electric chair malfunctioned the first time.) The seed for *A Lesson Before Dying*, however, was planted in the '60s in San Francisco, where Gaines's apartment is near Alcatraz. When he knew an execution was to take place there, he became so agitated that he had to go for a long walk. "Knowing when a man was going to the gas chamber made work impossible," he notes. Then he discovered that in Louisiana in the '40s, electrocutions were always held in the parish where the capital crime was committed, and always on Fridays between noon and 3 p.m. "Everything clicked for me then. Friday between 12 and 3, [the time of] Christ's crucifixion!" For a writer whose work attests to the endurance of the human spirit, the message was clear.

BOB SUMMER
May 24, 1993

WILLIAM GIBSON

THE WEARY RESIGNATION that William Gibson sometimes feels in his role as information-age guru and novelist may have been reflected in his recent cameo on television's *Wild Palms* miniseries. Introduced therein as "the man who invented the term 'cyberspace,'" Gibson now quips: "And they'll never let me forget it."

There are good reasons for his renown. Gibson's first novel, *Neuromancer* (1984), commissioned by the late Terry Carr for his Ace Specials line, electrified the science fiction field. He also laid the groundwork for his vision of a cybernetic future in a series of short stories published in *Omni* magazine. Gibson helped to inspire the creation of the label "cyberpunk" to describe an evolving genre. And while cyberpunk's popularity has waxed and waned over the years, attended by controversy, the rise of virtual reality and computer networks is helping now to give it a second wind. Bantam is about to publish Gibson's latest novel, *Virtual Light.* While not directly related to *Neuromancer* or other cyberpunk, the book shares enough with his earlier work to reward renewed interest.

Hackers the world over consider Gibson their prophet. As such, he's attracted the attention of *Time, Mondo 2000, People,* the *Wall Street Journal,* the *Village Voice* and *USA Today.* Artists, writers and musicians from Robert Longo and Kathy Acker to Donald Fagen and Billy Idol make no secret of their admiration for Gibson's work and the influence of his vision on their own.

But, like many pivotal figures, Gibson did not set out to be one, and in some respects he doesn't seem to fit the role. We meet over lunch at an informal corner restaurant near Lincoln Center in New York; he is here for one day to give a reading with novelist Steve Erickson in Central Park. Strikingly tall at 6'6", thin, amiable and unprepossessing, a drawl creeping in and out of his conversation, Gibson views himself and his notoriety with a healthy measure of irony and self-mockery.

With some amusement, for example, he recalls that he wrote *Neuromancer* and *Count Zero* (1986)—which, along with *Mona Lisa Overdrive* (1988), form a loose trilogy—on a manual typewriter. Though computer techies regularly invite him to their conferences, he admits that he knows relatively little about technology. "People are invariably disappointed to discover my lack of technical expertise," he notes drily.

By and large, Gibson prefers to maintain a low profile as a cyberpunk spokesman. From the first, however, he wanted to play with and subvert the dominant assumptions of science fiction. Heavily influenced by the "New Wave" writers of the 1960s and early 1970s who tried to tear science fiction from its pulp roots and inject a dose of literary, even experimental, technique into the genre, Gibson turned the traditional science fiction viewpoint on its head. From his first published story, "Fragments of a Hologram Rose" (1977) through his early *Omni* stories and the *Neuromancer* sequence, he rejected the self-assured, well-heeled heroes who then populated most science fiction. He brought the genre down to street level.

Hip, visual and packed with gritty detail, Gibson's stories are set among the disenfranchised—pimps and prostitutes, petty thieves and tattoo artists, computer cowboys and bike messengers. In his work, the future world, shaped by science and high technology, by impersonal multinational corporations and enigmatic artificial intelligences, serves as background to the lives of real people who can no more control events in that world than we can in ours. However, cyberpunk homes in on interfaces between human brains and computers; Gibson's characters can "jack in" to "cyberspace," a kind of virtual reality representation of data and programs in a vast computer network.

The emergence of cyberpunk ignited a furious debate in science fiction circles between those who saw cyberpunk as the genre's only hope and those convinced that it betrayed science fiction's principles. Gibson feels, in essence, that science fiction has remained pretty much unaffected by the movement. "Look what's won the genre prizes since *Neuromancer*," he observes. "Extremely traditional work." Nevertheless, he believes that cyberpunk writers have accomplished something important: "It's not that we opened up *new* territory, but that we kept a particular conduit open" for other writers and for readers.

Whatever his demurrals, it's clear that Gibson set out as a writer to make changes. While growing up in the small town of Wytheville, Va., he was "totally obsessed" with science fiction. He wrote and drew cartoons for various "fanzines"—amateur publications—that circulated among science fiction aficionados. But when, as a teenager, he was sent to boarding school in Arizona, he lost touch with the genre. "I was able to operate there much better as a regular teenager," he recalls. "My interest in fandom waned." Throughout the early '70s, having moved to Toronto and later to Vancouver, where he lives today, Gibson drifted from one odd job to another; after his marriage, he became "househusband and principal caregiver for our first kid." In such circumstances, writing was one of the few careers he could attempt.

"When I decided [as an adult] that I wanted to try to write something, science fiction seemed like the natural choice." In a sense, he came back to his beginnings. "It's funny," he muses. "I guess I have this image as the cyberpunk antichrist, deeply antithetical to the traditional values of science fiction, but actually, I've sprung from science fiction soil."

Moreover, Gibson is hardly a technophobe. Since he got his first computer, a now-archaic Apple IIc, in 1986, he's been hooked. Writing on the computer has radically changed his creative process, and for the best. Now, when he begins work for the day, he skims through what he's already written, making revisions as he goes, until he reaches the "work space," where he's generating new text, carrying the story forward. "With the computer, the concept of drafts is gone," he says. At times, however, he finds that the ease and freedom of word processing can be dangerous. "The earlier parts that I've gone over so often may be too heavily revised and overwritten," he admits.

Gibson has also embraced the idea of electronic books. Voyager is issuing electronic versions of his three cyberspace novels to tie in with the simultaneous release of *Virtual Light* on disk. And last year, Gibson collaborated with artist Dennis Ashbaugh and art-book publisher Kevin Begos Jr. on a project entitled *Agrippa: A Book of the Dead.* Inside a specially crafted oversized book illustrated with Ashbaugh's evocative engravings is a $3\frac{1}{2}$-inch computer disk containing a long poem by Gibson addressing his feelings about his father, who died when the author was very young. The trick comes when you read the poem from the disk: an encryption program, functioning like a virus, devours the text, so you can read it only once. Published in a very expensive limited edition, *Agrippa* caused fierce argument in the art world and also among museums and libraries. The text's disappearing act challenged ideas about the permanence of art and literature, and raised serious problems for archivists interested in preserving it for future generations.

Though it wasn't the main attraction of the project for him—"The techno side of it was for me the least interesting part; what I was dabbling with there was performance art, and the New York art scene"—Gibson thinks it was a good idea to shake up people's ideas about the printed word. "I'm in the vanguard of the death-of-print crowd," he readily admits. "I love books, and books as objects, but when you think about it, a library is just a pile of moldering organic material—it's literally rotting. Soon enough the library will become something at the end of a modem." Then will the electronic age doom publishers? Gibson thinks they'll adapt to it.

Despite the fact that some readers (and the media) are interested in his work, though they consider themselves largely outside the world of science fiction, Gibson still feels strongly connected to the genre. *Virtual Light* may be, on one level, his most accessible book so far, set as it is in the very near future (California in the year 2005). But, says the author, "in order to read it with anything like full comprehension, you have to approach it as a science fiction novel—in a sense, as a science fiction novel about science fiction. There are levels at which it is a very self-conscious book." Then again, the success he's had in crossing the genre border has always surprised Gibson. "I didn't think *Neuromancer* would find much of an audience. I sort of assumed it required a grounding in the genre to get what I was doing."

Perhaps readers who are less than familiar with science fiction find Gibson's work comprehensible and relevant because so many of the concepts he treats as science fiction have become (or already were) elements of contemporary reality. Early on, he was hailed as a "hard" science fiction writer because readers recognized that much of his work was grounded in realistic, emerging technologies and evolving social trends. "Often I find myself wondering how one could write a contemporary novel that wasn't, in effect, a science fiction novel," Gibson muses. "How can we write about the world we live in today without embracing science fiction to deal with certain material?"

He recalls a recent interview at his Vancouver home in which the interviewer took the position ("I think mostly to draw me out") that the world hadn't changed much over the years, that all the trends and shifts addressed in Gibson's work were "bells and whistles," mere details. "We were out in my garden," says Gibson, "and he said, this is the same way it was back here in 1951. And I looked at him and said, 'In 1951, you could lie on the grass in the sun with your shirt off and not get skin cancer.'" He points to other recent developments, such as AIDS (which figures prominently in *Virtual Light*), that in some ways require "the tool kit of the science fiction writer" to deal with in depth, and he has noticed non-genre writers taking cues from science fiction in order to deal with the modern world. Martin Amis's *London Fields* is a notable example. "Amis is clearly depicting late-'80s London, but there are these things going on, weird weather patterns, some sort of war, possibly a world war—they're just flickering in the background, but I think it works because that's how people *feel* now."

In *Virtual Light*, Gibson tries for a similar effect in reverse. "One thing I tried to do was use as much real stuff—existing today—as possible, but by presenting it out of context in a science fiction novel, make it seem quite strange and creepy."

Does Gibson feel, as some other writers do, constrained by the cyberpunk label? Would he ever like to break away from it, to try something entirely different?

Though he admits that, at times, "it's possible to feel a little claustrophobic about" cyberpunk, he isn't sure he could leave it behind him. Before *Virtual Light*, he collaborated with Bruce Sterling on *The Difference Engine* (Bantam, 1991), an "alternate history" novel in which Charles Babbage, the great 19th-century mathematician, succeeded in building the wood-and-brass computer of the title, thereby transforming the course of history. "I thought that we were doing something as stylistically different as it was possible to be, but its concerns are exactly the concerns of our previous work. It's talking about a lot of the things *Neuro-*

mancer is talking about, and it's doing it a lot more coherently, and coldly." He pauses, considering. "That was my vacation from cyberpunk, but I don't know if I went that far away."

When all is said and done, Gibson admits, cyberpunk and its concerns may just be in his blood. "Maybe the challenge for me is to write a William Gibson novel that does all the things that a William Gibson novel is purported to do, but set it in 1993, in the real world," he suggests. He pauses, turning the idea over. "I suspect that it could be done—and it might actually prove something."

ROBERT K. J. KILLHEFFER
September 6, 1993

ELLEN GILCHRIST

A CREEK RUNS THROUGH Ellen Gilchrist's front hallway. No, it's not the residue of some catastrophic flood; noted architect E. Fay Jones carved a channel for the site's groundwater when he designed the house in 1957. Nature is an honored participant in this serene structure, nestled in the hills of northwestern Arkansas, which admits the midwinter sunlight through floor-to-ceiling glass that constitutes much of the outer walls, and uses wood and stone to define its flowing interior space. "It's so Japanese!" approves the author, herself a student of Zen.

Although she bought it only recently, the house suits Gilchrist perfectly. She has created a tranquil, productive life for herself in Fayetteville, Ark., after a childhood spent uneasily alternating between the Midwest and her parents' native South, followed by turbulent decades that included several marriages and three children born when she was very young—a personal history the general outlines of which she shares with Rhoda Manning, protagonist of many short stories in Gilchrist's American Book Award–winning collection *Victory over Japan* (1985) and of her new novel, *Net of Jewels,* issued by Little, Brown.

Gilchrist has lived in Fayetteville off and on since the mid-1970s and now seems firmly settled in this small university town. At lunch in the Old Post Office Restaurant, she knows half of the people in the dining room and interrupts her meal at one point to give a big hug to a friend recently returned from Texas.

Human connections are important to the author. Her first story collection, *In the Land of Dreamy Dreams* (1981), contained four tales featuring Rhoda Manning, one of the group of interrelated characters who now, Gilchrist complains jokingly, "come over and demand a role whenever I think of a new dramatic situation." Rhoda's cousin Crystal and her black housekeeper Traceleen made their first appearances in *Victory over Japan.* Another cousin, the writer Anna Hand, turned up in *Drunk with Love* (1987), her third collection of short fiction, and dominated Gilchrist's novel *The Anna Papers* (1988). A second generation of the Hand-Manning clan became prominent in the three novellas of her most recent book, *I Cannot Get You Close Enough* (1990).

As Gilchrist got more involved with this extended family, she found that short fiction was no longer a comfortable genre. "The thing about the short story form," she says, "is that in order to do a good job with it you've got to concentrate on no more than two characters; you've got to pretend that nobody has any children or parents, that only this moment in these two or three lives is of any real importance. I would corner off two people to write about, but I would immediately have to connect it to a bigger world to be satisfied with it. I think that in order to serve the vision I currently have of reality, I'm going to have to have at least five or six characters interplaying."

The author faced some problems of consistency and overlap when she wrote *Net of Jewels*. A harrowing scene in which Rhoda undergoes an abortion was lifted in large part from "1957, a Romance," found in *In the Land of Dreamy Dreams*. "There are certain pieces of my work where I know I got it right the first time," she comments, "and I just decided to use it the way it was." Gilchrist unabashedly rewrote Rhoda's history to make her a 19-year-old virgin at the beginning of *Net of Jewels*, although "Music" in *Victory over Japan* showed her having a sexual encounter at age 14. "At the time [of "Music"] I believed that a story had to have a dramatic ending, so I had her sleep with the boy even though it really violated my internal sense of Rhoda's personality. It works to get you out of the story, but it never seemed true to me; it was just a trick, like riding a bicycle with no hands.

"You can't go back to the easy fix you learn as a short story writer, where you kill somebody off or get somebody laid to create a climax. What I'm trying to do now is make a study of existence—that's the high ground, but I perceive it as that. I want it to be as true to what I know about human beings as it can be. When I was writing *Net of Jewels*, I thought: The more I've written about Rhoda, the more I know about her, and I'm going to serve that knowledge in this book. This is the difference between writing novels and writing short stories; there aren't any tricks."

Seated at her dining-room table, casually dressed in a light brown wool turtleneck and a pleated navy skirt, her legs drawn up nonchalantly underneath her, the author seems as free from artifice as she hopes her work is. Chin-length, blunt-cut blond hair (showing gray at the temples) frames the pretty, apparently makeup-free face of a woman happy to be and look her age (57)— so much so that in *Net of Jewels* she found it "really hard to revisit the mind of a 20-year-old girl in the late 1950s."

It was a difficult book to write, she says, partly because there was little room for the humor that has always enlivened her work. "I would hope that I would always know what comedy is—if you can make people laugh, what else can anyone ask?—but I knew this novel would not be funny. I think what I've done here is written a little piece of history, a portrait of a time and place that is going to be, for young women reading it, like me reading Jane Austen, because young women really can't comprehend a world where if you got pregnant you *had* to have the baby; the only way you could get out was by putting your life in danger. I hope that I have recreated the intensity of the desperation of somebody who is pregnant and doesn't want to have the baby."

She's also captured the slow, tentative transformation of a spoiled, self-absorbed young woman who begins to learn there is a world outside her family, a world whose moral challenges and dangers are incarnated for Rhoda in the civil rights movement. Gilchrist herself took part as an adult in the struggle to bring racial justice to the South, but she knew long before that there were a lot of things wrong with the privileged life her parents accepted as their birthright.

"I spent a lot of my formative years in public schools in Illinois and Indiana; a big part of me is an old Harrisburg, Ill., cheerleader from a town that was a real democracy. I didn't have the words 'racism' and 'sexism,' but I was fighting against them all my life, because I was fighting to be free. I was one of the lucky ones, because I'm a reader; I had the literature of the world and the library as my backup staffs. You teach someone to read and they're not going to be encapsulated; they're going to find like minds. I always knew there were other places; I always wanted to go to them."

Yet, she acknowledges, she is unquestionably a Southern writer. "Both of my parents are from the Deep South, and everyone I knew growing up could speak proper, perfect English on formal

87

occasions but could also speak a sort of mixture of English and the beautiful, inventive things that black people had done and are still doing in the South with the language. I was taught to speak by people who take a long time to say things, and it's heavily voweled and full of adjectives—it's Faulkner's language. When I first read Eudora Welty and Faulkner, I almost fainted; I couldn't *believe* that you could write things and have them published in this language that I spoke."

Gilchrist was nearly 40 when she began writing seriously. "I had a newspaper column—in a real newspaper—when I was a sophomore in high school. But after I started getting married and having babies, I stopped. I was raised in a world in which you didn't have ambitions after you had children; the moment you had a baby in your arms, the ambitions were transferred to your child. When the boys were young I studied with Miss Welty for a year [in the mid-1960s at Millsaps College], and I had written a lot of poetry and been reasonably successful in publishing it. But then I got married again and forgot all about it."

When she was in her late 30s, a close friend took up writing poetry and asked for her help; editing the poems, Gilchrist says, "I was jealous of what she was doing." Just how remote writing had become from her life became apparent a few days later when another friend casually referred to the excitement of meeting a poet, and Gilchrist realized that "my best friend in New Orleans didn't even know I had ever been a poet." Long-suppressed feelings were stirred up: shortly thereafter, reading Anne Sexton's *45 Mercy Street* in a public place, she found herself weeping uncontrollably.

"I began to have this recurrent dream of being in my house in New Orleans and opening a door to find all these rooms that I didn't know were there, full of chests with the drawers full of treasures. Nothing had been touched in a long, long time, and I had this feeling that I wanted to get other people in the house and show them these rooms. So I began to write. I was going on a vacation with my husband, scuba diving with some friends. We were out the door, walking down the steps to the car, and I walked back in the house, opened up a coat closet in the hall, got out a Royal portable typewriter I hadn't touched in about seven years, and took it with me to the islands. I don't think I ever went in the ocean."

Poetry got her up to Fayetteville; her friend Jim Whitehead, director of the University of Arkansas writing program, told her that she needed to be in a community of writers. Bill Harrison's short story course convinced her to try a new form, and a National Endowment for the Arts grant helped her complete *In the Land of Dreamy Dreams*, which the University of Arkansas Press published in 1981. That brought her to her agent, Don Congdon, and her editor, Little, Brown's Roger Donald.

"A young man in the writing program here was working as Don's assistant; he read *Dreamy Dreams* and gave it to Don, who called me up and asked if he could be my agent. He told me all the people he'd represented, which included most of my favorite American writers, and we talked for about an hour. I didn't know anything about agents; I said, 'Do we have a contract?' and he said, 'No, we just trust each other. If you get sick of me, you can quit.' "

A number of New York editors wanted to sign Gilchrist, but she was most attracted by Roger Donald's offer of a contract for a novel and a collection of short stories. She has worked with both men ever since. "Don reads the manuscripts, too; he's a very fine editor. Roger and I don't mince words with each other; he doesn't tiptoe around my feelings, and I don't tiptoe around his. My strength as a writer is that I can accept criticism and learn from it. I don't think what I've written is etched in stone; I know it's a draft, and I feel free to write that draft because I know that Roger or Don or both will tell me what part of it is bullshit and where the story really begins."

The first draft currently occupying Gilchrist is of a new novel about Olivia, the illegitimate, half–Native American daughter of Anna Hand's brother. "A friend of mine told me that the government is now giving scientific grants based on the security of the computer systems, so everyone decided to code scientific information into computers in Navaho. The big idea for a book is always kind of like a vision, and as soon as I heard this I knew exactly who was going to get this information and exactly what she was going to do. Because Olivia's on the make; she has to find a place in the world, and she wants a job. So it takes place in Tahlequah, Okla., in the summer of 1991, when Olivia goes back to learn the old Indian languages."

Although Gilchrist is "really looking forward to writing a book set in 1991 after this long morass of the 1950s," she didn't deliberately set out to give herself a change of period. "You can't really plan fiction," she says. "You just turn it loose. Whatever the muse gives me, I serve that. I can't afford to care whether it's the right thing to do—it's just what I'm doing next."

WENDY SMITH
March 2, 1992

JOHN GRISHAM

THIS IS WHAT HAPPENS when you cross that line between relative obscurity and international recognition: actor Wilford Brimley, who's playing a pivotal role in a forthcoming movie based on your bestseller, takes stock of your 70-acre spread and decides a quarter horse is just what you need. So he makes a selection from his personal stables at his Utah ranch and ships it all the way to Oxford, Miss., where you live.

Makes no difference that you don't know the first thing about equestrian matters. It's the thought that counts, and the knowledge that once you've arrived, life is full of grand gestures and surprises.

"At first I wasn't sure if the bridle was supposed to go on me or the horse," admits John Grisham, recipient of Brimley's gift and author of the phenomenal bestsellers *The Firm, The Pelican Brief* and *A Time to Kill.* "The guy who delivered him had to give me a few lessons on the spot. But now we're going to buy three more so the whole family can ride together."

What Grisham lacks in horse sense, however, he certainly makes up for in the ability to write a suspenseful story. If early reviews are any indication, his newest effort, *The Client* (Doubleday), promises to follow in the triumphant footsteps of his three previous books, which topped 1992 bestseller lists in cloth and paperback.

At 38, a relatively young age to have it all, John Grisham appears remarkably untouched by the whirlwind success that has made him one of America's hottest writers. When *PW* meets him at his Victorian home in Oxford on a slate-gray January morning, he's your basic ordinary guy, marked with a stubble of beard and dressed in a blue denim workshirt that matches his eyes, fretting about some mundane concerns. His wife is weathering the flu, party plans for his daughter's seventh birthday are under way and

Bo, the lumbering chocolate Labrador, has abandoned his assigned security role and is smothering the visitor with sloppy dog kisses instead. Oh, and Grisham also is trying to figure if he can juggle plans to attend his distant cousin's inauguration.

"Bill Clinton and I may be distantly related," he says matter-of-factly, in a measured Southern drawl. Grisham also shares political affiliation with his relative, having served seven years as a Democratic member of the Mississippi state legislature. Politics, he learned, was much like his first career, law: at times exciting and challenging, but for the most part, downright frustrating.

He could say the same for writing, at least in the early days. In 1984, just three years out of Ole Miss law school and running a one-man criminal defense practice in Southhaven, Miss., Grisham got the itch to write a novel. Specifically, a courtroom drama, based on a gut-wrenching case he had observed involving a young girl who had to testify against the man who had brutally raped her. Watching the girl suffer, Grisham could not even imagine the nightmare she and her family had endured. He became obsessed with the idea of retribution and yearned to shoot the rapist. "For one brief moment, I wanted to be her father. I wanted justice. There was a story there."

That tale of paternal revenge became *A Time to Kill*, written in the predawn hours over three years as he juggled a taxing 60- to 80-hour work week plus three months a year in the state House of Representatives. A son, Ty, now nine, then a daughter, Shea, joined Grisham and Renée, the girl next door whom he married after law school. Looking back, he admits that much of the 1980s is now a blur, and that he was just too busy to worry about whether the book would ever get published.

Recalls Grisham: "Because I have this problem of starting projects and not completing them, my goal for this book was simply to finish it. Then I started thinking that it would be nice to have a novel sitting on my desk, something I could point to and say, 'Yeah, I wrote that.' But it didn't consume me. I had way too much going on to make it a top priority. If it happened, it happened."

In the beginning, it almost felt as if it wouldn't happen. First, there was the task of finding an agent. In early 1987, Grisham sent off the manuscript to dozens of agents and got a few responses, but nothing concrete. Finally in April, Jay Garon of New York called and told Grisham he wanted to represent him. Why did he accept? "He was the only one who said he'd mail a contract immediately," Grisham says.

Garon says there was no doubt he had discovered a natural-born storyteller with immense talent. "I smelled a winner right off the bat," he says. "That was the easy part. The hard part was trying to convince a market that is leery about new writers to give him a chance." Garon peddled *A Time to Kill* for about a year, amassing a slew of rejections before finally making a deal with Bill Thompson of the now-defunct Wynwood Press for $15,000—the same Bill Thompson who had bought *Carrie* from a newcomer named Stephen King years earlier (and who now runs a packaging company called The Literary Group). *A Time to Kill* was published in June 1989, in a 5000-copy printing.

"I bought 1000, and another 1000 were sitting in a warehouse, so you know not many were out there," Grisham acknowledges. But now he was halfway into his second novel, *The Firm*, a story that he was only lukewarm about but that "made Renée go berserk." Because she is his best editor and most vocal critic—"She makes those people in New York look like *children*"—Grisham stayed with the project. He completed it in September, and Jay started the peddling process again.

Only this time, the story took a different twist. Grisham had no idea that a bootleg copy of his still-unpublished manuscript had landed in the hands of West Coast filmmakers, so he was caught completely off guard that first Sunday in January 1990 when Renée tracked him down at church. Garon had called from New York, she relayed breathlessly, and John needed to call him immediately. Apparently Hollywood wanted to buy *The Firm.*

Grisham went to bed that night a rich man. Paramount had plunked down $600,000 for the movie rights to a manuscript that no publisher had yet seen fit to buy. The following day, news of the deal lit up phone lines on both coasts. Within two weeks, Grisham had a contract with Doubleday—one of the many houses that had passed on *A Time to Kill* two years earlier. "I still have the rejection letter," he says, with a hint of a smile.

The year 1990 evolved into one of Grisham's most memorable. First there were the deals surrounding *The Firm*; then Renée's father, a contractor, began building the house of their dreams on a former horse farm in Oxford; and finally, Grisham decided to quit the legislature and close his law practice so he could write full time. He did all this without the guarantee that *The Firm,* scheduled for March 1991 publication, would fulfill its promise.

Not to worry. *The Firm* enjoyed a whopping 47 weeks on the *New York Times* bestseller list after it was released; in 1992, it topped *PW*'s list of longest-running paperback bestsellers with 48 weeks. His next book, *The Pelican Brief* (Doubleday), became 1992's longest-running hardcover bestseller, staying on the *PW* list for 42 weeks. And after Doubleday acquired the paperback rights and republished *A Time to Kill*—the novel that remains dearest to Grisham's heart—it claimed the No. 2 spot last year on *PW*'s longest-running paperback bestsellers list at 27 weeks. To date, combined sales worldwide for the three books have topped an astronomical 17 million copies.

If that isn't enough good fortune, three of Grisham's books will hit the screen within two years. *The Firm,* directed by Sidney Pollack and starring Tom Cruise, Brimley and Gene Hackman, is slated for release in July; filming on *The Pelican Brief,* directed by Alan Pakula, will begin in May. Director Joel Schumacher wants cameras rolling in June for *The Client.*

Grisham hasn't written the screenplays for any of his books, nor does he wish to. Hollywood, he says, isn't his scene. "I sell the film rights for a lot of money, I kiss it goodbye and I move on. No one puts a gun to my head. If the movies bomb, you won't hear me moaning and mouthing off."

Grisham still considers himself a lawyer, but he is ecstatic that he doesn't have to practice anymore. In fact, he says, "Most lawyers I know would rather be doing something else." It appears at least half of them are budding novelists, as evidenced by the glut of attorneys turned writers these days. About this, Grisham is not surprised: "Law provides lots of juicy material, lurid situations, scummy characters. The plots are practically handed to you." In his humble opinion, only three are masters of the genre, which means handling the legal terminology without bogging down the reader: himself, Scott Turow (*Presumed Innocent, The Burden of Proof* and *Pleading Guilty*) and Steve Martini (*Compelling Evidence*).

"Turow's *Presumed Innocent* was the first, and it's a classic," says Grisham of the legal-suspense wave. "People make a big deal over comparing us. We're both lawyers and we're both writers, but that's where the similarities end. I think people would like to see us duke it out, but that's not going to happen. There's plenty of room for both of us. And in the end, the good books sell and the bad ones don't."

Not one to take success for granted, Grisham is nervously anticipating reaction to *The Client*, the first book in a three-book deal he has with Doubleday. Even though *The Pelican Brief* sold millions, some critics blasted it. That hit Grisham hard, because he had placed so much importance on repeating his earlier acclaim. "It's the American way," he shrugs. "As a rookie, people were really pulling for me with *The Firm*, but the second time around, those same people were secretly wishing I would fail so they could rip me to shreds."

This time, Grisham has vowed not to get upset by critics, and to focus on reader reaction instead. In writing *The Client*, he concentrated mainly on character development—an effort that shouldn't go unnoticed, says Doubleday's David Gernert, Grisham's editor since *The Firm*. "This was a very brave, very smart move for John. It is different from his other books, yet he doesn't lose the twists and elements that make him such a compelling writer. He has that ability to combine suspense with subtle and effective humor, and create characters that are just human, not extraordinary. In the case of John's books, it's really true: you can't put them down."

Grisham, who always begins writing his next book at 5 a.m. the morning after he sends a completed manuscript off to New York, says he follows three rules in developing his stories: A beginning that grips readers and hooks them for a ride, a middle that sustains them with narrative tension, and an ending that sets them on the edges of their seats. The characters tend to be ordinary people sucked into a conspiracy that puts their lives in danger. "And always, there's something dark, shadowy and sinister lurking in the background."

If Grisham has any regrets about his meteoric rise, it is that success has come so fast he hasn't had the chance to savor it. He has slowed his pace considerably from last year, giving fewer interviews and making fewer appearances so he can spend more time with his family. In April, he heads to a remote location in Brazil with fellow members of the First Baptist Church in Oxford on a mission to help erect buildings for the villagers. It will be a delight, he says, to be around people who have no interest in books or movies.

Story ideas continue to race in his head, which is good news for Grisham fans. He compares a writer's career to that of an athlete, noting that at some point, it's time to retire the uniform. "There's nothing sadder than a sports figure who continues to play past his prime," Grisham says.

But if and when the words run out, John Grisham will probably do what he does best—change careers. In 10 years, he has already done what most never accomplish in a lifetime, having mastered three professions—lawyer, politician, bestselling author— with enviable ease. What next? Without hesitation, he answers, "A Little League baseball coach. Now that's where you can have some *real* fun."

MICHELLE J. BEARDEN
February 22, 1993

PETE HAMILL

NEW YEAR'S DAY 1994 marked the 21st consecutive year of sobriety for Pete Hamill. And in what must have seemed like the perpetrator returning to the scene of the crime, Hamill agreed to meet for an interview at one of his old drinking haunts in Greenwich Village, the Lion's Head on Christopher Street, to discuss his new book, *The Drinking Life: A Memoir* (Little, Brown).

Hamill settles in at a table in the back dining room, orders a BLT and a diet Coke, and lights up the first in what seems like an endless string of cigarettes ("They don't affect my writing," he laughs). *The Drinking Life* is autobiography from afar because it traces Hamill's life only until the time he stopped drinking in 1973. "It's the kind of book about drinking that you can give to your friend with the problem," claims Hamill. "It's not saying: 'For Chrissakes why don't you get with the program?' Here's a guy talking honestly about it, as straight as he can, about facing your life. How do you want to live? Do you want to get old, or do you want to die?"

It's hard to imagine the soft-spoken man who gently proselytizes against drink as the wild Hamill of *The Drinking Life*—kicking in whorehouse doors in Mexico City and spending time in the local calaboose. "I started early," he says. "If you start when you're 15 and you stop when you're 38, that's a lot of drinking." He's 58 now, and though his short-cropped beard is graying, he still looks youthful and vigorous.

"One of the things I didn't want to do with the book," Hamill continues, "was to make it into a sermon. I was saying, 'This is how you begin to get into the culture of drinking,' because I think it is, in a sociological sense, a culture. What I have come to learn is that you can't solve something like a drinking problem or a drug problem without examining the entire life."

Hamill stopped drinking on his own. For him, there was no

Betty Ford Clinic, AA meetings or, as the Irish put it, "whiskey school." "Somehow I knew that if I went to encounter groups, or to 12-steps, or to a shrink, or whatever, no matter what, *I* had to do it. It's all up to you in the end, it's your will that's involved and your determination. It wasn't a conscious thing: 'I will not go to AA.' I just said 'I'm going to stop.'

"And I then began to use what I had," he continues. "I was a writer. I began to keep a journal in which I tried to analyze the problem, which was the equivalent of standing up in front of a group. There were things I couldn't figure out, or I thought I'd figured out, and didn't realize until much later that I was wrong. But it ended up a benefit. I ended up kicking this thing.

"After the first year," Hamill emphasizes, "you get to a point where you say, 'Jesus Christ, I can't even think about doing it again.' The first year was far and away the hardest, the first six months in particular."

There's a lot of Ireland, a lot of the rebel in Hamill. He expresses enormous pride in his family, his city, his Irishness and his love of the written word. All seem to emanate from his father Billy, a Belfast man—and fellow rebel. A large part of *The Drinking Life* deals with facing up to the triangle of love, conflict and alcohol that marked their relationship. Billy Hamill was a member of Sinn Fein. After a British soldier was blown up, "he went on the lam to Liverpool, and from Liverpool he came here." Soon after arriving in America, Billy lost a leg in a football accident. Despite his handicap, he worked to support his wife and seven children. He also drank. "His mother signed his birth certificate with an 'X.' To go from an 'X' to having all these crazy writers in the family [Pete's brother Denis is a columnist for the *New York Daily News*; his brother John is a screenwriter] was just too much for this poor guy."

Hamill blames his environment—namely boozy, Irish Brooklyn—not his father, for his own alcoholism. "My brother Denis said it best one time. 'It wasn't that we grew up in a dysfunctional family, we grew up in a dysfunctional neighborhood!' "

As the son of an immigrant, Hamill sees a distant connection between drink and ethnicity. "I think it's no accident that there's a lot of drinking among conquered peoples—American Indians, Poles, other Eastern Europeans and, of course, the Irish. It has something to do with defeat."

Hamill thinks of his father, Belfast, the drink, and laughs. "I remember a party in London where the guest of honor was Lord Mountbatten and the only other Irish person in the place was Edna O'Brien. It was one of these long, formal dinner tables with Mountbatten in the middle. And Mountbatten starts telling jokes. He's one of the most boorish people I've ever met. And he starts to tell Irish jokes. And he starts to tell Irish *drunk* jokes. And at one point I lean back like this, and Edna leans back like this and looks at me and we laughed. He had no idea. To him I was a Yank and Edna O'Brien was someone who lived in London. But I did have a feeling: I'll never give these bastards the satisfaction of getting drunk in front of them."

Drinking proved to have a deleterious effect on Hamill's relationships with women. He blames the breakup of his first marriage, and the ensuing problems he had with his daughters Adriene and Deirdre, on alcohol. His present wife, Fukiko Aoki, never knew the boozy Hamill. "I've been married for seven years," he says, "and it's hard for my wife to imagine that I was once *that* guy. Not the kid, not the boy—*that* she can imagine. But the 20-year-old, the guy rolling around in the whorehouse in Mexico City, it's hard for her to imagine that."

Hamill dropped out of high school when he was 16. After working at the Brooklyn Navy Yard and doing a stint in the Navy, he used his talent for cartooning to make a living as a graphic artist in an ad agency. In 1960 he read *Reflections of an Angry Middle-Aged Editor* by James Wechsler, editor of the *New York Post*, in which Wechsler discussed his experiences as a newspaperman. Hamill wrote him a long letter especially critical of the lack of "working-class" journalists at the paper. Wechsler invited Hamill to the *Post* for a chat and asked him if he had ever thought about becoming a newspaperman. On June 1, 1960, Hamill reported to work at the *Post*, he says, "clumsily disguised as a reporter."

Hamill knows he probably couldn't get in the front door of a newspaper today with his educational background. "I think that goes back to this immigrant mentality, that this is America and you can do anything. And I believed it! Today, in my case, with two years of high school, it's not that you wouldn't get to the editor, you'd never get past the personnel directors, who are making decisions based on resumés, which is insane. Jimmy Wechsler was a great man. He made my life possible."

In 1963 Hamill left the *Post* to satisfy his relentless wanderlust, living in Spain, Italy, Ireland, Puerto Rico and Mexico. He returned to the paper as a columnist in 1965, covering the incendiary events of the '60s—civil rights, Vietnam and the 1968 presidential election. Asked if he sees any connection between writing and drinking, he replies, "I think newspaper writers and drunks share a similar need for the instant reward. You're attracted to the newspaper because your story will be in the paper tomorrow. Sometimes that night. You finish, you go to the bar, the first edition comes in and there it is. You get the instant kickback. You get the same thing with drinking.

"Fitzgerald was right when he said that there are no second acts for American writers," Hamill says, "mainly because they can't remember the fuckin' thing. You have a first act in which you have full consciousness, then either fame or drinking or some combination of factors ends up attacking the thing that made you gifted in the first place, so that you're not seeing as clearly, you're just not. I can remember unbelievable details about being 12, but maybe only three lines from when I was 32. The reason is that drink starts to attack consciousness.

"My feeling was that if I was going to be any kind of a writer, it was going to take me a long time. I'd probably have to wait until my 50s to write my best stuff. Maybe 60s. But I couldn't do it unless I could remember. Writers are rememberers or they're nothing. And that remembering means remembering the pain and the grief and lousiness along with all the joys and triumphs and everything else."

Hamill began writing novels because it was different from newspaper writing and he wanted to learn the form, how to write longer than 3000 words. "Before me and Jimmy [Breslin]," he says, "there was very little tradition of American journalists writing novels. The instinct to make fiction was always there, even after I started to have some successes at journalism."

His first novel, *A Killing for Christ*, came out from NAL in 1968. Then he switched to nonfiction with a collection of journalism pieces, *Irrational Ravings* (Putnam, 1971). Ironically, the title was suggested by then–Vice President and media basher Spiro T. Agnew, who had held up a Hamill column and exclaimed, "Listen to these irrational ravings!" Between 1973 and 1989, with Jason Epstein ("a good friend") as editor, Hamill published six novels with Random House (*The Gift, Dirty Laundry, Flesh and Blood, The Deadly Piece, Guns of Heaven* and *Loving Women*) and two short-story collections (*The Invisible City* and *Tokyo Sketches*).

Finally deciding it was time for a change, Hamill and his agent, Lynn Nesbit, brought *The Drinking Life* to Bill Phillips at Little, Brown. Two additional books are under contract there. Hamill plans a second collection of journalism pieces, where he'll recall his short-lived and often hilarious stint as editor-in-chief of the *Post* in 1993. (Fired by aspiring owner Abe Hirschfeld, Hamill refused to leave and subsequently made New York journalism history by receiving an unsolicited front-page kiss from the contrite Hirschfeld.) "It was one of the greatest times in my life. It was just a ball," he recalls. There will be a novel, too, about New York City in the present. "*The Drinking Life* and *Loving Women* are set in the past. I don't want to end up stuck there forever, so I'm doing a very contemporary novel."

Originally, *The Drinking Life* was not a book about alcoholism. "It went through an odd evolution," says Hamill. He had started out to write a book about the '50s, and was surprised, as he looked back at that time, to see how much drinking there had been. "I got excited thinking about that and the '50s book began to fade, thank God, because I didn't know that [David] Halberstam and [Dan] Wakefield were writing '50s books, too."

Hamill, who has an apartment in Greenwich Village and a house in upstate New York, keeps to regular writing habits. "I write every day, one thing or another," he says. "I usually don't function very well in the morning. I get most of the serious writing done from 7:30 p.m. to 2:00 a.m." He cites the telephone as a major distraction during the day. "Basically I write at night because of the peace and quiet. If it's baseball season I can work with the ballgame on—because it's got no plot. And I'll play music that has to do with whatever it is I'm writing. One of the things I learned with *Loving Women* was how useful music can be to trigger memory."

Besides the two books owed Little, Brown, Hamill is working on a screenplay about Pancho Villa for Turner Entertainment. He also is a contributing editor for *New York* magazine. He'll soon be returning to *Esquire* to write a monthly column and to the *New York Daily News*, where he'll work on special projects.

Since *The Drinking Life* ends in 1973, we ask if Hamill plans another autobiographical volume covering his Vietnam experiences and his friendship with Robert Kennedy, which were hardly mentioned at all in this book. The idea is one he already entertains. "I hope that in another 10 years I can write a book called *A Writing Life*, and tell what the rest of my life was like." One suspects that the second half of Hamill's life will be just as interesting as the first half—and definitely more clear-eyed.

DERMOT KAVANAGH McEVOY
January 10, 1994

CARL HIAASEN

STANDING UP in Carl Hiaasen's 17-foot skiff, as it skims the glass-like saltwater of the Florida Bay flats, is definitely a no-no. Even if it means a better view of the frolicking porpoises swimming side by side with the boat. "You could fall backwards into the engine and literally be decapitated," Hiaasen warns his passengers above the din of the motor. Pause, evil smile. "And it would take me weeks to clean up the mess."

For Hiaasen, Miami's worst nightmare since Don Johnson, the very notion of a headless body or a severed appendage of any sort is liable to bring on fits of maniacal laughter. His twisted imagination is legendary, having produced a lineup of macabre characters: a one-eyed ex-governor who lives in the swamp and dines on roadkill; a giant named Chemo with a face like Rice Krispies who wears a Weed-wacker in place of an amputated hand; a torso-less pit bull permanently attached to a man's forearm, its decaying head stubbornly maintaining its death grip even in decomposure.

Such is Hiaasen's reputation that fans can't wait to see what he has devilishly conjured up in his fifth novel, *Strip Tease*, published by Knopf. For the record, they won't be disappointed. In tackling the rollicking subjects of sex, politics and topless creamed-corn wrestling, the *Miami Herald* columnist steps into terrain familiar to a muckraking journalist. There's a corrupt congressman consumed by a stripper, a slimy lawyer out for a scam, a pint-sized lobbyist with strong cologne and weak morals. In other words, Hiaasen says, "regular people, just out of real life."

Who is Carl Hiaasen, once described by a reviewer as "Elmore Leonard after several hits of nitrous oxide," and why does he write such terrible things, particularly about South Florida?

To find out the ultimate truth, one must travel to the Upper Keys, a two-hour drive from Miami's concrete-and-crime madness, to the modest stilt house where the 40-year-old Hiaasen lives most of the time. Thanks to such modern-day conveniences as computers and fax modems, he can write his twice-weekly column for the *Herald* in the comfort of his own book-laden digs. When the urge for bonefishing strikes, he's just two blocks from the dock where his trusty skiff, *Final Edition*, awaits.

Hiaasen endures interviews but is not thrilled about them. He is far more cheerful on a boat trip around the bay's mangrove islands in search of the elusive bonefish. It is abundantly clear that Hiaasen gives not a hoot for media attention and the trappings of his accelerating popularity. In a perfect world, he would be left alone to write, fish and enjoy the company of his small circle of friends.

Hiaasen's uneasiness with fame is transcended by his sense of duty to protect what little wilderness is left in South Florida. Inevitably, every conversation leads to the topic that consumes him: the obliteration of the land by greedy developers, paid-off politicians and a stampede of new residents. A third-generation Floridian, a rare distinction in this state of transients and migrants, Hiaasen has witnessed the sad disintegration of his stomping grounds, and uses his column to fulminate against further destruction.

Chuckling in disbelief, he shows us a newspaper story about a woman claiming to have been attacked by an eight-foot barracuda that rocketed onto the deck of her boat. Barracudas neither grow so big nor demonstrate such ferocious temperaments, he announces. But, he adds, "Let the public believe this stuff. If it scares even one carload of geeks out of Florida, then I'm all for it. I'm in favor of putting out any kind of propaganda to keep people away from here."

Indeed, this is the same man who appeared on *Good Morning America* and bragged that Miami led the country in the number of bodies found in automobile trunks. He went on to say that there was nothing wrong in South Florida that a force-5 hurricane couldn't fix. Those remarks prompted a furious letter to the *Herald* from Miami's mayor, claiming that Hiaasen "displayed a one-dimensional, exponential hatred of South Florida. . . . He owes an apology to the entire human race, in which he has lost faith."

The memory of that outburst brings a smile to Hiaasen's boyishly handsome face. "I understand the city council passed a resolution condemning me," he says. "I've always wanted to track down a copy of it, and put it with the rest of the blurbs on the back of one of my book jackets. It would be a wonderful endorsement." Deep down, doesn't it bother him, just a little bit, that he is the object of such rancor? "Naw. This town is so fractured, so tense, so bizarre, that if I wasn't making enemies, then I wouldn't be doing my job."

Hiaasen grew up in Plantation, a suburb outside Fort Lauderdale, the oldest of four children of a lawyer and a homemaker. His grandfather, born just after the family migrated from Norway to North Dakota, left the biting Midwestern winters in 1922 to establish Fort Lauderdale's first law firm. From the stories he later told his grandson, old South Florida was nothing but untamed wilderness: Indian trading posts, swamps, pasture, scrub and wetlands. Although the younger Hiaasen recalls tubing down Alligator Alley, hunting for snakes in the Everglades and fishing for sea bass, he can't forget the terrifying sounds of bulldozers and concrete mixers.

"Air-conditioning and mosquito repellent were the ruination of Florida," he says, his piercing blue eyes snapping with anger. "Now we've got malls, malls and more malls, and too many people and too much traffic. It's gotten so urbanized and so unacceptable." His wife, Connie, a lawyer, still lives in the house they own, two doors down from Hiaasen's boyhood home. But Hiaasen prefers the solitude of the Keys, and travels north only when absolutely necessary.

His love of nature was matched by his fascination with words. At age four, he was reading aloud the *Miami Herald* sports pages to his parents; later, he devoured the works of Florida's renowned mystery writer John D. MacDonald, whose novels contained environmentalist themes long before they were fashionable. Hiaasen's talent for satire and irreverence emerged at Plantation High School, where he wrote for the anti-establishment newspaper *More Trash*. "Law never held any interest for me," he says. "I never got any pressure from my dad or grandfather to follow in their footsteps. It was accepted all along I'd go into writing."

Hiaasen enrolled at Emory University in Atlanta as an English major, where he was introduced to Dr. Neil Shulman, who asked him to ghostwrite two books loosely based on the doctor's experiences. One of those eventually was sold to the movies and released as *Doc Hollywood*. In 1972, Hiaasen transferred to the University of Florida's journalism program; he earned his degree in 1974, then took a job at the *Today* paper in Cocoa. Two years later, he was hired by the *Herald*.

His meteoric rise there—from bureau reporter, to member of the award-winning investigative team, and finally to columnist—has not surprised his colleagues. Through his tenacious reporting and his sharp-edged writing, Hiaasen earned the respect of his peers. "Most reporters can be divided into two groups—those who can write and those who can report. Carl is the rare journalist who can do both," says Jeff Leen, a *Herald* reporter and coauthor of *Kings of Cocaine*. "His mind is like a laser beam: intricate, flawless and fair."

In addition to exposing underhanded developers and drug dealers, Hiaasen collaborated on three thrillers during the 1980s with fellow reporter William Montalbano. *Powder Burn*, *Trap Line* and *A Death in China*, all published by Atheneum, sold modestly well for the duo, who divided up characters and chapters and managed to remain friends through the process.

In 1986, Hiaasen broke loose with his first solo effort, *Tourist Season* (Putnam), the story of an iconoclastic newspaper columnist driven mad by developers, a chamber of commerce president asphyxiated by a toy alligator, a kidnapped Orange Bowl queen and snakes on a cruise ship. It was, as Leen puts it, "the dark side of his Dr. Jekyll–Mr. Hyde personality, the one you don't see as a reporter."

His demented wit was also evident in his next two Putnam works: *Double Whammy* (1987), a slam-dunk account of good ol' boys who commit murder over bass-fishing tournaments in Central Florida, followed by the uproariously funny *Skin Tight* (1989), in which a villainous South Florida plastic surgeon kills a woman during a nose job, disposing of her body in a tree-shredding machine.

It's no wonder that some readers are disappointed when they show up at a Hiaasen book-signing and find just a normal guy: no scars, no drooling and all body parts intact. They ask him where he comes up with his outlandish plots, and he honestly can't answer. "I always start with the characters, pulling together traits of people I've encountered, and then the story takes over."

An admitted workaholic with little interest in the business side of publishing, Hiaasen is unabashedly grateful to his longtime agent, the woman he calls "the amazing Esther Newberg" in his *Strip Tease* dedication. Hiaasen was Newberg's first client when she left politics in the late 1970s to work for ICM. The two have grown professionally together, and they remain close friends. "Esther works as hard for a $10,000 book as a $1 million deal. If she likes you and believes in your book, she'll bust her butt for you," Hiaasen says.

Newberg is equally admiring. It was Pete Hamill who alerted her to "this kid at the *Miami Herald*, possibly the most talented columnist in the country," she recalls. "When people like Hamill and [Jimmy] Breslin give you information like that, you'd better listen." She loves his twisted sense of humor and says he's a joy to edit. "Really, I consider Carl a national treasure. He's finally getting that special attention he deserves."

It was Newberg who found a new home in 1991 for Hiaasen with his fourth book, *Native Tongue*, a scathing indictment of Florida's fascination with theme parks, condos and championship golf courses. Although not unhappy with Putnam, the agent wanted a publisher who wouldn't box her writer into a particular category. She found that with Knopf.

"I picked up a couple of Carl's books in an airport about four years ago on my way to Frankfurt [Book Fair]," recalls Sonny Mehta, Knopf's president and editor-in-chief. "Those books kept me sane during an appalling week. . . . I couldn't wait to get back to my hotel to read them." After learning Newberg was Hiaasen's agent, Mehta made a persuasive pitch to lure him over to Knopf. His reward was a contract for *Native Tongue*, which to date has sold nearly 50,000 copies in hardcover, then a two-book deal beginning with *Strip Tease*.

"I'd like to think we don't publish category writers at Knopf. Carl's got that individual voice we look for," says Mehta, a crime-mystery buff who personally edits Hiaasen's books. "I'm a huge fan of his. And it's pretty incredible in this business to work with somebody and still remain a fan."

Although Hiaasen won't disclose his target in his next project, Newberg gives us a hint. "If you're in the construction industry in South Florida, I'd be worried about the next book," she warns.

Hiaasen knows he won't be able to keep up his double career forever. One day, when he decides to devote himself full time to books, Hiaasen hopes that the *Herald* will find a voice of similar outrage and discontent. There is not much to salvage in Florida, he concedes, but he wants to preserve what little is left for the generation that includes his son Scott, a 22-year-old University of Florida journalism major, and those to follow.

"The one good thing about book tours is meeting the readers. Everyone has a story about a place from their childhood that has been paved over, whacked up, torn down in the name of 'progress,' " he says.

"What I've learned is that I'm not alone in how I feel. The resentment over the rape of the land is universal, and that feeling of betrayal and anger expressed by my characters is felt all over the world. If we can stay made enough, maybe we can beat the bad guys at their own game."

MICHELLE J. BEARDEN
August 16, 1993

JANETTE TURNER HOSPITAL

J ANETTE TURNER HOSPITAL is, simply put, a natural Scheherazade.
It's not just that she saw in Scheherazade, who told tales to save
her life, "the perfect narrative framework" for her 1989 novel *Charades*. It's that the primitive force of her fiction, its command of
the sensuous as well as the spiritual, leads a reader of her five novels and two collections of stories to believe that she, too, is telling
tales to stave something off, to "negotiate" her own life. In *The
Last Magician*, her newest novel, released by Holt, Hospital explores the secrets of the Queensland rain forest as well as life in
the demimonde "quarry" of Sydney, Australia, the country of her
birth, and she uses a hooker who quotes Milton and a Chinese-
Australian photographer who quotes Lao-Tze to tell a harsh and
desperate tale about what she identifies as "the murky underside
of respectability.

"Various establishment systems—the law, the academic world,
the literary world—are put on trial and found severely wanting,"
she says of her new novel, while sitting on the deck at her home
in Kingston, Ontario. The house sits in a thickly wooded spot
where the St. Lawrence River meets Lake Ontario, at the point
where the magnificent Thousand Islands begin to dot the river.
"But it's wider than that. I locate the quarry, a metaphor for the
underside of the city, in Sydney, but I don't mean it to be specifically Sydney or even specifically Australia. It's really about the underside of Western society."

Hospital was born in Melbourne and grew up in Brisbane. A
small, blond dynamo of a woman of almost 50 years, she left Australia for the U.S. in 1967 together with her husband, Cliff, a com-
parative religion scholar whose specialty is Sanskrit and who now
teaches at Queens University in Kingston. And so began a nomadic life that has led her to Boston and Cambridge, to India,
London, Los Angeles, Canada, Australia and back again. She has

taught writing at MIT and Boston University as well as in Ottawa, Sydney, and Monash, and now she spends half of every year teaching at La Trobe University in Melbourne.

Hospital's first novel, *The Ivory Swing*, received Canada's prestigious Seal Award in 1982; it was issued here the following year. *The Tiger in the Tiger Pit* (1984) and *Borderline* (1985) confirmed her talent and her prolificity. All three were published by Dutton and reprinted by Bantam. Bantam published her fourth, *Charades*, in both hardcover and paperback, and Louisiana State University Press issued two volumes of stories, *Dislocations* (1988) and *Isobars* (1991).

The Last Magician is Hospital's first book with agent Molly Friedrich, and her first with Holt and editor Marian Wood, whom Hospital describes as "an immensely alert and intelligent reader. She also has an absolutely extraordinary photographic memory. I really want an editor who I feel has deep empathy with the manuscript and with me," she explains. "When I bleed she bleeds— and it's always been 'she' with me. I've never had a male editor." Her longtime Canadian editor is Ellen Seligman at McClelland and Stewart. In London it's Lynn Knight at Virago, and in Australia it's Rosanne Fitzgibbons at the University of Queensland Press. *The Last Magician* received keen reviews in England, and was reported to be "widely tipped" for the Booker Prize.

"The fact that I was mugged once in inner-city Boston, and then went to live in inner-city Sydney while teaching at the university there, also had a big bearing on the shape the novel took," Hospital reveals. "I talked to male and female street prostitutes and street kids, and sat on the steps of soup kitchens for the homeless and talked to people there. The story I kept hearing again and again was that among their regular clients were people whose faces they saw in the newspapers—politicians, judges, lawyers, and cops—and that paradox fascinated me. Law keepers, the guardians of law, order and morality, consort all the time with the lawbreakers—that was what I wanted to explore."

"The world is thick with messages, . . . crowded with absences," observes Hospital, who traces both views in this novel. Many of the other themes familiar to readers of her earlier work will be found again in *The Last Magician*. There are people who disappear, people who are dislocated, people in transit, people who cross borders, people who can't speak. There is the potency of place, particularly the lush and wanton Australian rain forest. There are preoccupations with judgment, power, atonement, revelations, love and memory. There are old wounds, absences, secrets, silences, and open endings. We all inherit plots and then ride them like treadmills, as Hospital has written elsewhere.

But the theme of being silenced, of being without a voice, is especially powerful in the new novel. "That's always been of interest to me in my writing—to give a voice to the people who don't have one in the normal media channels or in literature. But I also felt in a rather scary way that I was writing about my own silencing, which was just engulfing me. I was writing about my own experience as an intellectual and literary figure in Australia. It certainly has to be said that Australia's not a nurturing environment either for intellectual or literary women, and in fact it often sets out to be incredibly destructive.

"I didn't think I'd be able to finish the book. I had to make little deals with myself, trick myself into finishing it. I knew there were going to be terrible penalties for saying the things I wanted to say about the hostility of authority systems. I felt that when I finished I'd probably never write again. It was the first time ever that I finished a novel and was not already in the space of the next one. But I've reached the stage now where I'm *yearning* to write some stories that were brewing in Australia, especially about my trips through the outback. It's a good sign."

Hospital has written one mystery novel, *A Very Proper Death*, published under the pseudonym Alex Juniper by Random House in Canada and by Scribners in the U.S. But *The Last Magician*, she says, is also "an intricate murder mystery. The last magician is the one who out-magics all the others, who's in possession of the truth, who removes all the illusions. He's a photographer who simply monitors, records and stores things, which I think is a metaphor for the artist. He doesn't always know the significance of a photograph when he takes it, and in fact the murder is solved 20 years after it took place, from a photograph, from the retroactive significance that a viewer realizes years later." But there's more than one murder mystery to this novel, and the solution to the second is not nearly so incontrovertible as the first.

The story's ending is genuinely ambiguous. "Right from my very first novel I have always had open endings," Hospital acknowledges. "In *Borderline* I wanted to make the reader feel the real hor-

111

ror, the trauma of refugees who never know for sure if their loved ones are dead or alive. But it is very much the basic experience of my much-dislocated life that relationships end, and years later open again. There is no such thing as a final chord until the last final chord, until we die."

But the opening chord of *The Last Magician* is emphatic. It is a clear allusion to Dante's *Inferno,* and so it should come as no surprise that Hospital is also a scholar of medieval literature. She says she was "electrified on multiple levels" five years ago when she saw some photographs by Sebastião Salgado in the *New York Times* of the Serra Pelada gold mine in Brazil—thousands of peasant slaves swarming up and down the steep sides of a huge pit, like a vision of hell. "It seemed like a Bosch canvas, it was so arrestingly horrific. And it resonated with my inner landscape of nightmares and night terrors after being mugged. But I am also steeped in Dante, and the image of the pit immediately made me think of Botticelli's drawings of the *Inferno.* It was two portrayals of the same scene, one in the 15th century and one in the 20th century. It's not that I really thought it out. I just knew from the kind of humming I got in my head and the vibrations in my body that all of this had something to do with a novel. But I had no idea what, or where I was going to set it.

"Then I went off to teach in Sydney and lived on a street on the cusp between being semi-slum and being gentrified. One end was burned out, boarded up, abandoned buildings lived in by squatters and derelicts—'derros' in Australian slang. Kids lived in the basements and on the sidewalks. They lived in the subway station, which was tunneled into the rock cliffs in the ravines [beneath the city]. I felt I was somehow moving in the landscape of these photographs and the Botticelli drawings. By that time the ferment level in my mind was quite high. I was zipping back and forth as I constantly do when I'm in Australia, from Brisbane to Sydney and back to the rain forest, putting it all together.

"Ideas and subjects just grab me by the scruff of the neck. I get the abstract central conception of the novel first, and a vivid sense of place and locale comes early on. Then the characters, and last of all the plot. It's just something I simply discover. Once I've got my central conception, my place, my characters, I set out, and I literally don't know where I'm going. I find out when I've written the novel what's going to happen."

In Hospital's imagined world the powerful emotions and events of childhood are often played off against those of adulthood, and *The Last Magician* is no exception. Asked about the moving, terrifying childhood games and taunts that enter into the narrative, Hospital confesses, "I lived opposite a cutting in the railway line both in Melbourne and in Brisbane, and we played daredevil games as kids. We used to lie on the tracks, and the boy next door always claimed that if you would lie parallel, inside them, the train could pass over you. I suppose there are certain little fragments, splinters of yourself, that do get into characters," she allows.

"I suppose I remember the past so well because in primary school I was, by imposed necessity, a loner"—she came from an intensely conservative and fundamentalist religious family—"so you become a very acute observer. You're always trying to translate to yourself what's going on, and you play things over in your mind, trying to figure out their meaning, because it's all foreign to you, trying to learn behaviors, what other kids do. You become a very close and sharp observer. Then, too, when you're wrenched from and geographically dislocated from your past, you have an intense motivation to hang onto it, to recall it. Plus there's just loss. I miss the Queensland rain forest so much. You hang onto the images of the things you pine for."

But Hospital is adamantly not an expatriate writer. "That's a label other people put onto you," she says. "There's the whole issue of nationality. I'm constantly being asked to account for this— 'Do you consider yourself an Australian writer? A Canadian writer?' I am just someone whose life has been exceedingly nomadic, but unintentionally so. I am deeply and viscerally attached particularly to Brisbane, also to this spot in Kingston, to Boston, to a village in South India—all these places leave permanent grooves in my life, and they matter to me. The countries that vilify their writers who leave, and regard it as a species of treason if you go—Australia, India, Canada, Ireland—it's a sign of post-colonial cringe. England and America, countries that have a strong enough sense of themselves, never do it and don't feel threatened, but the colonies do."

One way to handle the pain of life, of course, is to write. "That's why it's so difficult to write," Hospital admits. "It's so painful to reactivate the old pains; it's a risky thing to do for one's own well-being. But these things lurk. They catch you off guard, and their potency is not lessened for lying dormant. And the safest way to deal with them is in coded form, in as labyrinthine and transposed a way as possible. You try to let the pain seep away."

For this passionately Australian writer who has shown that she has the straight-out gift for telling a story, perhaps even the silences, in the end, will speak.

MISSY DANIEL
September 14, 1992

ROBERT D. KAPLAN

ROBERT D. KAPLAN lives in a D.C. suburb, dresses nattily and drives a late-model foreign compact. In themselves these are banal facts of the sort that Kaplan has spent his career eschewing in his pursuit of more elusive quarries: from 1975 to 1991, he lived abroad and traveled incessantly, reporting from more than 40 countries and writing three books, most recently *Balkan Ghosts* (St. Martin's Press). Here in America, though, such details seem oddly telling. As the athletically built writer meets us at a Metro station in southern Maryland and we drive to the condominium where he lives with his wife and son, one can't help but remark on the surface differences of his American life from that of reporting on the famine in Ethiopia or traveling with the *mujahidin*, or freedom fighters, in Afghanistan. As if to dispel his own claim that he has settled down, Kaplan notes that soon he will be off to Turkey to write a piece for *National Geographic*. It becomes obvious that he combines an adventurer's zeal for what he calls "unsimulated experiences" with the unromantic professionalism of a seasoned political journalist.

Add to that his dogged prescience, which had him reporting on the breakup of Yugoslavia when most opinion-makers still regarded the Balkans as part of an abstraction called the Soviet bloc. *Balkan Ghosts*, which *PW*, in a starred review, called a "vividly impressionistic travelogue," is the fruit of what Kaplan describes as a 15-year "obsession" with the Balkans. In dense, engrossing chapters, he treats religious conflict in Croatia, rural strife in Romania, and nationalist pandering in Greece, which he calls "the place that best sum[s] up and explain[s] the Balkans."

Kaplan's basement study is decorated with art acquired on his travels—a Hungarian drawing, a miniature from the Khyber Pass, a photo of Calcutta at dawn—and a framed *Atlantic* cover illustrating his story "Tales from the Bazaar." Perhaps the most revealing decoration, though, is a photo of his father at the Texas State Fair in 1933. "He bummed around the country for 10 years during the Depression," Kaplan explains. Clearly he has inherited his father's wanderlust. Born in New York City in 1952, he wrote for the college newspaper at the University of Connecticut, and after graduating in 1973 he worked for 18 months as a reporter at a Vermont newspaper. "I covered everything from criminals to the governor's office," he recalls. "It was all very interesting, but I was supremely bored. I had studied languages in college, I had gone abroad as a student, and I wanted to write overseas. So I quit my job and bought a one-way ticket to Europe, and I didn't come back, essentially, until last year."

In summarizing his long writerly sojourn, Kaplan tells of shrewdly working his media contacts to build a career. Starting out as a stringer for the *San Francisco Examiner* and the *Christian Science Monitor*, he first wrote about Tunisia; then he spent time in Egypt, Sudan, Syria, Jordan, and Israel, where he stayed a few years. Finally he moved to Greece, where he married in 1982. Maria, his wife, is a Portuguese-born Canadian.

Eventually Kaplan became a "super-stringer"—regularly relied upon by media outlets, in his case the *Atlanta Journal-Constitution*, Toronto's *Globe and Mail*, and ABC Radio. Soon he began to indulge his burgeoning interest in the Balkans—a fixation that began as a hobby, he says. Twice a year he went from Greece to Yugoslavia, to Bulgaria, to Romania and to Hungary. "I thought, this is far more interesting than Ethiopia or Afghanistan and the rest put together. Traveling around, I saw that this was a region where communism was an artificial reality that had nothing to do with people's true emotions, a place where a lot of political grievances remained completely unsettled."

Already Kaplan envisioned a book about the region, but he was unable to interest even newspaper editors in the subject. By this time, too, he had realized that he was drawn less to hard news than to the sort of analysis that requires long articles and books. "I'd always wanted to write for intellectual journals," he says. Finally, in 1984, he sold a piece on Tunisia to the *New Republic*; a year later, he interested the *Atlantic* in an article about Sudan.

The famine there and in Ethiopia became the subject of Kaplan's first book, the travails of which make an emblematic hard-luck publishing story. "The hard-news media does not cover the world; it covers the foreign extensions of America's domestic obsessions," he says. "And America's obsession with Ethiopia was with beautiful, starving, El Greco–like kids, but the famine was just a side effect of a war that had been going on for a decade. The media rushed in and covered the famine but didn't cover the war or any of the history or politics that had produced it." Kaplan decided there was a need for a book to clarify the situation. But though the *Atlantic* bought a 10,000-word essay, the book he wrote found no buyers.

After trying in vain to sell his work himself, Kaplan signed on with Andrew Wylie, who impressed him mightily. "He gets a lot of flak, but all I can say about him is: I was nobody, and he read the book and even memorized parts of it. But he couldn't sell it." Finally Wylie placed the book with Westview Press of Boulder, Colo., which paid a $2000 advance—far less than the *Atlantic* had paid for the essay excerpt. Coming out from a small press after the mass coverage of the famine had subsided, *Surrender or Starve: The Wars Behind the Famine* (1988) was passed over by most review sections, and the book sold poorly—although Westview has kept it in print.

So Kaplan was back to square one—except that now he had a book to his credit. Plus, crucially, he had gained a footing on the often rocky terrain of foundation grants, having gained one from the conservative Madison Center for Educational Affairs. To do so, he drew on his aptitude for analysis and his willingness to buck convention. "I applied to both liberal and conservative foundations," he recounts, "and I discovered that in the 1980s the liberals had absolutely no interest in the communist world—they were interested in exposing the iniquities of American policies in Central America. They'd been in operation for decades and had become bureaucratized. They had very defined credentials that I didn't meet: I didn't go to an Ivy League school, I wasn't a former AP correspondent. The conservative foundations knew they had to expose Communism, but the kinds of people who'd go backpacking in Afghanistan and Ethiopia were not the kinds of people socially and culturally who would apply for grants from conservative foundations. So I had something original to offer them."

Kaplan still longed to write a book about the Balkans, but after the famine debacle he knew that such a work had little chance of being published, and this time even the conservatives weren't interested. For his next book, then, he decided to drum up funding in the way he knew best. *Reader's Digest* had asked him to go to Afghanistan to report on the guerilla war against the Soviet forces. Relying on the *Digest's* lucrative fees and another assignment for the *Atlantic*, he made two long trips into the Afghan hills, traveling with the *mujahidin*. Ultimately, he got another Madison grant. And acting on a tip from a *Digest* editor, he acquired a new agent, Carl D. Brandt. "Carl covered the Balkans in the '50s, so we hit it off," Kaplan says. They have worked together ever since.

When Brandt began shopping around Kaplan's book on Afghanistan, he swiftly received an offer from Michael Janeway, then executive editor of Houghton Mifflin's adult trade division. "It was the easiest sell, just a month from the time I sent Carl the pages to the time he said he had a publisher. I was ecstatic," Kaplan recalls. His high spirits turned out to be premature. Janeway left Houghton while the book was in production, bequeathing it to Henry Ferris, now of Times Books ("who did a good job," says Kaplan. "I have no complaints"). *Soldiers of God: With the Mujahidin in Afghanistan* (1990) "sunk without a trace."

By now Kaplan had gotten wind of major changes in Eastern Europe. When he visited Hungary early in 1989, he found it "incredible. People weren't even paying lip service to the Communist Party." An old friend there, Gabor Tarnai, told him the citizens were waiting for the system to collapse. "I'd learned to trust Gabor. I knew something was going to happen, and I knew if something happened, the Balkans were going to go nuts."

Returning to the States in April, Kaplan met with *Atlantic* editors Cullen Murphy and William Whitworth in Boston, and told them that East Germany was at a flashpoint. By now they had confidence in his advice, and they sent him to Germany to write a long piece. "I spent three weeks there, rushed back, wrote a 60-page article. They had it by October, and they slated it as a cover story for March or April. Then the Berlin Wall collapsed. I was in Macedonia, and Cullen called and said, 'Bob, we can't run this. We've been overtaken by events.' "

Kaplan's disappointment was eased by the fact that at last he was at work on his book on the Balkans, traveling on another

Madison grant. "I went to Croatia in 1989, and it was clear war was going to break out at any moment. I was saying, 'The world is collapsing where I am.' But nobody believed me. Every network camera crew was in Berlin, in Poland, or in Russia. Yugoslavia was where nobody was."

Meanwhile, back in the States, Carl Brandt was having trouble selling Kaplan's Balkans book. "Fourteen houses either rejected the manuscript or didn't even want to read it," Kaplan recalls. David Sobel at St. Martin's, however, snapped it up immediately, unable to believe other editors had passed on it. (Sobel has since left the house, and *Balkan Ghosts* is now a Thomas Dunne Book.) The book began to gain a reputation even before publication. "Paul Kennedy read it and gave it to his friend Jason Epstein," Kaplan recalls. "He said, 'I wonder why I didn't see this manuscript. I would have bought it in two minutes!' "

With hindsight, *Balkan Ghosts* seems to be a serendipitous book, a rare confluence of talent, logistics and events. Even so, one can see why so many deskbound editors had trouble with it. Unlike most journalists covering the Balkan conflict, who will dispose of old ethnic rivalries in their opening paragraphs in order to get to current events, Kaplan makes such rivalries his subject, and sets them out in complex fashion. Writing in the spirit of Rebecca West—whose massive *Black Lamb and Grey Falcon* is the *Ulysses* of the genre—he makes palpable the extent to which the past bears down on the present in a region that has been called "history's cauldron."

For his part, Kaplan has already moved on to his next book, a study of State Department "Arabists"—odd and influential members of the U.S. diplomatic corps—that will be published by Adam Bellow at the Free Press. And his recent admirer Jason Epstein has signed up his proposed magnum opus, in which Kaplan will try to predict the crises of the coming decades. "Whereas in the Balkans book I used the travel genre as a vehicle to explore the historical process, I'm now going to use travel as a vehicle to explore the strategic flashpoints of the 21st century, based on environmental stress and demography. I'm going to go to the Maldive Islands, which are sinking, to the worst sections of Lagos, to the threatened Indians of Central America—to where real big conflicts can happen because of too many people and too few resources, and because of culture clashes. I believe we're going from a time of nation-state war—the first part of the 20th century—to ideological war, and now into a time of culture war."

As he talks, his voice is animated by his wanderlust, an irrepressible longing for another trip, another story, another chance to ride the wave of history. "When I leave for Turkey, a part of my life is finished," Kaplan says. "I'm already putting the Balkans behind me. It was fascinating when you were the only one there and you could predict what was going to happen. Now it has reached the realm of the obvious."

PAUL ELIE
March 29, 1993

RHODA LERMAN

WHEN INTERVIEWING an author for whom linear logic holds little attraction, one must expect a certain scattered, intuitive slant to the conversation. Talk may link up, loop back, make sense later, but if it does it's by chance, not by design. Words are important, of course, and humor, and, nowadays, her "dog children." But logic definitely takes the backseat with Rhoda Lerman, who, with six novels under her belt, including the just-released *Animal Acts* from Holt, is about to write her first nonfiction work, a straight-ahead, first-person, linear narrative about Newfoundland dogs and the dedicated passion they've aroused in her.

In contrast to the work in progress, the novels are idiosyncratic affairs, wildly inventive, lusty and fabulistic, tackling subject matter that, however related at its core by humor, feminism and mysticism, has a wide variety of surfaces ranging from earth-goddess mythology (*Call Me Ishtar*), contemporary mating rituals (*The Girl That He Marries*), fictional autobiography (*Eleanor*), psychological transformation (*The Book of the Night*), Jewish theology (*God's Ear*) and animal consciousnes (*Animal Acts*). The novels are also, it turns out, works of intense inquiry, during which time Lerman studies her subject for long periods. *God's Ear*, for instance, about an insurance salesman named Yussel Fetner who struggles to follow his father's bidding to "circumcise his heart," inspired Lerman to learn Yiddish, study the Kabbalah and immerse herself in Jewish life for two years. *Eleanor*, a fictional account of Eleanor Roosevelt's life, involved spending three years with Roosevelt family members, including grandson Curtis. For *Animal Acts*, a hair-raising adventure about a woman fleeing her husband and lover with a carnival gorilla for company, which evolved from her fascination with animals, Lerman befriended gorilla keepers at zoos across North America, went to their conferences and carefully observed their charges.

"I keep reinventing my wheel and wiping out my fan club," says Lerman, wryly acknowledging that although each of her books has received extraordinary praise from the critics, each since *Eleanor*, which was a popular success, has experienced consistently mediocre sales, a situation that has led her devoted but wary publisher to offer smaller and smaller advances for each book. Only three, *The Girl That He Marries, Eleanor* and *Book of the Night,* had paperback editions, and only *Book* is still in print, in a small British edition.

"It's been downhill since *Eleanor* into anonymity," Lerman says, prompted to reflect on her literary history. *The Girl That He Marries,* Lerman says, was optioned by Hollywood repeatedly and sent her three children to college; and Norman Lear hired her to write a TV docudrama about Eleanor Roosevelt called *First Lady of the World* after *Eleanor* was published, though surprisingly few others have beaten a path to her door. "But my books have gotten better," she says. "It would be nice if they could be commercially successful, but I won't write them in order to be. I want to keep traveling into new worlds." What *is* disappointing, she says, is the attitude she encounters among the male writers who live near her in upstate New York. "They say, 'We don't read women.' "

Lerman appreciated the recognition she received when she was invited to give the opening speech five years ago at a Harvard conference on women's leadership. She spoke from personal experience on the power of the imagination and on using imagination as a leg up in a masculine world. "Being invited to the conference was one of the biggest moments of my life, because what I had to tell the women was really important. It's fortunate that I can live as I do, have what I want now, and want what I have. I can still write what I want to write.

Lerman, who is 58 and the possessor of a robust ruddiness and a voluble, earth-mother manner, has lived in the small town of Cazenovia, N.Y. (alternately "a charming old town with rich old families") and "Stockbridge without the visitors"), for the past 30 years, leaving periodically to teach or to research her novels. Her husband, who works in the floor-covering business, comes from nearby Syracuse; this summer they celebrate 36 years of marriage. ("Either we're very much in love or lazy," Lerman quips.) They have two grown-up daughters and a son no longer living at home, and eight Newfoundland dogs. A handler-groomer lives with them.

Ten years ago, no books or bagels were available in the area, but currently, boasts Lerman, there are both (a Barnes & Noble has even opened). On the day we visit, rain obscures the gentle green landscape, and a highly billed encounter with the Newfies is described as likely to be very sloppy. When it actually takes place, after lunch in one of Cazenovia's landmark inns, Lerman proffers a well-worn sweatsuit as the ideal outfit in which to visit the animals, who, though trained, are very affectionate and very large. This day they are allowed into the house, a 17-room mansion built in 1892 by Stanford White, only in shifts.

Living so far from the publishing center and having no interest in or aptitude for self-promotion has, she feels, been partly responsible for her lagging reputation, but has also given her room to flourish as a writer, with no clamor to fend off and only her own curiosity to answer to. She approaches each book as a chance to indulge this curiosity.

For *Animal Acts*, the driving question evolved from a story she had once heard about a gorilla in mysterious circumstances. A friend of one of her uncle's—one of four she grew up sharing jokes with—had rented a gorilla at Coney Island—why, she doesn't know. "Only, the animal couldn't be returned, because the pet shop was closed. I never found out what happened to the gorilla, but the book explains what might have happened, if." In the story, Linda, the 50-ish heroine, takes a feverish ride south from Coney Island to Florida with the fearsome but tractable gorilla, named Moses, who sits in a cage at the back of the truck and serves as a focal point for Linda's obsessions over the "irreconcilable differences" between men and women. "Men and women are different species, not gender differences," Linda says. "Gorilla is of the same material. Women think in puddles, men in straight lines."

Lerman's fascination with gorillas increased as she further explored their natures. Then, a keeper at the Toronto Zoo—one of the people to whom *Animal Acts* is dedicated—informed her that gorillas can have fantasies, citing as evidence a female in her care who would mate only in the presence of a particular (human) boy. After spending more time with gorilla keepers and gleaning more understanding of gorilla behavior, she was invited to watch a live birth at the Calgary Zoo. "I had seen dogs give birth," she says, "but this was different. This was 'us.' Not 'them.' They allowed me to stay in the back with Kikinga [the father]. He was lonely because his wife was giving birth. He made a nest next to me. I was thrilled out of my mind. In the book's acknowledgements, Lerman credits Dian Fossey's *Gorillas in the Mist*, Elaine Morgan's *Aquatic Ape*, and George Schaller's *Year of the Gorilla* as indispensable to the writing of the book. She tells *PW* that Anne Moir and David Jessel's *Brain Sex: The Real Differences Between Men and Women* provided the theoretical framework for the male-female dichotomies she speculates about in the novel.

Lerman says she was careful to avoid mythical references in *Animal Acts*, any mention of Osiris or "Hamlet, the pig god" or anything else that might mystify a potential reader, as is her wont in her other books. "I could have gone on for pages. I had starred reviews on *God's Ear*. It went noplace but the waiting list in libraries; it didn't sell. I'm tired of people saying, 'I don't understand your writing.' I do want people to understand. Often the mythology is daunting. But it is hard to leave out."

Lerman was born on Long Island, grew up in Connecticut and considers herself a Floridian, having moved to that state with her family after her father died and attended junior high, high school and college there. She has a fraternal twin sister, Judith, who, she says, "is very, very smart, much more logical, whose specialty is learning disorders and who has also been married to the same man forever." They are very close and talk daily. Of having a twin she says, "You're never alone. You've always had that other person, that other relationship."

She discovered her literary bent in the second grade. "We'd taken a trip, and the teacher asked us to write down afterward what we had seen. I was the only one who'd remembered the water fountain. As if there's just one way to be a writer." In college she majored in geology but was requested by the chairman to leave the department because, Lerman contends, she was a woman. Math was her favorite subject at one point, and she taught herself trigonometry when she was a teaching assistant. "I can think like that, but I don't like to."

She describes her early life as "good," "sweet," "Country Club Jewish." She says it provided no material to a writer until after she married and her husband took over the management of a rock 'n' roll band in the '60s. Then she was stimulated to words by the tension she observed between the world of sex, drugs and rock 'n' roll and her life as a suburban wife—and came up with *Call Me Ishtar*, her first novel, which is about the reincarnation of the goddess Ishtar in the body of a suburban Jewish housewife.

The book was published by Doubleday after an editor there, Julie Coppersmith, read a story Lerman had published in the *Nickel Review* and got in touch with her to see if she had anything else. "*Ishtar* did very well," Lerman says. "It had a cult following." After *Ishtar* Lerman wrote a script for 20th Century Fox about a man who wanted to be a woman. "Then Dustin Hoffman brought out *Tootsie*, with the same plot. Then *Ishtar*. I felt a little abused." Since the plot lines of the book and the movie are different, the connection between the two, other than the title, is virtually nil.

When Coopersmith left Doubleday and become an agent, she took Lerman with her and sold her next book, *The Girl That He Marries*, a comic romance, as well as hardcover rights to *Ishtar*, to Holt. She has been with Holt ever since, edited by Marian Wood. "Marian wasn't hot on the gorilla book," Lerman says. "She's a challenge, but she's loyal. I'm part of the house, though Holt has not always understood me. There's frustration at not having made me rich and famous." Her current agent is Owen Laster at William Morris.

Lerman says that she writes fast once she's finished with her research and her long spells of dreamy thinking. She works in pencil for her first drafts, then moves on to the typewriter and uses a computer only for final editing. "A computer assumes the thing you do second is better, but often the first is what has muscle," she says. "I love good writing. It's music to my ears. I was brought up in a musical household. Everyone played cello. A truly great sentence has music coming out of it. I read my stuff aloud to myself. It has to sound right." She adds that her family constantly indulged in wordplay, banter and jokes. "Toilet jokes crack me up," she says. She writes erratically, preoccupied with her work in progress even when not actually at her desk. When she is ready to get serious, she goes off to a pay-per-day retreat run by Colgate University or to the downtown Sheridan Inn, where there are no distractions or responsibilities. Nowadays she spends a fair amount of time going around to dog shows and bringing home ribbons.

"You can listen to animals and they'll make every effort to talk to you," she says, eager, like all animal lovers, to explain the magnetic attraction to an alien species. Her book on dogs should explain more. "This is the first time I can write from my own experience," she says, visibly relieved to be tackling a subject so plainly in sync with the rest of the world, and of interest to it.

SUZANNE MANTELL
August 1, 1994

DAVID MCCULLOUGH

"PEOPLE CAN ARGUE whether Harry Truman was a great man and whether he was a great president, but there's no argument at all about his being a great story," says David McCullough, who has spent the past 10 years on that great story. The result is *Truman*, a 1,117-page biography published by Simon & Schuster.

But the word "biography" seems almost too small to describe *Truman*; perhaps "historical novel," though a misnomer, better conveys the breadth and vigor of this Tolstoyan narrative about the so-called "little man from Missouri" whose presidency is central, both literally and figuratively, to this country in this century.

Truman begins before the beginning—Harry isn't born for nearly 40 pages—and stretches past the end, beyond Harry Truman's death in 1972 to the death of his "Dear Bess" a decade later. McCullough planned it that way.

"It has become fashionable," he says, "to begin biographies midway through the subject's life, or even at the end. I briefly considered opening with Truman, back home in Independence, Missouri, after leaving office, on one of his walks around town, remembering the past. Then we would cut to his birth and childhood . . . But no. I wanted the form of the book to be a measure of the man, and Harry Truman never did anything in an inverse or clever or fashionable way. Therefore, for a straightforward life, a straightforward beginning."

Elaborating on Truman the man and Truman the subject of his book, McCullough says, "He saw himself in the presidency as part of a chain of being, as one of many presidents. I wanted to convey his strong sense of history not only in the writing, but in the form of the book.

"I also wanted to establish the Americanness of the man— Truman's frontier, middle-American roots, because chief among his attributes is authenticity. His life is an authentic American story. And it's a big book because it's a big life."

The book seems to have been waiting for McCullough, though its genesis took him by surprise. After the 1981 publication of *Mornings on Horseback*, about Theodore Roosevelt's early years, he wanted a change from "the milieu of blueblood New York aristocracy. More important, I wanted a change of *form*—I wanted to do a whole life, not just a section."

McCullough chose Picasso as his next subject, and worked at the project for months before realizing that he had made a false start. "I grew to loathe Picasso very quickly," he says with a wince.

Then, McCullough had a meeting with his agent, Morton Janklow, his editor, Michael Korda, and S & S CEO Dick Snyder. Korda suggested that since there was then no good one-volume biography of Franklin D. Roosevelt, McCullough might consider writing one.

His response was, " 'If I were going to write a biography of a 20th-century president, it wouldn't be FDR, it would be Harry Truman.' " McCullough recalls. "I don't know what made me say that. I hadn't thought about it at all, though I've always found Truman the most appealing president of this century."

Korda, Snyder and Janklow responded: "Why not?" McCullough, still somewhat dazed, echoed, "Well, why not?" and asked for time to look into it. And the rest was history, in the most literal sense.

McCullough began by reading "the obvious books," such as Merle Miller's *Plain Speaking: An Oral Biography of Harry S. Truman* and Truman's own memoirs. He also consulted Truman's daughter Margaret Truman Daniel to ascertain whether she knew of anyone working on a similar project and to ask if she would be willing to talk with him at length about her father. From their conversation he learned that she would welcome such a project.

"It's unbelievable," McCullough says, "that my book is the first full-scale, life-and-times [treatment] of Harry Truman. There are others, and some good ones, but they're thin books."

On his first visit to the Truman library in Independence, McCullough realized what an enormous task he had taken on. He read thousands of Truman's letters (liberally quoted from in the book); papers and documents from Truman's long life and long political career; and, in addition, the papers of Dean Acheson,

Clark Clifford and many others who served during the Truman administration. McCullough must have been stunned; even now he shakes his head, declaring, "One could spend an entire life at the Truman library and not cover all of it."

During his own "Truman years," McCullough conducted 125 interviews; these acknowledgments alone read like a White House gala list: Lauren Bacall, Jimmy Carter, Gerald Ford, John Hersey, Lady Bird Johnson, Jacqueline Kennedy Onassis, Ronald Reagan, Franklin D. Roosevelt Jr. et al. When interviewing the three former presidents, McCullough says, he asked where they were when they heard that President Roosevelt had died; their feelings about FDR and about Truman, his successor; and their evaluation of Truman now that they have occupied the White House themselves. McCullough also approached former President Nixon, who declined to be interviewed.

McCullough says that earlier in his career his method was to complete all research before starting to write. "But I don't work that way anymore. Now I do what I consider to be 60% of the research; then I begin writing. It's when you write that you learn what you don't know—and what you need to find out."

McCullough lived in Missouri on and off during the course of his project. In 1983 he was asked to become host and narrator of the PBS series *Smithsonian World*, which required that he move to Washington. This move was a fortuitous event, for it deepened his understanding of Truman's Washington years.

"Life in the capital," he says, "enabled me to observe the living model in the way a paleontologist studies living forms to understand fossils better. I was able to see present-day politicians and bureaucrats in the living form while writing about those of an earlier era."

In France, he retraced Truman's World War I experiences. He traveled to Key West, a favorite Truman vacation spot. At Lamar, Mo., he made drawings of Truman's birthplace and the surrounding landscape.

"I must immerse myself in a subject," McCullough says. "I reach the point where I know the people I'm writing about—not only the subject, but the full cast of characters—better than I know people around me. I know who said what, I know exactly what their rooms looked like. It's not until I reach this state that I'm ready to write. When someone says, 'I hear you're working on a book,' I often think the preposition is wrong; I'm working *in* a book."

Although known as an historian and a biographer, McCullough says he prefers to call himself a writer, because "the real problems I work with are writing problems." He sees himself as "part of a school of history writers" that includes Bruce Catton, Barbara Tuchman, Robert Caro, William Manchester and others characterized by McCullough as "writers first of all, none of them trained historians. Most of them are, as I am, lapsed journalists. In our apprenticeship as writers we learned about the elements of *story*. About the elements of narration, and how to hold an audience. As a consequence, I believe we write—I hope I write—in a way that transcends the academic plodding of so much that readers think of as 'history': dreary, deadly, to be avoided at all costs."

McCullough, 58, a native of Pittsburgh and a graduate of Yale, states rather proudly that his major was English, not history. After college he worked at Time Inc. from 1956 to 1961, first writing circulation promotion for *Sports Illustrated* and later serving as a staff writer for *Architectural Forum.* In 1961 he went to Washington to work with Edward R. Murrow at the U.S. Information Agency, a job he calls "one of the great breaks of my life."

In 1964, during Murrow's final illness, McCullough returned to New York, where he spent the next six years as a writer and editor at *American Heritage.* "My greatest accomplishment there," he says, "was the *American Heritage Picture History of World War II,* which I edited and which is still in print almost 30 years later."

During that period, he began writing his first book at night and on weekends. *The Johnstown Flood* was published in 1968 by Simon & Schuster. It was well received, and in 1970 McCullough decided to leave his job to write full time. "It was a difficult decision, because by then my job at *American Heritage* was a very good one. I couldn't have done it without the support of my wife, Rosalee, and her belief in me."

The McCulloughs, who live on Martha's Vineyard, are momentarily in New York staying in the genteel precincts of the Yale Club. Tanned and relaxed after a trip to Hawaii to visit with one of their five adult children, they evoke the family closeness of earlier eras. And one understands better why Truman family loyalty occupies such an important place in McCullough's book.

His publishing family—S & S—is also important to McCullough.

It's the only one he has ever belonged to. "You hear about the tumultuous publishing business," he muses, "but most of the principals I met when I walked in the door almost 30 years ago are still right there—Frank Metz, the art director; Sophie Sorkin, director of copy editing. Richard Snyder and Michael Korda were there at that time, too." Peter Schwed, now retired, was McCullough's editor before Korda.

Not long after publication of *The Johnstown Flood*, McCullough had lunch with two friends at a restaurant on Manhattan's Lower East Side. One of the friends, an engineer, began talking about the nearby Brooklyn Bridge and about the various things its builders *didn't* know when they embarked on the epic project.

"Immediately I knew that this was the subject of my next book," McCullough recalls. "I went directly from the restaurant to the New York Public Library at 42nd Street, took those marble stairs about four at a time to the card catalogue, and found over a hundred cards on the subject of the bridge, but no card describing the book I'd already begun to work out in my mind." *The Great Bridge*, the story of the construction of the Brooklyn Bridge, was published in 1972.

The Path Between the Seas, the story of still another epic feat of engineering, was published in 1977. Examining the creation of the Panama Canal, the book appeared just as debate in Washington over the canal's future reached the boiling point. Owing to the work's vast historical and political panorama, it played an important part in shaping national policy with respect to the canal. McCullough recalls that "there was a copy of the book on virtually every desk in the Senate." President Carter read the book and required everyone on his staff to read it. McCullough was invited to the White House to advise the President. Later, when the treaty was signed, giving Panama eventual control over the canal, McCullough and his wife traveled to Panama with President Carter for the ceremonies.

While writing *Truman*, McCullough was involved in the creation of the PBS series *The Civil War*, which he also narrated. He is host of another PBS series, *The American Experience*, and found time as well to collect some of his journalism and speeches into a volume called *Brave Companions*, which S & S published in 1991. (All of McCullough's books are still in print.)

He is often asked, especially by teachers, "How can we increase interest in history?" McCullough's answer: "There's no trick—it's all there. The real story is the most gripping story of all." And every one of his books proves his point.

SAM STAGGS
June 8, 1992

ALICE MCDERMOTT

IN 1979 A NERVOUS graduate of the University of New Hampshire's writing program handed literary agent Harriet Wasserman's secretary a few short stories and 50 pages of an unfinished novel. Wasserman read them, called the writer and said, "I want you to give me everything you've got." Not too long after that, she invited Alice McDermott to her office and asked, "Would you like a male editor or a female one?"

The astonished 26-year-old, who would have been happy with "any living, breathing literary editor," wound up under the wing of Jonathan Galassi, then a rising star at Houghton Mifflin. She followed him to Random House, which in 1982 published her first novel, *A Bigamist's Daughter*, to the kind of critical enthusiasm most beginning writers only dream about. Next McDermott went with Galassi to Farrar, Straus & Giroux, which released *That Night* in 1987; it was nominated for a National Book Award and later made into a film.

Given this prompt and warm encouragement, it's surprising to discover that, for McDermott, "the hardest thing I had to do even to become a writer was believing that I had anything to say that people would want to read." She began with short stories, she explains, because "I felt I had to apologize for wanting to write fiction for a living, and with a short story there was this sense of, well, it's just a little bitty thing!"

On the even of the April publication of her third novel, *At Weddings and Wakes* (Farrar, Straus & Giroux), the author, now 38, continues to display a certain diffidence about her work. Discussing the brevity of her books, none of which runs to much more than 200 pages, she comments, "I still have that sense of apology: Look, I'm not going to waste your time; I'm going to tell you what I need to tell you, then stop. When I'm composing something I'm always looking for that point where I feel everything I and the reader need to know is there, then that's enough. Sing your song and get off—before they bring out the hook!"

She traces the origins of this feeling to her childhood in suburban Long Island, "a place where writers were all dead people, not knowing anyone who was even close, who even worked as a secretary in a publishing house. It just seemed so remote. I remember discovering the *New York Times Book Review* when I was at Oswego [a campus of the State University of New York], sitting out there on Lake Ontario with the *Times,* which we had started getting because we all realized we were going to have to begin thinking about jobs, and finding that they had this whole section about books!"

"We didn't have the *New York Times* around much at home. I think my family, with completely good intentions, discouraged me [from becoming a writer] because it seemed so removed to them; they saw me starving in a garret and tried to steer me away from it the same way they tried to steer me away from cocaine: 'I know it sounds very appealing right now, but believe me, you'll regret it!' Their big thing was that I should go to Katie Gibbs and learn shorthand: 'If you really love books, you can get a good job in publishing if you have your secretarial skills. Then maybe you can be an editor and if you really want to write, you can write at night. But you'll have health insurance!' "

McDermott laughs without resentment as she mimics her parents' advice. She knows how tough a writer's life can be; after earning her B.A., she worked briefly as a clerk-typist at a vanity publisher, background she drew on for some hilarious but ultimately sad scenes in *A Bigamist's Daughter.* She was still uncertain enough about her choice of career when she enrolled in the University of New Hampshire's graduate writing program to declare, "I'm going to give myself these two years, and if I haven't published anything by the time I leave then I'll know I'm not a writer."

UNH gave her the confidence she needed. "For the first time in my life I was in a community of people who were writing, and that was wonderful. I don't want to make my family sound like a bunch of philistines; we always read at home, and books were important. But to be involved in the process in any way was remarkable to me—that people said 'I am a writer' without apologies. I went there filled with the idea of inspiration in the middle of the night: you jump out of bed and type for a while, then in the next scene you're at Sardi's. Here people read what I wrote, talked to me about it and told me what to do. It showed me how to be a working writer."

She credits her teacher Mark Smith with pushing her toward professionalism. "In my second year, he asked me what I had sent out. When I admitted I hadn't submitted anything, he said, 'Look, you've got the talent, but you've got to take yourself seriously. Is this a career, or just something that you're doing?' He treated me as a colleague, which was a wonderful confidence-builder; he helped me see myself as something other than apologetic about what I did."

All her talk about confidence-building and feeling apologetic may make McDermott sound neurotically self-deprecating, which she isn't. On the contrary, she's confident enough now to candidly reveal her insecurities and laugh gently at them, knowing that they're an inevitable part of the process. "One of the best things about New Hampshire was that when you said, 'This is really tough to do,' people said, 'Oh, yeah, I know.' Whereas once when I was home on vacation and all depressed about whatever I was working on—as I usually am when I'm writing—I came down to get a cup of tea and, when my mother asked me what was wrong and I said it was going really badly, she said, 'Well, don't do it!' "

Fortunately, McDermott didn't take her mother's advice. She started sending out her short stories, which were published in *Redbook, Mademoiselle* and *Seventeen*. After *A Bigamist's Daughter* was released, she and her husband moved to the West Coast, where she taught at the University of California, San Diego, and completed *That Night*. Another transcontinental move, this time with a young son in tow, to Bethesda, Md., delayed work on a book that she eventually put aside to write *At Weddings and Wakes*.

"I had started a novel trying to deal somehow with Irish Catholic things, and I just wasn't settling into it right," she explains, seated in her publisher's downtown Manhattan offices. Her fair, faintly freckled skin and light brown hair suggesting her own Irish descent. She is relaxed and extremely articulate about the craft of writing as she discusses the genesis of her current book.

"I was sitting in my son's room, and he has that poster of *In the Night Kitchen* [Maurice Sendak's loving tribute to his native Brooklyn]. I thought, that sort of dark Brooklyn street, that's it exactly— clearly it's not an accurate drawing of any real place, but I liked that sense of giving an almost impressionistic feel, just the darkness and the strangeness of it. That gave me the idea for the opening chapter of *At Weddings and Wakes*."

That chapter describes the twice-weekly journey taken by the three Dailey children and their mother from their Long Island home to the Brooklyn apartment where their grandmother and aunts live—a vivid rendering so evocative in its use of physical and period detail (the time is the early 1960s) that the reader only gradually realizes that no specific subways, streets or neighborhoods have been identified.

That's the way the author wanted it; she had tried for the same impressionistic effect in *That Night*, which was set in a suburb most critics identified as Long Island but McDermott intended as "very much a generic suburb. I think when I write I take detail or image from absolutely wherever I can get it. I don't dare stop and think. It's just: 'That'll do. That'll do,' " she says, stretching out her hands to mime snatching individual "thats" out of the air. "It's only afterward that you sit back and say, 'Yes, this is that place.' "

McDermott, in fact, dislikes drawing those parallels. "If I was going to crusade for anything in literature, it would be that sometimes I worry that we're forgetting how to read fiction by relating it too much to real things, by saying, 'How do you do this?' or 'How autobiographical is it?'

"What really brought this home for me was when I went to the set of the movie of *That Night*. They took me into the room they had built for the girl who's the narrator. They had made this wonderful early '60s girl's bedroom: every detail was just right, things I hadn't thought of in years. And I had the feeling that all these details I had wrested from reality and tried to make something else entirely had been pulled back into reality.

"I think we have to remember that fiction is in its own world—it's a new world every time you open a book, and what its relationship is to the real world is almost beside the point. And isn't that wonderful? It's giving you an opportunity to see life not actually portrayed but as something else entirely. Not to get highfalutin, but it's a work of art that's complete in some way. The thing I took away from my morning on the movie set was that revelation: It's not that you remembered or found the right source to tell you what kind of advertising was in the subway in 1962—

it's easy to find that out. It's what that advertisement means in the context of the whole work that's important."

When McDermott sets a novel in the past, as she has done with her two most recent books, evoking a particular period is not her primary interest. "The past gives you a perspective where you can see connections. I think with *A Bigamist's Daughter* I was resisting seeing connections—I said, 'No, there aren't any connections, goddammit,' and using the present was a way of proving that. Maybe just with age, I've started hoping there were connections, and it seemed that one way to find them was to look at some part of life as a whole. Generally that would be the past; that kind of closure seems to define the area you're working in. So it's a matter of trying to make sense rather than being proud of proving that there is no sense!"

Making sense of the past, for McDermott, involves a complex time structure in which the narrative circles around certain key events, which are not necessarily presented in chronological order. "That seems to me to be true to our experience about life; it's all seen through time. You don't look at the past just once, and you look at it with the knowledge of the present, which was the future. I like that going over, seeing an event through other events that have occurred since, seeing it again and seeing it in a different way, from a different perspective as time goes on—to me that's very much what fiction does. I see so much of the process of fiction in memory, and I guess that appeals to me."

"Also, I'm interested for my own writing in structure; I find myself more and more intrigued with the way novels are put together. Straight, realistic narrative seems to leave something out for me; I like the puzzle of it, the game of putting things together in unusual ways that somehow, I hope, come together. I guess this is why I've moved away from short-story writing. I remember saying in graduate school, although I'm not sure what I meant by it—I probably read it somewhere and thought it sounded good—'Life is lived in short stories; we live in moments.' Well, at 21 it feels like a short story, but the older I get, the more my life feels like a novel!"

With a three-year-old daughter and a six-year-old son demanding her attention, teaching responsibilities at American University and a new novel under way, McDermott's life is full enough for a Victorian three-decker. "The new novel is contemporary, but there are relatives to remind us of the past, and there's a sense of future as well—that's different, and that's what keeps me with it. The battle is always to keep yourself interested; I'm as easily distracted as the reader. My office is right through the laundry room, so I can always think of other things that need to be done! But a good thing that comes with having children and being busy is that it gives me energy, because it makes me use my time more efficiently."

WENDY SMITH
March 30, 1992

TERRY McMILLAN

TERRY MCMILLAN blows into the Viking offices like a cool breeze off the bay in San Francisco, where she lives. She's toting two over-stuffed carryalls, while her cab driver staggers under a garment bag crammed to bursting. She directs him to a nearby closet, warmly greets the Viking receptionist, then flings her arms around her editor, Dawn Seferian, and publicity director Paul Slovak. Introduced to her interviewer, she says, "Oh, God—can you give me a few minutes?" and disappears into a maze of cubicles.

When she reappears, she's shed the carryalls and her coat, acquired some coffee, but not yet found an ashtray—a scarce commodity in Viking's smoke-free environment, but an essential accessory for someone who finds it easier to talk with a Kool in her hand. One is finally provided by a helpful staffer, and she flings herself with a sigh of relief into the nearest chair.

It's a hectic time for McMillan. Her third novel, *Waiting to Exhale,* will soon be published with an 85,000-copy first printing and a $700,000 floor for the paperback rights. Viking is sending her on a 20-city, six-week tour that begins with a breakfast speech at the ABA in Anaheim and includes nearly 30 bookstore appearances, closing with a July reading at Central Park's Summerstage festival.

"I don't even believe the stuff that's happened so far," she says. "It's wonderful, it's a writer's dream, but it doesn't really feel like it's happening to me. 'There's this chick I know named Terry McMillan and, gee, I can't wait to read this *Waiting to Exhale*—it sounds like a good book!' "

But McMillan has never been one to hang around waiting for things to happen. Growing up in Port Huron, Mich., the daughter of working-class parents who didn't read to their children, she discovered the magic of books as a teenager shelving books at the local public library for $1.25 an hour. (A biography of Louisa May

Alcott excited her because the writer, like McMillan, "had to help support her family at a young age.") She started reading furiously, soaking up most of the classics of African American literature while studying at a community college in California, and began writing poetry after a romance went sour. Pretty soon, the lines of verse turned into sentences; she published her first short story in 1976, when she was 25. She wrote her first full-length work, *Mama*, while working as a word processor and raising her infant son alone.

When *Mama* was released by Houghton Mifflin in 1987, she refused to let it meet the usual fate of the first novel: scattered reviews, zero publicity and minimal sales. "I had seen it happen before to friends of mine, really fine writers, whose publishers did nothing except send out a little press release and the galleys. My publisher had come right out and told me what they couldn't do, and I said, 'Fuck this! I'm not just going to sit back; I've never been passive, and I'm not going to start now.' "

Indeed, it's hard to think of a less passive figure than McMillan, dressed dramatically in black stretch pants, a bright purple sweater and a boldly patterned jacket with a matching black-and-purple design, sporting fuschia lipstick and nail polish. With her vibrant brown eyes, wide smile and dimples, she fills the room with personality even before she begins to speak, leaning forward and stabbing the air with her finger when she wants to emphasize a point.

"I wrote about 3000 letters," she continues, on the subject of her promotional efforts for *Mama*. "When I was at some writers' conference I read this book, *How to Get Happily Published*, and I was so grateful; I wrote the authors a letter. They talked about how to promote your own book, and I went to the library, copied these different pages, then I wrote to the chains and the independent booksellers, universities, colleges. I did it all summer long: my friends were hanging out at the beach, and I was licking envelopes. Luckily I worked as a word processor, and the guys in the mail room were so sweet; they mailed my stuff for me.

"I got a shitload of readings, so I set up my own tour, because the publisher wasn't going to send me anywhere. Every week I sent my itinerary to my publicist—and it should have been the other way around. *Mama* sold out its first printing before pub date; my editors called and said, 'Terry, we don't think this would have happened if you had not done all this.'

"It wasn't that I was stroking myself and thought I had written this incredibly strong, powerful, wonderful book, but if somebody thinks something is good enough to publish, then show your support! I know every book can't get a $100,000 publicity tour, but if you spent $5000 on all of us, it might sell a few more books."

McMillan continued to display a strong-minded attitude during debates with Houghton Mifflin over her second novel, *Disappearing Acts*, which was structured as a series of alternating first-person monologues by the book's lovers, Franklin and Zora. "They were so impressed with Franklin's voice and the fact that I was pulling it off that they wanted me to write the whole book from his point of view. It was going to be this coup: black woman writes story from black man's point of view, it's never been done, blah, blah, blah, blah, blah. Well, I didn't write *Disappearing Acts* to prove anything; that was the way the story had to be told. When my editor told me Zora sounded kind of preppy, I said, 'Look, she's not barefoot and pregnant, living in the projects and getting her ass kicked. I cannot apologize because some of us have been to college, okay?' "

Her already strained relations with the publisher reached a breaking point when Houghton Mifflin indicated it would like to see a completed manuscript of *Disappearing Acts* before making an offer. McMillan's agent, Molly Friedrich, promptly sent the existing chapters to Viking's Dawn Seferian, who bought the project two days later. Published in 1989, the novel received generally excellent reviews and went on to sell more than 100,000 copies in paperback for Washington Square Press.

It also provoked a lawsuit. Leonard Welch, with whom McMillan had had a child in 1984, claimed the portrait of Franklin libeled him. The case was decided in the author's favor last April, and Welch's subsequent appeal was denied.

"I was more embarrassed than anything else," McMillan says, "because I was concerned that people would think I really didn't write fiction, which *Disappearing Acts* was. I relied on some of my experiences with him, but Franklin Swift and this man are two different people. I worried about the effect on other writers, because everybody relies on their own experiences—even the ones that say they make it all up: they're lying! It's not; it's still fiction."

141

The ongoing lawsuit was only one of the factors that slowed the writing of *Waiting to Exhale*, which wasn't finished until December 1991, a scant five months before scheduled publication. "I had not been under this kind of pressure before," says McMillan. "I get tons of mail about *Disappearing Acts*; I'm so sick of that book I don't know what to do. After about 90 pages [of *Waiting to Exhale*], I'm saying to myself, 'Are they going to think this is as good as *Disappearing Acts*? Are they going to be disappointed?' Eventually, I just had to say, 'I cannot think about my audience; I can't guess what people are going to like.' "

Once she got into the thick of the novel, not even a move from Tucson to San Francisco could stop her. "I had the movers take my computer last; they were putting books in boxes, and I was sitting there writing. I get to California, I'm sitting in my sister's fiancé's office going blind writing on my little laptop that's not backlit, I'm looking for a place to live while my furniture's on a truck somewhere, it's the end of August and I'm supposed to be finishing the book by September 1st! I finished the first draft November 20."

There was still a lot of work to be done. "I'm not one of those writers who just edits, especially when I'm working on a first draft. Sometimes I actually delete an entire chapter from the memory so I have to type it all over, because that's the only way I can relive it. I have to stay close to these people, I have to have their experiences, too, and the only way to do that is to start all over—that stuff is cumulative. It can be very exciting, and it can be very painful, but I have to make the emotional investment."

Staying close to her characters means reproducing their salty, often profane language, which later dismayed reviewers. "I was criticized for this with *Disappearing Acts* too," the author responds, "but basically, the language that I use is accurate.

"I said to Dawn when I read that review, 'You know, it's not on every fucking page!' Then I picked up the galley when I was on the airplane coming to New York, and when I got here I called Dawn and said, 'You know, I think you're right: it *is* on every fucking page!' But so what? That's the way we talk. And I want to know why I've never read a review where they complain about the language that male writers use!"

She braced for criticism about *Waiting to Exhale*'s depiction of black men, who are seen only through the often exasperated eyes of her four central female characters. "The men are on the periphery, they're not the focus of this story, therefore they don't get the three-dimensionality that the women do. Periodically, I would stop and say, 'Oh, they're going to be pissed off at me now!' But I said exactly what I meant, and I'm not apologizing for any of it. This book is not meant to represent or portray any gender or group of people. Nobody thinks that a Czech writer is representing all Czechs, or a Russian writer is writing for all Russians."

In her introduction to *Breaking Ice*, the anthology she edited of contemporary African American writing, McMillan argued that her generation of black writers "are a new breed, free to write as we please . . . because of the way life has changed." Her own fiction, which often portrays successful middle-class professionals, is a case in point.

"This is 1992. I appreciate and value all the protest literature of the '60s, but I am tired of carrying this plantation on my shoulders. I know that if it wasn't for Martin Luther King and Malcolm X we wouldn't be able to do some of the things we do now, but I don't need to constantly remind you of that. I'm not trying to prove anything to white folks, and I'm not trying to make them feel guilty—my editor didn't enslave my ancestors. So why do I have to keep belaboring the point?

"Unfortunately, the black people who are the most militant are the ones who seem to be more hung up than anybody on what white people think. 'We're airing our dirty laundry, why can't we portray ourselves more positively?'—to me, that's stuck in the same '60s stuff. They make the assumption that we are anthropologists, sociologists, psychologists, when all we are is storytellers. They try to put this weight on our shoulders, which I totally dismiss. I'm prepared for them with this book: 'Why you make the brothers out to look like they ain't shit?' I say, it's only two of 'em in here, not two million. I want to tell my stories on a much more personal level, more intimate. It's not just the black man pitted against white society; it's deeper than that."

Characters drive a novel for McMillan, and right now, despite her commitment to publicize *Waiting to Exhale* and to write a screenplay for *Disappearing Acts*, she's eager to get back to the group of people waiting to be given voice in her new novel. "I'm stacking up stuff about the story and thinking about these people—I've known who they are for a while, I see them and I sort of know the story, but they haven't started talking to me yet. It's like a picture that's out of focus. I don't force things on my characters; I wait and watch them grow. While I'm writing the screenplay, these people keep intruding—and I'm so glad! I can't wait for this summer to be over so we can play some more."

WENDY SMITH
May 11, 1992

PAUL MONETTE

T HERE'S SOMETHING COMFORTING and familiar about the lavender-painted house on King's Road above the Sunset Strip in West Hollywood. The walls are lined with elegant black-and-white vintage photographs; each room is littered with books. The sun-dappled pool and brick patio seem peaceful and cool under the trees. Outdoors somewhere are the gardenias that Paul Monette planted during his lover's struggle with AIDS, when the man had lost his sight and the scent of the blossoms seemed to soothe him.

This home was once filled with a gallant love; it was a place of elegant dinner parties, where witty conversation and laughing men held sway. The house became a kind of literary symbol in Monette's memoir *Borrowed Time* (1988) and in his collection of poetry, *Love Alone: Eighteen Elegies for Rog* (1988), illustrating at some points all that was ideal in a homosexual relationship, and at others showing the darker side, when the bedroom became the final battleground against a vicious disease.

Monette still lives in the house where his longtime companion, Roger Horwitz, died seven years ago. Now, only a few months after being diagnosed with AIDS himself, Monette is at once living with the disease and readying himself for the release of *Becoming a Man: Half a Life Story*, published by Harcourt Brace Jovanovich, which recounts Monette's lonely, often bitter years as a closeted homosexual. "It is about how I came to understand the complexity and crucialness of love," he says.

Monette's road has not been an easy one professionally or personally, but as he has traveled it life and art have eventually become one. In 1975, with the help of agent Wendy Weil, *The Carpenter at the Asylum*, his first volume of poetry, was published by Little, Brown. Three years later, the same company published its first gay novel, Monette's *Taking Care of Mrs. Carroll*. Avon published his next three novels: *The Gold Diggers*, *The Long Shot* and

Lightfall. His editors were Roger Donald at Little, Brown and Bob Wyatt at Avon.

In 1981 he entered a four-year period of frustration. Seemingly at loose ends, he wrote novelizations of the films *Nosferatu, Scarface, Predator* and *Midnight Run*; drafted 10 scripts, never produced, which he describes as "high-priced memos for 10 people who had idiotic things to say"; and began two novels, which went nowhere. Then, in 1985, Roger was diagnosed as having AIDS, and although Monette went through the motions of working on a screenplay for Whoopi Goldberg, he virtually stopped writing.

"AIDS changed everything for me," says Monette, 46. "For 19 months I took care of Roger. I genuinely said things like, 'I'll never write again.' Certainly writing a sweet, comic, realistic book didn't seem possible anymore. It would have been like going back and writing *Little Women.*"

Three weeks after Horwitz's death on Oct. 22, 1987, Monette flew back east to see his family. He realized that if the plane crashed, he would have left behind no record of his feelings for Roger. He wrote a poem before takeoff, then another during the flight. Four months later, he had written 18 elegies, which would be published by Stonewall Inn Editions, an imprint of St. Martin's, as *Love Alone.* At the same time, he began writing *Borrowed Time: An AIDS Memoir*, which would eventually be edited by Daphne Merkin and published by HBJ.

Just as AIDS shattered Monette's personal life, *Borrowed Time* reconfigured his professional life. It was, for example, his first book to be reviewed by the *New York Times.* He became highly sought after as a speaker. "The 10% to 15% of the audience who is gay will get what I talk about," he says. "I'll make no inroads with the 50% who hate or fear homosexuals. But then there's another 20% to 30%—mothers, wives, children and co-workers of gays—who want to understand and don't want to be lumped together with the hatemongers."

The success of *Borrowed Time* also meant that his new works might be better appreciated. Working with editor David Groff at Crown, Monette published *Afterlife* (1990), a novel about three AIDS widowers, and *Halfway Home* (1991), a novel about AIDS with a happy ending. For this body of work, he has been recognized by academia (an honorary degree from the State University of New York), traditional writers' groups (awards from PEN

Center West and the ALA) and gay and lesbian groups (awards from Words Project for AIDS, GLAAD and *Lambda Book Report*). But the greatest satisfaction comes, he says, from the "humbling" letters he has received from young gays and lesbians who feel disenfranchised and alone. "There's a point with a book where it leaves you as the author and then has a capacity to touch someone," he says. "This happened especially with *Borrowed Time*. You teach and write and hope that you can do something considered worthy by people whom nothing usually touches."

Ultimately the inspiration for *Half a Life* came from those who repeatedly told him that, as described in *Borrowed Time* at least, he and Horwitz seemed to have had a perfect relationship. In *Half a Life*—which was edited by Drenka Willen—Monette writes of his motivation: "I ought to tell how impossible such happiness looked from the prison of twelve to twenty-five years. Convinced I was the most unloved, the most unloved man who'd ever lived. No window in my cell and no chance of release till I faced the truth that I was queer."

In *Becoming a Man*, Monette recalls those years of growing up in Andover, Mass., a child of '50s white-bread blandness. What emerges is a painful portrait of a guilt-ridden, confused, outwardly asexual boy who suffered constantly, apparently irrevocably, from not being able to be himself. He was accepted at Phillips Academy in Andover—a prep school that he calls the bastion of "white genes, ramrod posture, and hearty comradeship"—as a "day student, non-athlete, on scholarship." During the day, he grew to love Latin and poetry. His evenings, however, he spent poring over his Elizabeth Taylor scrapbooks.

On to Yale, where he edited a newspaper, a poetry magazine and the literary magazine, and took over administration of the Yale Arts Festival. After graduation he taught at two prep schools and ended up on probation at one for becoming involved with a male student. He tried women. He tried interior decorating. He continued to write. Finally, just as he published his first volume of poetry, he met Horwitz, the "laughing man" of his dreams.

Given Monette's tortured past, *Becoming a Man* must have been difficult to write. "Was it easy? No. But life isn't easy. I tried to avoid self-pity in the book. I wanted to be honest. In that way it's like *Borrowed Time*. There's no smiling ending."

The language of the book will present challenges to some readers. On page after page, Monette describes himself with words like *fairy, queer, queen, homo* and *faggot.* By doing so he takes his stand in the ongoing "politically correct" debate among gays and lesbians. "There's a school of thought that says this language which apartheided us should be reclaimed," he explains. "It's been isolating, hurting and denigrating to us. It can now become a way of exalting us, a way of demystifying the words."

Beyond the sometimes painful words are Monette's own sexual experiences, which began when he was nine and a half years old. At one moment in the book, after a particularly graphic sexual episode, he queries the reader: *Is this more than you want to know?*

An interviewer who is also the mother of two small boys replies in the affirmative. Hearing this, Monette laughs, mentions that a friend has made him a T-shirt printed with the quote, then again turns serious: "A gay person will be riveted by that scene. I was virtually sexless for so long that it was important to get all the incidents right."

For some, *Becoming a Man* may seem a bitter book. When asked about this, Monette first shows surprise, then says, "I guess I do feel bitter. I have a right to. But the book isn't just a way of settling scores." He doesn't view his parents as enemies, although he did wait until his mother died to write the book. His father, once a conservative Republican, now works as a "buddy" running errands for people with AIDS. "They did the best they could in a stupid and savage society," Monette says of his parents.

In *Becoming a Man* Monette also recounts his evolution as a writer, revealing that he chose to be a gay writer rather than a writer who happened to be gay so that he might be able to "tap into that sensibility." He says, "I see myself being gay as more important than being white or male, even. Being gay and writing about the gay experience was a great liberation."

On the other hand, he scoffs at the idea that some gay novels, his own included, are "crossover" works intended, in part, for a heterosexual audience. "People used to say that *Borrowed Time* was 'mainstream,' but no one ever talked about Updike's books being a crossover from the New England culture. I think that if you write well and from the heart, then people will be drawn to your work."

In speaking about future projects, Monette is as forthright as he is in his writing. "I don't know if I have another book in me.

After my diagnosis last December, nothing has been the same. AIDS is a full-time job. When it gets to the dying part, that's *really* a full-time job. I feel well. I have the best medication. But I don't want to leave a book in the middle."

Through his literary success, Monette has become one of the senior statesmen on AIDS and gay rights issues. The bad news continues to be immense and daunting. "The backlash from the political right has been more severe than everyone anticipated, and our society still has done nothing to combat AIDS," he opines. "It hasn't changed in 12 years. We've had two administrations in a row that have ignored their own AIDS commissions. Two hundred thousand people have died in this country, and the government continues to say that a million people are infected. So far, nothing has made a difference. Money for research has been cut back, and the drugs are coming from Europe. I wish I could be more optimistic, but I see how vicious the religious people are—petty, destroying, homophobic. I don't expect these things to be resolved in my lifetime."

Will recent, hotly disputed studies suggesting that being gay is a product of biological rather than cultural imperatives change how people view homosexuality? "I would hope so," he muses, "but we live in a world where amniocentesis is used in China to determine the sex of girls. Therefore, selective abortion is practiced more and more specifically. If scientists could identify the gene for gays and lesbians, women could have an abortion just on that basis."

His hopes are few and cautious. "Colleges have remarkable organizations for gays and lesbians," he notes. "People are going out to law firms and saying, 'I'm gay. Will you have a problem with that?' I exult in that, because my Roger always had to be so careful." Gay and lesbian literature and bookstores also offer encouragement. "The future of gay and lesbian literature is certain because there is such a hungry audience. Gay and lesbian bookstores serve as a bulwark, a reference point, an anchor. You can't censor that level of ferment. I believe in the crucialness of freedom of speech above all else. Our humanity requires it. It even requires my listening to what homophobes like Pat Buchanan have to say.

Where does this leave Monette? "I would rather be writing glib Hollywood comedies than have gone through the holocaust of

149

AIDS. I don't know why other writers haven't written about it, but they will.

"Writing became the best way to save my life. For some, the tragedy has been so immense that they couldn't write. But literature is what transforms us. Do books save lives? At best, they can. The truth may be too late, but it's better than no truth at all."

LISA SEE
June 29, 1992

MARY MORRIS

"THERE'S A TIME in your life when it's the right thing to go off to a jungle for a year and there's a time in your life when it's the right thing to live in a brownstone in Brooklyn." For Mary Morris, whose new novel, *A Mother's Love*, has been issued from Doubleday under Nan Talese's imprint, it's brownstone time.

After 20 years of wandering the globe, Morris lives on a side street in a determinedly residential neighborhood. The interior of her brownstone is largely white and wood, accented by a few plants, her daughter's drawings and copies of Morris's own books on the mantelpiece. It is a warm, bright, cheery setting, thoroughly domestic. But Morris, a petite woman with a vibrant, forthright personality, has been somewhat suspicious of domesticity. "For a long time I saw independence and stability as an either/or situation: either you travel, write and lead a completely independent life or you have family and stability—but you can't have both. Now I actually think that given the right kind of circumstances you *can* have both, but it's complicated."

Her latest novel reflects the strong, often conflicting compulsions to independence and domesticity that have marked much of Morris's work. In alternating chapters, *A Mother's Love* tells the story of Ivy Slovak. We see her in the present, as an unwed mother struggling with the deeper meaning and practical application of motherly love, and in flashbacks as an insecure child overwhelmed by her mother's desertion.

Although it might seem that Morris conceived her story to meet the crest of a timely topic, nothing was further from her mind when she began writing the novel. "I didn't write *A Mother's Love* thinking it was going to become a hot sociopolitical issue. I wrote it because the story interested me. Then Dan Quayle came down on Murphy Brown and single motherhood. With every article that appeared last spring, I thought 'Ohhhh, this is going to ruin my book.' "

Nan Talese convinced Morris that the original title, *The Night Sky*, was too opaque. She approved when Morris chose *A Single Mother* for its double meaning, suggesting both an individual mother and a woman who is raising a child by herself. Talese has been Morris's editor for more than a decade now, since the publication of *Crossroads* in 1983. Lynn Nesbit, Morris's agent at the time, had shown the manuscript to "several top male editors, who did not respond well." Talese, then at Houghton Mifflin, was more receptive. Morris remembers being "terrified" when she walked into Talese's office for the first time. "But she was very warm. She asked me if I was looking for overnight success. Of course I was; who isn't?" But Talese observed that she was not interested in an author's flashy debut, but instead wanted to make a commitment to a writer's career.

"I think that was the most important thing anybody's ever said to me," Morris muses. "I still want overnight success, but after 15 years, what's overnight success? In fact, I just dropped Nan a line asking, 'Have I been patient long enough?' "

Though Morris followed Talese from Houghton to Doubleday, she decided to stay at ICM when Nesbit left to form Janklow & Nesbit Associates, opting to be represented by Amanda "Binky" Urban. "I think Binky and Nan are a wonderful balance. I need some reality grounding, and Binky gives me that. I also need some sort of nurturing and babying, and Nan does that. I couldn't ask for a better balance in my professional life."

Morris's personal life has fallen willy-nilly into its own kind of balance as well. "I came to domesticity backward," Morris explains. "First I had a child, then I had a husband." Morris was not married when her daughter Katie was born in 1987. In 1988, she met Canadian journalist Larry O'Connor at a conference in Virginia. After surviving the difficulties of a long-distance relationship, the two married in August 1989, spent a year travelling around the southwest, and finally settled in Brooklyn. Recently O'Connor decided to try his hand at writing a book; now he too works at home.

Morris's office on the ground floor is like the rest of the house, clean and functional with no extravagant touches. When she is not teaching creative writing at Princeton, where she has been affiliated since 1980, Morris's ideal schedule consists of getting her daughter off to school, doing the day's errands, then anchoring herself at her desk by 9:30 or 10 and writing until late afternoon.

"Once I start working, I never go out, ever," Morris announces. But once she starts working, she's not necessarily, well, working. "I piddle, I straighten up, sweep." Likewise, when she's not "working," she may well be. "At 4 o'clock every day I take a walk or do something physical in order to change gears. I always carry a small notepad and usually end up writing a line or two." When the odd line strikes, anything will serve to record it. Included among the rough materials for a just-completed draft of a novel is "the lid of a cereal box with extensive notes."

Morris usually juggles several projects at once, often putting some things aside to germinate. "I much prefer my work to have a period of fruition—about 10 years," she says, only somewhat facetiously. The longest delays are involuntary as she waits for her work—be it travel writing or stories or novels—"to take a certain internal shape." Her first travel book, *Nothing to Declare*, crystallized a full seven years after she had visited Mexico. *The Waiting Room*, her second novel, about the effects of the Vietnam War on those who stayed at home, took nine years. For Morris, much of the waiting has to do with what she calls "fictive distance." She explains, "If a tragedy happens to you on Saturday, you shouldn't try to write about in on Monday."

Even when she is not writing, Morris bubbles with energy. She holds a notepad as we speak, emphasizing her answers with accompanying doodles. "I guess there are writers who finish one thing and move on to the next," she says, drawing one line, ending it abruptly and drawing another. "But things don't happen that way for me." *A Mother's Love*, for example, was originally two different books. In 1987, when a teaching stint at Princeton came to an end, Morris moved to California with her newborn daughter to teach at U.C. Irvine. In those surroundings she was struck by the idea for her character Ivy, "who seemed to me like so many of the people I met there, people who grew up in desert towns, and had itinerant youths, and who wanted to be artists." But the piece she wrote was more a fable than a real story, says Morris, and though she loved the material, Nan Talese "really didn't like it." At the same time, she was at work on another novel about a single mother in New York, a book that, though not specifically about her life, drew on her year and a half as a woman living alone raising a child.

"I was interested in this character, but she was flat, didn't have a history," Morris recalls. "Then one day I was looking at the 'Ivy' material and the other story, and I conjectured, what if the woman raising a child on her own was herself abandoned as a child . . . and it became perfectly clear what I wanted to write."

A conspicuous lack of linearity makes unraveling Morris's life and career a bit of a challenge. Born in 1947, she spent her entire childhood in the same house in suburban Chicago before heading to Boston's Tufts University for her B.A. While a graduate student at Columbia, she began writing short stories. "I wrote one and sent it to *Redbook*. They bought it and paid me a phenomenal amount of money. I wrote another and they paid me *more* money. I thought, this is great; I'm going to make a living as a short story writer. Then for 10 years I didn't sell another story commercially.

"I was just about to give up and go to law school when I got an NEA grant," Morris says. At around the same time, she got a call from a friend who was working as a reader for David Godine. Although he asked to see the novel she was working on, Morris instead sent him 27 stories that "nobody in America wanted to publish." Godine liked 12 of the stories enough to sign Morris up for a collection. So in 1978–79, armed with both the grant and a contract from Godine, Morris took off for a lengthy visit to Mexico.

"That was a year I changed immensely," Morris observes. "I was lonely, totally isolated—without even a telephone—but in the end the experience completely transformed the way I felt about being a writer and about my work." While she was in Mexico she wrote a few more stories for *Vanishing Animals* (Godine, 1979) and continued work on the novel that would become *Crossroads* (Houghton, 1983), but that period was probably most important as the inspiration for a book that would not be published for another decade, *Nothing to Declare* (Houghton, 1988).

"I had no intention of writing about that trip," says Morris. Even when she began considering a travel book, *Nothing to Declare* wasn't what she had in mind. Originally, she conceived of the book in three parts. It was to start with her travels through the Middle East in 1967–68, then proceed to Mexico and finally end in Russia, where she planned to visit her grandmother's village in Ukraine. "But when I opened up the notebooks and started writing, I ended up writing just about Mexico," Morris says.

"I feel I've lost a little of my innocence from writing *Nothing to Declare*," she adds, somewhat ruefully. "What used to happen and what I still try to insist will happen is that places would call to me for various reasons: I felt a need to go to Mexico, a need to go to Ukraine. Then people started *wanting* me to go places. That's a whole different experience, and one I don't really like. It's like somebody sending you to a party and saying, 'There's a guy you're going to fall in love with.' What are the chances of that happening?"

Still, Morris's travels continued to inspire her: she wrote about her sojourns in China and Russia in *Wall-to-Wall* (Doubleday, 1991), and has planned another book on her 1988 travels through the Southwest with Katie. The latter would complete a trio on the theme of "how women move through the world differently from men." It's a project that began with her experiences as a single woman in *Nothing to Declare*, continued with her thoughts on family and roots in *Wall-to-Wall*, and, if all goes well, will end with a work containing insights on mothers and daughters.

Another result of her time in the West was an entirely different nonfiction project, now gestating: a look at what she calls "the systems of coping" used by the more fringy elements of California's population. She was enduring a lonely start to her stay on the West Coast when a friend pointed out that California was a hotbed of the strange and wonderful, and suggested that Morris should investigate. "I spent a year infiltrating groups as a believer," she confesses. She became a member of the Earth-Based Unit of the Ashtar Command and the L.A. UFO Abductee Support Group. She also posed as a high-level reporter for a major newspaper to fly with the angels in Reverend Robert Schuller's holiday pageant at the Crystal Cathedral.

Future fiction projects include a new story collection and a novel due out in the fall of 1994, which concerns "a woman who is afraid of her house." Her nonfiction notwithstanding, fiction is where Morris wants to turn her focus. "I feel ill at ease with the notion of who I am. There are really three parts: who I am as a person, who I am as a writer, and then there are the characters in my books. I think my fiction and nonfiction get blurred together in readers' minds. It may be that the parts people think are the most autobiographical are the least so, and the parts they think are the least [true] may—on another, disguised level—be the most faithful."

There's no question that Morris's readers are intrigued by the person they meet in her pages; by now, they think they know her very well. And if the "real" Morris continues to blur her fictive and actual selves, the portrait can only grow in perspective and depth.

MARIA SIMSON
March 15, 1993

WALTER MOSLEY

"I'D LIKE TO BE REMEMBERED in the canon of genre writers in this field," says crime novelist Walter Mosley. "I'd like my name to be mentioned with Raymond Chandler, Hammett, Ross Macdonald, people like that.

"If people mention my race, I wouldn't be unhappy," continues Mosley, author of four murder mysteries based on the character of black detective Easy Rawlins, his reluctant but always gallant sleuth. "I'd like to think that I'm breaking new ground, not doing something completely new like Hemingway or someone like that, but doing something different in an interesting new way. I'm using a wide range of black characters and trying to reflect life in America. I'm talking about black life as if it were human life in America, taking the point of view that black people are insiders rather than standing on the outside looking in."

Judging from the success of Mosley's books to date, the author seems likely to achieve most of his goals. Easy Rawlins, the laid-off aircraft worker who becomes an L.A. detective with a knack for finding some semblance of meaning behind the murder and mayhem he probes, has garnered both critical and popular acclaim. The mysteries have been praised by a wide variety of reviewers and publications; Mosley has been profiled in *Vanity Fair* and *People*; and the author's consistently high sales (particularly in paperback) are notable. Three of the titles have been nominated for Gold Dagger Awards, presented by Britain's Crime Writers' Association, including his third novel, *White Butterfly* (1992), which was also nominated for an Edgar by the Mystery Writers of America.

Moreover, Mosley's new book, *Black Betty* (Norton), is one of the most eagerly awaited summer fiction titles. His first novel, *Devil in a Blue Dress* (1990), is currently being made into a movie produced by Jonathan Demme and directed by Carl Franklin, with

Denzel Washington starring as the laconic, perceptive sleuth. Finally, no less an authority than First Mystery Fan Bill Clinton has declared Mosley to be his favorite practitioner of the genre.

In person, Mosley is an affable, thoughtful man with an almost jovial nature. As he fields questions during an interview at the midtown office of his agent, Gloria Loomis, his expressive face frequently lights up as he considers his replies; he shifts restlessly in his chair as he reflects on the implications of his answers. Indeed, it's easy to imagine the amiable author as a more intellectual version of his fictional alter ego, pondering the literary landscape for clues about how he fits in and the meaning of the various twists and turns his career has taken. Mosley is a presence in the literary community in New York City: he turns up frequently at readings and parties; he is a member of the Executive Board of the PEN American Center, where he chairs the Open Book Committee; and he is on the Board of Directors of the National Book Awards.

Mosley's background certainly qualifies him to write about a character whose adventures both define and transcend the limits of racial boundaries. He was born in South-Central L.A. in 1952, the son of a mixed marriage between a black school custodian and his white Jewish wife, both of whom stressed the values of education. He has repeated the pattern in his own mixed marriage to dancer and choreographer Joy Kellman. In conversation, however, Mosley emphasizes his identity as that of an African American writer, discussing both himself and his character in terms of the way they reflect the black community.

"Easy's response to racism is just to work harder," Mosley comments. "He doesn't believe in justice, and he doesn't believe that the black man is ever going to get a fair shake, so he knows he's going to have to do more to overcome that. I think that Easy's attitude reflects the conditions in that neighborhood [South-Central] even today. It's gotten better in some ways, but it's also gotten worse, and I believe that overall it's worse there than it ever was. There are more opportunities there, but they're for fewer people, and that translates to fewer chances."

Despite the fact that he's a relative latecomer to the writing game, Mosley has certainly capitalized on his chances. He came east to college, attending two Vermont institutions, Goddard College and Johnson State, where he earned his B.A. Mosley eventually moved to Manhattan, supporting himself for many years as a freelance computer programmer. When he enrolled in the City College writing program, he came under the tutelage of novelist Frederic Tuten. Though he worked on a novel in class, Mosley gave his mentor a copy of the already completed *The Devil in a Blue Dress,* and Tuten submitted it to his agent, Gloria Loomis, without telling Mosley.

Loomis then called Mosley, officially acquiring him as a client before sending the manuscript to Gerald Howard at Norton. "The funny thing about Norton taking the book is that Jerry was halfway through it before he realized it was a mystery," Mosley says. "My relationship with Norton has worked out very well," he continues. "Most people think that there's a lot of financial pressure on me to write bestsellers because of Easy's commercial success, but detective fiction isn't really something Norton does a lot of, so there's less pressure than one might expect."

Howard also expresses satisfaction, observing that the house had confidence in Mosley from the start. "We contracted for two books in the series right away," he says. "Unlike anything else I've ever experienced in publishing, it actually worked out the way we planned."

Of late, Mosley's attention has been drawn back to the West Coast of his origins—he returned to Southern California in recent weeks to watch and participate in the filming of *Devil in a Blue Dress.* Mosley hasn't experienced the horror stories that are frequently told by writers who must deal with the Hollywood studio system to get their work adapted for film. Quite the contrary.

"I had an incredibly positive experience," he relates of his movie-making junket. "Carl Franklin [the director] came up to me and asked me questions about the script and story, and it was pretty clear to me that what I said mattered. I also talked to people like Denzel, Eddie Murphy and Wesley Snipes, who were all very encouraging and interested in the character. There's a real shortage of male role models in black culture right now, and Easy seems to have hit a bit of a nerve in that sense."

There are a number of other aspects to Easy's character and Mosley's fiction that separate his work from other books in the genre. Mosley consistently returns to what he sees as the bleak fatalism of 20th-century black life in America. He also thoroughly explores the notion of being an insider or an outsider in society, using characters of all races and social strata. This dark vision of limited opportunity, accurately reflecting the economic and social realities of black communities, especially in the decades Mosley has covered so far, has a wider relevance that does not escape Mosley's readers. By the 1990s, this urban blight extends well beyond the edges of minority neighborhoods, and Easy's struggles with forces that seem overwhelmingly ranged against him can be translated to other members of society; his resilience and his triumphs, small and compromised as they may be, can be claimed by readers of any background or circumstance.

Mosley takes pains to maintain chronological continuity in his novels, covering the late '40s, the '50s, and the early '60s to date by setting each new book approximately five years after the previous one. In *Devil in a Blue Dress*, Easy is an unencumbered man in his 30s. By the end of his third appearance, in *A White Butterfly*, he's been through a broken marriage and seen the tenuous real estate empire that he established from a windfall profit in the first book whittled down to a financial house of cards. In between, in the 1991 entry, *A Red Death*, Easy endures the pervasive atmosphere of fear and loathing in the McCarthy era as he grapples with the issue of betraying (to the FBI) a Jewish Communist who's working to help black people in the community. *Black Betty*, the new book, finds Easy confronting many of the changes ushered in during the early '60s.

While some authors might recognize a fatigue factor in spending a career with a single character, Mosley acknowledges an ongoing fascination with his protagonist. "I love writing about Easy," he says with a smile. "He's always changing—his life, his children, his friends—and I learn more about writing with each book. There are certain things I enjoy about writing mysteries, creating the tension, the idea of the first-person narrative. I think it's something I'll always do."

Working toward that end, Mosley has two more Easy Rawlins novels waiting in the wings, the just-completed *The Little Yellow Dog* and *Bad Boy Bobby Brown*, which the author intends as a homage to Malcolm X. He indicates that he has plans for as many as nine or 10 Easy books, enough to chronicle the entire spectrum of postwar urban black life in America and bring the character into his 70s. But Mosley is also branching out into a literary life beyond Easy: he has recently completed *R. L.'s Dream*, a novel about the blues, which Norton will issue in 1995.

"It's a modern novel in the sense that it's set in the '80s, but it's about a blues musician who played with Robert Johnson," Mosley relates. "Johnson [a legendary pioneer blues singer and composer] is someone I find tremendously intriguing. To me, he represents the negative space in the blues, and there are all these amazing similarities between Johnson and Christopher Marlowe—they both died in their 20s, they both elevated their art into a higher form and they were both murdered in bars. I'm trying to bring together different characters from different walks [of life] and describe a life informed by the blues sensibility, and to bring a sense of mystery to the blues."

Stretching out beyond the restrictions of the mystery genre has brought Mosley face-to-face with the links between music, language and character writing. "Music is fiction, and fiction is music," he says. "This isn't a music novel per se, but there's a rhythm to language and a beat to it, and there are words and passages that just invite you in, so that you get buoyed up by language. The more I go into that the farther I can work my way into the images, which in turn allows me to go deeper into the characters."

No believer in the cloistered life, Mosley works for approximately three hours every morning before beginning his social rounds, which normally consist of a day full of visiting his Manhattan colleagues and friends. He remains preoccupied with the ongoing notion of self-improvement and testing his own limits as a writer, attempting to strike a balance between what must be said and what must be left unsaid.

"If you're writing a scene, you're writing about one particular thing that's going on, whether it's a conversation, a murder, sex between two characters, whatever," Mosley explains. "But to write that scene, there may be 99 other things going on at that time that are assumed, and you have to know about every one of them. I find that when I'm unhappy with what I've done, most of the time what's happened is that one or two of those things that needs to be assumed has crept into the writing."

Mosley's growth as a writer can also be measured in his determination to break more boundaries with genre-stretching future books. In addition to giving Easy Rawlins fans their near-annual fix, the author has other works in mind. He mentions a play about Mouse, Easy's violent sidekick, a coming-of-age novel about a black man living in Harlem and even a science fiction novel. Whatever the outcome of these germinating ideas, it is already clear that Mosley is a writer with a unique voice and perspective.

ROBERT McCULLOUGH
May 23, 1994

MARCIA MULLER

Never mind that they don't look anything alike, that one works at home, alone, while the other's job takes her into dangerous company and life-threatening circumstances in places often far from her San Francisco base. Never mind that award-winning mystery author Marcia Muller, sitting demurely on a sofa in her suburban northern California home, says that her groundbreaking series heroine Sharon McCone "will always be taller, braver, younger, thinner." Undeniably, the diminutive, reddish-blonde-haired author of 20 novels and her resilient, dark-haired, part Native American PI are sisters under the skin. It shows in the character.

Slight and ladylike, dressed in beige jeans and a tweedy sweater, Muller welcomes us into her impeccably orderly, redwood paneled home high on a hill in Petaluma. With a view of the Sonoma mountains behind her, she speaks thoughtfully about her writing career. Mysterious Press has just published the latest Sharon McCone story, *Till the Butchers Cut Him Down*. Following the 1993 Edgar-nominated *Wolf in the Shadows*, this is the 14th entry in the series that began in 1977 when Muller introduced the young female private investigator in her first novel, *Edwin of the Iron Shoes*.

With a deep fund of short stories to her credit as well, and a number of mystery anthologies co-edited with her husband, mystery writer Bill Pronzini, Muller has convincingly overruled the judgment of a creative writing professor at the University of Michigan, who told her she'd never be a writer. "He said I had nothing to say, which of course, at 19, was true. It was devastating and I backed off completely."

But only for a while. In retrospect, her meandering pre-Sharon career aimed her directly toward her life's work. Raised in Michigan, the youngest in her family, Muller had tried her hand at fiction before (including a novel written at age 12, about her dog), but after that discouraging pronouncement, she switched to journalism. "I thought I could slot myself into a particular area and do well," she recalls with a laugh. "But I was not a good journalist. I was always putting quotes into people's mouths."

She moved from Michigan to California in the late '60s with her first husband, who was in the Navy, returning to Ann Arbor for a year to finish her journalism degree. After returning to the West Coast for good, she had a number of different jobs. In one, she conducted field interviews for the University of Michigan's Institute for Social Research. "That required writing very detailed character sketches and descriptions of living conditions. It got me into parts of San Francisco and the Bay area where I never would have gone, and meeting people whom I never would have met."

At the same time, she was reading. "I picked up a Ross Macdonald mystery and I fell in love with his work. I went back to Chandler, to Hammett and then moved forward. I couldn't put them down. I read Christie, Sayers, Ngaio Marsh, P. D. James. I also read a lot of American women, two in particular, Dorothy Uhnak and Lillian O'Donnell, who were doing police procedural series with very tough, very strong women characters. I had finally found the form I wanted to write."

At the time, there was not a single featured woman PI on the American mystery scene. In England, P. D. James had just introduced her young apprentice investigator, Cordelia Grey, in *An Unsuitable Job for a Woman* (1972). Cordelia, however, had inherited her agency on the death of her boss and wasn't yet a confident, unapologetic PI. "There were a few perfectly horrible female private-eye novels written by men," Muller recalls. "But the women were just men in drag, either obnoxiously aggressive or too clinging for words."

Muller started writing her first Sharon McCone story in 1972, without any real sense that she was breaking ground. "I thought that I was doing something different and that it might sell. I thought it could be a series and knew that's what publishers were looking for. I'd go to the library, pick out my ration of mysteries for the week and look at the shelves for the spot I'd be if I ever got published."

Her first manuscript made all the rounds and wasn't picked up. She sent a second to Michele Slung, then at David McKay Co., in response to an advertisement soliciting manuscripts that the

164

young and enthusiastic editor had placed in *Writer's Digest* maga-zine. Slung rejected the story but expressed interest in seeing any-thing else the writer might do with her character. "I had the com-pleted rough draft for *Edwin* sitting on my desk," says Muller, smiling.

David McKay took the story, she continues. "But they killed their mystery line with its publication: a death knell." For the next four years, Muller recalls, she "couldn't sell a word."

Slung had referred her first-time author to an agent who, Muller says, soon lost interest in her. Next, she landed with a woman who "did absolutely nothing" but had to be threatened with a cease and desist order before relinquishing the manuscript Muller had sent her. Muller alighted at the Curtis Brown agency, where she stayed until 1988, when she moved to her current agent, Molly Friedrich, at the Aaron Priest Literary Agency.

During this time, Muller met Pronzini, the author of the Name-less Detective series, through the Mystery Writers of America, and, through him, the editor who would usher in the next stage of her career. "Bill introduced me to Tom Dunne [of St. Martin's Press]. The funny thing about that was the manuscript I sold him, *Ask the Cards a Question*, had been rejected a year before by a differ-ent editor there."

Dunne remained her editor for the next six McCone novels, through most of the '80s. This was when, the author believes, she honed her writing skills. "Back then, you could learn to write while making a living at it. It's not as easy for new writers now. It's such a tough market, and publishers aren't willing to bring people along slowly, the way I developed. I think if I had had more and tougher editing then, I'd have come along a lot faster. But, St. Martin's allowed me to learn to write."

Muller was also writing two other series in these years and work-ing with editors, including Dunne, who have become major behind-the-scenes figures in the burgeoning mystery genre. Walker published Muller's three Elena Oliverez stories, about an Hispanic museum curator. The first was bought by Sara Ann Freed, with the next two edited by Ruth Cavin after Freed left the house. The Joanna Stark stories, about a partner in a San Fran-cisco security firm, were published by St. Martin's, the last two edited by Cavin after she moved there from Walker.

The Joanna stories were never meant to be more than a trilogy, says Muller, and the other series fizzled out on its own. "I never had time to devote to the Elena books," she recalls. "I was doing two books a year then and I simply cared more about Sharon."

In 1988, with the eighth Sharon McCone novel, *Eye of the Storm*, Muller moved to Mysterious Press, drawn there by her former Walker editor, Freed. "Sara's wonderful," Muller says without equivocation. "Even when rejecting a manuscript, she writes very detailed, encouraging letters. Between her and my agent and Bill, who of course gets first crack, I'm very well edited."

Mystery writers are known by the company they keep—mostly each other's. Occupied by work that of necessity keeps them solitary for long stretches of the day, many shake off that isolation with one another, both informally and professionally.

"Everybody in the mystery field either knows or knows about everyone else," Muller continues. "We telephone and fax. If you need a phone number or an introduction, there's always someone to call. I think almost every single one of us who is published today is so because somebody along the line helped out. Joe Gores got Bill into print; Bill got me. I told Sue Dunlap who to query with her first Jill Smith novel, and she sold it there. Bill and I introduced Julie Smith to Sara Freed, who was her first editor. It goes on and on.

"I don't think we're particularly competitive with other people. We're not imitators, we're not always looking to see what the other guy is doing. Originality is really the key to success in this genre."

Though Muller is rightly credited with being the first American mystery author to write a series starring a female PI, she's aware that the idea was in the air and being breathed by others. She notes that Sue Grafton was developing the character of her southern California detective, Kinsey Milhone, when the first Sharon McCone story came out, and that Sara Paretsky was defining her Chicago investigator, V. I. Warshawski, at the same time. "We wanted to write about people like us, like the women around us. The time was ripe."

Muller also points out that writer Maxine O'Callaghan, author of five books featuring the California PI Delilah West, had a short story about Delilah published in 1974 in *Alfred Hitchcock's Mystery Magazine*.

Harking back to Sharon's genesis, Muller recalls that her character was composed of "bits and pieces" from her own life. "Her appearance was [that of] an assistant I had at *Sunset* magazine. I used another friend's family circumstances." A few years ago, when she and Pronzini were moving into their house, Muller reread her first manuscript and found that "the voice is the same. She's the same person."

The detective only recently, in *Wolf in the Shadows*, pulled away from the security of her position as an investigator for the All Souls' Legal Cooperative ("in the 1970s, there really were such organizations") to branch out and work for herself. But originally, Muller says, she put Sharon in that environment so "she wouldn't just be sitting in an office with a bottle in the desk drawer. All Souls' gave her associates and friends. It gave her relationships." That, of course, proved crucial in establishing her credibility as a woman.

Sharon herself may have come fairly full-blown to the author, but plot problems were trickier. Muller remembers realizing, while writing *Edwin of the Iron Shoes*, that "with the solution I had in mind, I was going to be done on page 78. That's when I learned about plotting, to think, what can I do to complicate this? I did plot charts for two or three books, then I came to understand that flexibility is the key. Now I start out with a situation, a subject or even a title. I have a vague idea of what happens and where it's going to end and just start writing. If the author is only one step ahead of the detective, there's spontaneity and a sense of real life."

Muller's conversation consistently moves back to her character. "Sharon is like a real person to me. I'm not tired of her because I keep making changes in her life and her circumstances." One of those changes is, inevitably, aging; the PI is facing 40. "I'm interested in exploring what happens to her when she has to go to the chiropractor, like I did. Then there's hot flashes on stakeout, age discrimination, what it feels like when you think you're losing your looks."

Near one bookcase-lined wall of the living room stands a long, wide dollhouse. It's the All Souls' building, complete with the offices, kitchen and bedrooms that have been as much Sharon McCone's home as her own small house in San Francisco's Glen Park district. Built, decorated and even electrically wired by the author, who of course designed the fictional original, the carefully constructed model loudly declares the attachment between Muller and McCone. "Sharon is like the imaginary playmates I had as a child. We become more alike the more time we spend together." With a small, pleased smile, the author adds, "People will often call me Sharon."

DULCY BRAINARD
August 8, 1994

V. S. NAIPAUL

For someone who for most of his highly distinguished writing career has been a comparatively unobtrusive figure, Vidiadhar Surajprasad Naipaul has lately been making quite a splash.

Two months ago he made the trip from his quiet country place in Wiltshire, England, to Tulsa, Okla., for the formal presentation of his archives to the university there. He was back in the U.S. recently for a round of publicity that included a double appearance on *Charlie Rose* and a dinner thrown by Knopf for colleagues and press, all coinciding with the appearance of major interviews in the *New Yorker* (by Stephen Schiff) and the *New York Times Book Review* (by old friend Mel Gussow, his third in a decade).

The occasion for all this hoopla was the publication of *A Way in the World*, which, like each of the last few books in Naipaul's magisterial *oeuvre*, the author has declared despairingly to be probably his last.

However, at 62, sprouting a new beard that makes him look, if anything, even more forbiddingly stern than usual, the slight author seemed—in a talk with us in his Carlyle Hotel suite and at the Knopf dinner the following night—to be thoroughly enjoying himself. We have in fact known Naipaul from his undergraduate days at Oxford, when he arrived on the English scene in 1953 as a young scholarship winner from Trinidad. "Yes," the author says as he rises to greet his visitor. "I would have known you instantly. You still look the same. Yes, still the same. Absolutely the same." Almost certainly untrue, but, coming from one with a remarkably keen eye for the appearance and flavor of things, flattering nonetheless. The emphasis of the repetition—wittily characterized in Schiff's *New Yorker* piece as "Naipaul's *bis*"—is a habit of speech that may once have been unconscious but is now almost certainly studied.

For what strikes one most of all about Naipaul is the extraordinary force of his persona. It is an actorly one, enhanced by a remarkably deep and mellifluous voice, that seems to alternate constantly between sternness and playfulness. He says outrageous things very decisively, then seems to pause as if to weigh whether one is going to take them seriously or as a joke; and since levity always seems to lie close to his surface, the effect is of a hugely intelligent person playing sly games whose outcome only he can determine.

Even at Oxford, where one might have expected him to be a shy newcomer as a young man from a Hindu family in an obscure Caribbean outpost of the empire, he had remarkable self-confidence. "Why not?" he says now. "I was very intellectually alert, I felt cherished and admired. I knew French and Spanish literature, which none of the rest of you did, and I was extremely good at Anglo-Saxon. My tutor said Professor Tolkien [yes, *that* Tolkien] told him my language papers were the best."

But if Oxford was a happy time for him, the years that followed were not. He was desperately poor, and what work he could find—for the Caribbean service of the BBC, writing reviews for peanuts—was irksome. He worked very hard at his writing, knowing, he says, that it was the only thing possible for him. "I wasn't interested at all in doing anything else, couldn't imagine anything else." Still, he refuses to lament the hardship of it. "I was there voluntarily, after all, it was my choice, no one would be interested in my complaint. People now whine all the time, they make a career of complaint, Perhaps there should be a college course in it." A wintry smile.

It was during this time that Naipaul began to find his subject, his style and, eventually, a publisher. He wrote a long novel at Oxford, but the unpublished manuscript was destroyed, with all of his work up to 1970, by a workman's mistake in the London warehouse where the documents were stored. He is still bitter about this, and goes into one of his brief tirades. "No, I had no recourse. Deregulation means a company has no blame; this is a time of lawlessness when only big corporations with lots of lawyers have access to the law. If people hide behind the law, perhaps we should take the law into our own hands, and shoot them! Why not? Why not?"

His first three novels and story collections were centered on Trinidad as it emerged into political consciousness after WW II.

The Mystic Masseur, The Suffrage of Elvira and *Miguel Street* all were published by Andre Deutsch in London but took a while to reach this side of the Atlantic. "People here knew nothing of me, nothing! And why should they?" Was he grateful to Deutsch for continuing loyally to publish him over the years (until the mid-1980s, in fact)? "No, no. They got *Miguel Street* in the summer of 1955 and didn't publish it until four years later. And why should I be grateful? He wasn't losing any money. They sold 3000 copies of *The Mystic Masseur*. But he was very mean. I only stayed there because of Diana Athill [Deutsch's celebrated assistant, herself an author of some note]. She stuck with me even when she didn't understand my changes of style—*The Mimic Men*, for instance. But *In a Free State* lost her; she wanted another kind of book than the one I could write, and we drifted apart over *Guerillas*. I thought the black revolutionaries were scoundrels, and she couldn't accept that."

Naipaul is bitter about his early reception in this country. Even *A House for Mr. Biswas* (1961), regarded now as one of his finest fictional achievements, and certainly the capstone of his early career, made barely a ripple here, published, he says, in an edition of 1000 by McGraw-Hill. "The reception here was very strange. They saw it as native writing. Native writing!" he repeats with incredulous disdain.

A later history, *The Loss of El Dorado*, some of which prefigures *A Way in the World*, was rejected, says Naipaul, by the American publisher who had commissioned it ("They wanted carnival and Negroes, that sort of thing"), and Knopf bought it for $5000, thus beginning what has turned into a long association. But it did not begin auspiciously. "It had very good reviews here, but they didn't publish it properly. Yes, I was badly published at first, even by Knopf." He warms to the theme of author-publisher relations. "An author lives with editors who don't read him, publishers who don't read him, booksellers who don't read him. You need someone who reads the work well—I'm using 'read' in a technical way—someone who reads beautifully and sensitively. Writers need this. But you also need to be published aggressively. Sometimes it's difficult to combine the two."

Currently he is happy with his publishers on both sides of the Atlantic—Heinemann in the U.K. and, of course, Knopf here. "Yes, I was very pleased with Sonny [Mehta]'s reading. You can always tell when someone understands you. But, generally, why do publishers think of authors as half-wits? Perhaps many are, but I am of more than average intelligence."

This leads him to a consideration—or rather lack of consideration—of his contemporaries. "I am a writer, not a reader. I read for illumination, out of a sense of curiosity or inquiry, not to keep up, or to fill the time. And I don't feel I have to read something only once." In fiction, he finds himself constantly rereading Flaubert, Balzac, Conrad. "I would like to read only 20 pages a day—to read more is to throw away lovely things. Of course it depends on whether the writer is *worth* reading slowly. Many writers offer only one real sentence a paragraph or even a page. García Márquez, for instance, those Latin Americans—just so much fluff and lace. Fluff. Fluff."

Naipaul, in his 40 years of writing, has alternated novels, of an increasingly reportorial nature, with closely observed pictures of the post-colonial world. In his three books about India, subtitled respectively *An Area of Darkness, A Wounded Civilization* and *A Million Mutinies Now,* he has brooded on the persistence of what he regards as uncivilized behaviors. *In a Free State* took on the newly independent African states, *Guerrillas* the revolutionaries in the West Indies, *Among the Believers: An Islamic Journey* the fundamentalist Muslims.

His position is not that of the Blimpish neocolonialist, rather that of a man intoxicated with high civilization who deplores anything that drags life down to a baser level. "This is a marvelous civilization, so much is open to us now. But you can't think of what's happening in Rwanda and parts of Latin America without realizing these are terrible places, truly terrible places. Without much encouragement they'd start the slave trade all over again. Their writers should be talking about *that,* rather than lecturing us about the racism of Conrad. We should be spreading enlightenment to others, requiring the sort of self-examination that takes place in a high culture. But too many American universities now are encouraging shallow, *scoundrelly* folk. They're encouraging backward people to behave badly."

He is philosophical about his extraordinarily prolific and much-admired writing career. There have been 22 books and much journalism in those four decades, and he seems to have achieved a kind of weary apotheosis. "I never expected to make a lot of money writing, and for much of my life I didn't like to take advances for books; if I took one I felt I wouldn't write the book. I think this attitude has harmed me in the past. And for many years I had a frightful agent." The man is now dead, and Naipaul resides contentedly with Aitken & Wylie, though he still chafes: "I should have changed eight years before I did."

Through all the slow accumulation of the kind of reputation that inspires Nobel Prize talk, he remained confident. "I always felt the quality of the work would make itself felt, and it's turned out so. I had to wait, but I've been justified. You can't keep bad books on the market after five or 10 years. Quality survives. Yes. Good books don't die. You can take it from me. They don't die."

A Way in the World is a hybrid of fiction and autobiography, which Naipaul insists is "a work of the imagination—historical but also imagined." One of the most impressive sustained passages in the book is the story of a little-known Latin American revolutionary, Francisco de Miranda, whom Naipaul makes an exemplar of the con man who creates belief in himself as well as a universe around him. "I thought of the chapter as perhaps 25 pages, and the *conception* never changed, but I wrote on and on. I became inspired, and it took me six months. I was close to tears with the effort, and deeply moved. His story contains so many ironies about revolution and corruption. But wait till you hear the squeals from Latin America about his betrayal by Simon Bolivar! They won't be able to cope with that. No."

After the completion of each of his books in recent years, Naipaul has described himself as utterly exhausted and unlikely to write again. His current mood is no exception. "I am seven months into depletion, which makes me very vulnerable to other incapacities. But you need to be *fit* to write, and I exercise, I go for walks, I look after myself. The notion of the sickly writer is ludicrous." Still, he is slowing down. "I used to travel so prodigiously, taking hardly an aspirin, and now I've hardly been anywhere for five years. There are so many ailments now. My briefcase is like a doctor's case, full of ointments and pills!

"I'd like to travel some more before the body shuts down completely. But I can't travel without writing. I love to see things come out of the darkness, and if I can't do that I'll feel I've lost something vital. I *have* to do that."

How would he like to be remembered as a writer? Naipaul seems

173

genuinely taken aback by the question, and struggles to formulate a reply. "I'd like people to find my books . . . extraordinarily interesting . . . to find that in them the last half-century was well recorded, that the whole postwar period was *there*, in my work, described without prejudice. I hope they'd find them nice. Nice." He repeats it, seemingly unaware of its odd inadequacy. Then— "Rich to read—the way they're put together. And perhaps prophetic. *In a Free State* was condemned by Nadine Gordimer, but what I was saying was that we had to purge ourselves of those totalitarian impulses. And perhaps if they'd taken it seriously they wouldn't have found Idi Amin such a joke. Such a joke."

JOHN F. BAKER
June 6, 1994

LAWRENCE NAUMOFF

A STRIKING COUPLE meets us at the Raleigh-Durham airport: a handsome brown-haired man of average height and weight and a pretty, slender—and taller—blonde woman with an upswept hairdo. They are dressed in jeans and holding hands. She is smiling warmly, while he wears the pleasant but mildly worried look he will retain for the length of our day-long visit. Novelist Lawrence Naumoff and his best friend and sweetheart, Marianne Gingher (who also happens to be a writer), escort us to her black Honda and out into brilliant May sunshine for the 20-minute ride to Chapel Hill.

"There's something depressing about a happy woman," he says on the way, echoing his character Monroe in his last book, *Taller Women*. Gingher, who is driving, laughs appreciatively.

The route Lawrence Naumoff took to his current situation as a writer, as he awaits Harcourt Brace's publication of his fourth woman-centered novel, *Silk Hope, NC*, is not unlike one of the country roads of his native North Carolina that figure in his fiction: hilly and winding, shaded with overhanging trees, interrupted by splashes of sunlight, bumpy and washed out in sections, but reappearing in fine shape later on.

The golden boy of UNC–Chapel Hill writing instructors and English professors when he was an honors student in the 1960s, Naumoff received many prizes, including a Thomas Wolfe Memorial Award and a Discovery Award from the *Carolina Quarterly*. As an undergraduate, he published short stories and novel excerpts under the pseudonym Peter Nesovich. (Somewhat bemused, he says he can't remember why he felt the need for a nom de plume or why he chose that particular name.) Shortly after graduation, he was awarded an NEA grant.

Then he stopped writing altogether for almost 15 years.

In the interim he married twice, spent a brief time in Mexico, then took off for a remote farm in northwest Maine where he and his first wife lived for a year and a half in what he characterizes as a romantic back-to-the-land adventure. "There was almost no work to be had, it was so remote. We had to struggle. But young women are so happy to be in love. They ask no questions and will do just anything to be together. Looking back on that time, I'm so touched," Naumoff says.

When they scraped together enough money, the couple returned to North Carolina, and by 1969, when Naumoff was 23, they had bought a 26-acre farm and its old Victorian farmhouse in Silk Hope, a pre–Revolutionary War Quaker farming community where land was still cheap. Many years later it would be the eponymous setting of his new novel.

Naumoff farmed (wheat, corn, soybeans), raised livestock (chickens and hogs) and learned carpentry and building skills from old-line Quaker practitioners. "I had a big 4020 John Deere tractor and I would ride that thing for 12 hours at a time. I would think and contemplate things in a way that would be impossible if I were doing anything else. When you're riding a tractor, your mind is free to think."

From the Quaker carpenters Naumoff absorbed a timeless wisdom about work that would effortlessly transfer to the writing process when he eventually returned to it. "Their pace of life and orderliness ultimately made it easier for me to write a novel," he says. "I learned to work in a relaxed and thoughtful way. I learned to build novels the way they built houses. While I was not writing I had this rich life that was preparing me to write again."

For 10 years Naumoff lived, in his words, "in heavenly isolation, in a way that was a homage to an idealized rural life" on the farm in Silk Hope. The dream came to an abrupt end when the farmhouse was destroyed by a mysterious fire in the middle of one night. It was to prove a pivotal moment in his life. Naumoff had been 25 miles away in Chapel Hill on what he calls "a romantic errand, doing something I shouldn't have been doing," when "halfway through the night, I slowly realized . . . I was making a big mistake. I left. I drove back home on those dark country roads under a black sky until I saw the sky change and begin to glow orange in the distance." It was the fire consuming the old house and the surrounding 100-year-old maple and oak trees.

Though no one was injured in the fire, everything was destroyed, including three unpublished novels, dozens of short stories, family heirlooms and, ultimately, his marriage.

He built another house, this time with his own hands, on the same site, and married again. But neither the house nor the new marriage felt right. The idyll had been shattered.

In the throes of that unhappy second marriage, in which "just surviving each day" took all that he had, Naumoff began to write once more. "I had had 12 years of stupid mistakes," he says of his dry period. "Finally, I thought if I did not start writing again, I was going to die. I had enough money to live on for 11 months, so I decided to write a novel in that time. Writing saved my life."

His brief search for an agent included an interlude with Virginia Barber, whose reaction to the manuscript presaged some future reviewers' consternation over his frank and funny treatment of the battle of the sexes. "She said, and I quote: 'I read the manuscript in one sitting. It had a powerful effect on me.' But she went on to say that she doubted that she could find a publisher for the book," Naumoff recalls. Soon afterward he settled in with Barbara Lowenstein Associates, which has represented all his books. *The Night of the Weeping Women* (1988) was acquired for Atlantic Monthly Press by Morgan Entrekin. Well received, it marked the dramatic reemergence of his early promise and the beginning, as Naumoff puts it, "of an amazing six years" of productivity. *Rootie Kazootie* followed in 1990 from Farrar, Straus & Giroux; *Taller Women: A Cautionary Tale* was published by Harcourt in 1992. When the appearance of *Silk Hope, NC*, Naumoff is rapidly making up for time spent doing other things.

To date, Naumoff's novels always feature strong, spirited and frequently misguided women characters pitted against the system and sappy, self-absorbed men. The women inevitably take a fall for their feistiness and openhearted innocence, but they also emerge at the end as unwitting heroines and survivors. The novels are also belly-laugh funny. His friend and erstwhile employer Reynolds Price (Naumoff did construction and gardened for him in the lean years) offered a glowing pre-pub opinion of *Night of the Weeping Women*, saying that Naumoff "looks at marriage honestly. What he sees is outrageously—hilariously, tragically—undeniable; and he sets it all down with effortless-looking brilliance." Other reviewers concurred.

When *Rootie Kazootie* appeared two years later, novelist (*Bobby*

Rex's Greatest Hits) and short-story writer (*Teen Angel and Other Stories of Young Love*) Marianne Gingher wrote the review in the *Washington Post*, which served to introduce the writers to each other. Gingher said the book was a "brilliant comedy of errant romance . . . Plaintive, madcap, utterly seductive, Naumoff writes about marriage and faithlessness as if he were concocting an eighth Deadly Sin." Naumoff says today, "The review was better than the book. And she got right all of the things that were really important to me." One thing led to another, and his next novel, *Taller Women*, and the newest one, *Silk Hope, NC*, are both dedicated to Gingher, whom Naumoff calls his "longtime sweetheart."

Gingher teaches creative writing at UNC in Chapel Hill and commutes between her home in Greensboro, where her two teenage sons live, and Carrboro, a suburb of Chapel Hill, where Naumoff resides with his 14-year-old son Michael, the child from his second marriage, who has Down's syndrome.

When we reach the unimposing rented house on a quiet street that Naumoff now calls home, Marianne prepares lunch, and Naumoff repairs to the airy, high-ceilinged living room scattered with books.

Taller Women, which offered more stinging social commentary than his previous books, put off some reviewers. The *Los Angeles Times Book Review* savaged it, while *PW*, the *New York Times* and others sang its praises. Michael Dorris called it ". . . an unsparing tour of the complicated ways contemporary men and women connect, disconnect and generally drive each other to distraction." Yet Linda Healy, Naumoff's editor at Farrar, Straus & Giroux, which had issued *Rootie Kazootie*, had found it "disturbing" and "didn't want to be associated with it in any way." With an assist from his agent, Naumoff moved to Harcourt and his new editor, Alane Mason.

Naumoff is puzzled over the range of reaction to the novel and thinks its detractors are humorless ideologues who miss the point. "The idea goes all the way back to at least Herodotus," he says. "The book is about wantonness in women and how it is always, in the end, punished, whether they're just doing what the men are asking them to do or following their own impulses, however big-hearted and well-intentioned they may be."

Naumoff and his publisher think that *Silk Hope, NC*, is his most accessible novel yet. Certainly it is softer in tone than its predecessors, and the ending is more hopeful. The story concerns two sisters, wild and devil-may-care Franny and conventional and conservative Natalie, their old family home in Silk Hope and what it takes to live a virtuous life as modern independent women. "Something changed between the two books," Naumoff says of his treatment of the female characters. "I was more compassionate and tender with my heroine in *Silk Hope*. Franny is the first woman in my books to be visibly heroic. She achieves an accidental wisdom, a gradual clarity, that allows her to save her sister, save everything."

On the ride out to Silk Hope for a tour of the old farm in his red 1976 Datsun pickup, Naumoff considers his career. Something of his sensitivity to women must be attributable to having grown up the only boy wedged between two older and two younger sisters. He had a "happy, safe and normal upper-middle class Southern childhood," as the son of a prominent doctor (Philip Naumoff, M.D., who is still practicing in Charlotte at age 80).

A Jew in the Christ-haunted South and a youthful devotee of writers with outsider sensibilities such as B. Traven, Paul Bowles and William Burroughs, Naumoff relishes his marginal status in a traditional society. It is a stance he has maintained even with respect to organizations and institutions that might have boosted his writing career. "I've gone very far without being part of the MFA, writing conference, academic world, which is just not my way. Everything has happened on the strength of the writing."

Nearing the old farm, Naumoff pulls off the road and waves to an elderly woman in a field across the way, who is inspecting rows of cabbage and broccoli. It's his old neighbor Edith Campbell. He called the fire department from her home the night his house burned down.

"This is not one of my wives," he says to Edith, referring to our presence in the car.

"You've gained some weight," she says, teasing him.

As we walk the grounds of the farm on a glorious spring afternoon, memories are everywhere. Standing in the shade of a leafy maple tree, in his most engaging Southern manner, Naumoff is moved to sum up his writing credo. "I am not consciously a champion of women. I like the company of women. I like the way they think, I like the potential women have to offer the world. But it's very hard today to know what's the right thing to do. In the past there were universally accepted constraints and codes of behav-

179

ior. I do feel there are right ways to live involving duty and honor and virtue. It's the way I try to live and it's what I write about.

"I don't feel comfortable being called a writer of controversial books about men and women. There is so much more going on in my books," Naumoff says, referring to the larger moral and ethical issues he tackles in his novels. A fair observation from a writer whose true subject is the human condition and the difficulty involved in knowing—and doing—"the right thing."

MARGARET LANGSTAFF
June 13, 1994

JOHN NICHOLS

As DRAMATIC LANDSCAPES GO, Taos, N. M., rates near the top. Behind the town, mountains of an extraordinary purity rise abruptly, soaring 6000 feet above a broad, high-desert valley. To the west, sage-covered mesa, cracked by the zagged black chasm of the Rio Grande Gorge, stretches away to blue-hazed mountains on the far horizon.

This natural splendor, combined with the multicultural dynamic of the Native American, Latino and Anglo people who inhabit it, has long attracted artists of all stripes. But few have made the Taos Valley more thoroughly their own than author John Nichol, who, in his quarter-century of life here, has become one of the most vocal and effective champions of this special place.

It is John Nichols country, a locale integral to this versatile, 53-year-old writer's tragicomic vision of American life and culture. Evoked directly in his books of nonfiction and photography, unnamed or dubbed Chamisaville in his fiction, Taos and its environs inform most of Nichol's work, including his latest novel, *Conjugal Bliss*, published by Holt.

The Freudian slip of the book's subtitle—*A Comedy of Martial Arts*, with an editor's symbol for transposing letters that converts "Martial" to "Marital"—aptly defines the thrust of this often hilarious, sometimes bitter, look at love and marriage in the Great Southwest. It is the ninth novel and 15th book Nichols has published in the nearly three decades since, with *The Sterile Cuckoo* (McKay, 1965), he launched his literary life and, inadvertently, Liza Minnelli's acting career in the film role of Pookie Adams, the first of a long line of quirky, quixotic, immensely appealing Nichols characters.

He followed that initial success immediately with *The Wizard of Loneliness* (Putnam, 1966), another story of coming-of-age on the East Coast, but it is for *The Milagro Beanfield War* (Holt, 1974), the first book he published after moving to New Mexico, that he remains best known.

Reissued this year by Holt in a 20th-anniversary facsimile edition with a new afterword by Nichols, this cult classic, the basis of the 1988 film directed by Robert Redford, is the sprawling saga of a hardscrabble Latino subsistence farmer who, by illegally irrigating a small plot of parched desert, opens a pandora's box of troubling political and socioeconomic issues regarding the proper use of land and water. In *Milagro* and the two subsequent novels of his epic New Mexico Trilogy—*The Magic Journey* (Holt, 1978) and *The Nirvana Blues* (Holt, 1981)—Nichols, employing casts of thousands and wielding humor like a scalpel, dissects the politics of a rapacious, development-obsessed "Progress, American-style" that threatens to destroy everything in its path—traditional land-based cultures, history, human dignity, the earth itself.

New Mexico is the setting as well for Nichols's three other shorter, more self-contained novels, which address a broad range of subject matter—the Hollywood film world in *A Ghost in the Music* (Holt, 1979); the dark, death-haunted violence of American society in the aftermath of the Vietnam War in *American Blood* (Holt, 1987); a brief relationship between an aging, ailing writer and a much younger woman in the lean and lyrical *An Elegy for September* (Holt, 1992).

Interspersed with his novels, Nichols has also produced a series of nonfiction books—*If Mountains Die: A New Mexico Memoir* (Knopf, 1979); *The Last Beautiful Days of Autumn* (Holt, 1982); *On the Mesa* (Peregrine Smith, 1986); *A Fragile Beauty* (Peregrine Smith, 1987); *The Sky's the Limit* (Norton, 1990); and *Keep It Simple* (Norton, 1992)—all but the first illustrated with his own photographs. Fascinating partly for the insights they provide into the writing process, these books treat his experience of the Taos region in a very personal way and chronicle the places, people, and activities (notably trout fishing) that are important to him.

It's been a remarkably diverse and prolific career, and an often frenetic life, with two marriages, a son and a daughter raised to young adulthood, and immense amounts of time volunteered as a spokesman for a variety of environmental and political causes. In the last few years, a heart ailment has slowed Nichols's physical pace, but not his intellect or the compulsion to create—he estimates he's actually produced some 70 books—that has driven him for nearly as long as he can remember.

"The desire to write has always been there," he says, sitting, on a bright winter day, in the warm kitchen of his funky old adobe house on the outskirts of Taos. A recent illness has left his lean, muscular frame more rawboned than usual, his face slightly haggard, but his tousled hair is still dark brown and the toothy grin he flashes frequently, linked with a wry chuckle, is as warmly boyish as ever.

Nichols was born in Berkeley, Calif. His mother died when he was two, and he was raised all over the U.S.—in Florida, Vermont, Connecticut, rural Virginia, Washington, DC., and on Long Island, where he spent summers at his father's old family home and discovered early loves of both the natural world and verbal expression. "I grew up in a family of storytellers—loved tall tales, folk tales, magic stuff," Nichols recalls. He was already writing stories when, in 1954, he went off to prep school at Loomis, in Windsor, Conn., where he made his first attempt at writing a novel.

During his 1958–1962 undergraduate years at Hamilton College in upstate New York, Nichols blossomed as an athlete with a particular gift for hockey. But he also studied English literature and, though there were no creative writing courses available, continued to write. "I got hooked on long fiction at Hamilton—every year I write a novel or two," Nichols says, with a bemused shrug. "I just had this kind of fanatical energy."

Knee injuries, which would later make him ineligible for the draft during the Vietnam War, shattered Nichol's dream of a professional hockey career, so, after graduation in 1962, he accepted an invitation from his maternal grandmother to stay with her in Barcelona, Spain, where he taught English and wrote early drafts of what became *The Sterile Cuckoo*. He settled in New York in 1963, supported himself by selling drawings in the streets, playing guitar and singing in coffee houses, and submitted *The Sterile Cuckoo* over the transom to a string of publishers. With each rejection, he rewrote the book—probably 15 times in all, he says—until, in early 1964, David McKay accepted it.

But 1964 was also a pivotal year for Nichols in other ways. He signed with literary agent Perry Knowlton—"The first one through the door," Nichols says, with his hallmark grin—who has represented him ever since. Knowlton soon placed Nichols's second novel, *The Wizard of Loneliness,* with Putnam. And, on a lark, Nichols visited Guatemala, which changed his life, his work and the nature of his commitment to the world.

"I'd never been in a place so miserable, where you could so clearly trace the influence and domination of the U.S.," Nichols remembers. "It started the political wheels turning, led me to refashion my politics in a left-wing perspective. I got a social conscience, and once you get that, you're trapped by it—you worry about everything."

Back in New York, Nichols acted on that revelation, channeling his prodigious energy into politics. "My career had really been handed to me on a platter," he says, "and then I sort of shot myself in the foot, spent seven years writing bad books blasting capitalism, the war in Vietnam. I was torn between being a writer or giving it up to become an organizer, manning the barricades. But I couldn't stop writing—did seven or eight books that weren't publishable because they just weren't good."

In 1969, with his literary career in tatters, sick of his New York life and distressed by the apparently endless continuation of the war in Vietnam, Nichols moved to Taos. "I'd been reading about New Mexico," he says, "and it sounded almost like a colonial country, with a lot of possibilities for political action."

Nichols immersed himself in this new world, learning its history, getting acquainted with its multicultural ethos, and soon began contributing unpaid articles about the region and its problems to the *New Mexico Review,* a muckraking journal in Santa Fe.

"I owe my career to that publication," Nichols says emphatically. "It kept me writing, published me. It was a political writing life that was very important to me." That relationship continued until the *Review* died in late 1972 and, almost immediately, Nichols began recycling all that he'd learned about New Mexico into a new novel—*The Milagro Beanfield War.* In 40 days, he wrote a 500-page book, spent another six weeks correcting and producing a clean copy of the manuscript and then shipped it off. His agent took it to editor Marian Wood at Holt, and, at a stroke, Nichol's career was back on track. Wood has been his fiction editor and Holt the publisher of his novels ever since.

"It's pretty simple," Nichols says of that longstanding relationship. "I finish a book, send it to Marian, and she accepts or rejects it. I don't take it elsewhere. I admire her, trust her; she's rejected as many as she's accepted, but I think she's saved me a lot of embarrassment."

He now has a similar arrangement for his nonfiction/photo-essay books. On the last two volumes—plus another, *The Holiness of Water*, due later this year—he's worked exclusively with Bill Rusin at Norton. "I'm interested in loyalty to the editor and the publisher," Nichols says. "And, like my editors, my agents [Perry Knowlton for literature, his son Tim Knowlton for film, both at Curtis Brown] are friends, people who are important to me, who stand up for me—have kept me alive all these years."

Ironically, for a man who views "American capitalist consumerism" as one of the world's chief ills, Hollywood has been crucial to Nichols's survival, in the form of film options on his novels and a series of writing jobs that came, he says, "out of the blue," beginning with a script (not used) for director Alan Pakula's take on *Sterile Cuckoo*. Nichols worked on three projects with Constantin Costa-Gravas, including a rewrite of the Oscar-winning screenplay for *Missing*, and collaborated for eight years on scripts for Robert Redford's *Milagro*. He teamed with Karel Riesz on a film about Haitian refugees, with Louis Malle on a script for his own *Magic Journey*, and spent two years developing a CBS television miniseries about Pancho Villa and the Mexican Revolution—projects as yet unrealized. He's currently enmeshed in yet another script, set in the Amazon, for director Ridley Scott.

Productive as ever, he's also at work on a new novel set in New York in the summer of 1961, drafting his prose in longhand, often at a favorite local cafe, then revising it on the battered manual typewriter, an old Olympia portable that he's used since 1974, which sits on a cluttered desk in the corner of his kitchen. His schedule is haphazard, the only rule being that he write for six hours or so at some point during the day.

"I never lack thoughts for a project, always have some ax to grind," Nichols says of his creative process. "Things percolate a lot, and when I sit down to work it just comes out, though it's often very different from what I've been thinking. I do the first draft very quickly, then rewrite—and rewrite, and rewrite—trying to find the story, kind of by trial and error. I love the revision process, dwelling on lines, words—that final stage is really writing."

Whatever their precise nature, all his projects are animated, he says, by a social conscience, an unrepentant love of life and a fervent belief in the power of art to create change. "Literature teaches us to have sympathy and compassion for each other—makes possible a better world," Nichols says, and then, apparently embarrassed by the weight of that statement, he looks up, laughing. "But writing is *fun*—it means that everything in life is wonderful because it's all relevant to your métier. Everything is pertinent, interesting, meaningful—everything I observe is material. My work surrounds me and astounds me."

WILLIAM CLARK
February 14, 1994

LEWIS NORDAN

It took Lewis Nordan almost 40 years to find a way to tell the story of Emmett Till, a black teenager who was lynched in Mississippi in 1955 for whistling at a white woman. Nordan, too, was a Mississippi teenager at the time, and the day he heard about the murder was a day that changed his life.

"This story followed me through the years," Nordan says, "and it visited me in many forms. But all of them were so patently wrong that I never wrote it until now." Finally, two years ago, the haunting story materialized with the unexpectedness of a vision. Appearing on a TV talk show to promote his then-current novel, *Music of the Swamp*, Nordan was asked, "What is your next book about?" To his complete surprise he answered confidently, "It will deal with the death of Emmett Till." Nordan remembers that his next thought was an incredulous, "Who said that?"

He set to work immediately, wrote the first draft in six weeks and completed the novel in less than a year. The result is *Wolf Whistle*, his new novel from Algonquin.

Though the subject would seem to demand almost religious gravity, Nordan's version is astonishing: he conveys the horror of the murder and the injustice of the killers' acquittal in scenes that recall Gabriel García Márquez and other magical realists. Like a grotesque cartoon frieze drawn in mourning colors, the novel evokes gasps, disbelief, even pained laughter, without trivializing the tragic event which is its point of departure. No one will mistake *Wolf Whistle* for a docudrama; it's as far removed from journalism as Picasso's *Guernica* is from photojournalism.

Nordan was 16, "a little country boy in the football locker room at school," on the day he first heard about Emmett Till. "The other boys were making lots of jokes about the lynching, and I was laughing, too," he recalls. "Then an ol' redneck boy like the rest of us said something amazing. He said, 'That's not right. I don't like that kind of joke. That boy they killed was just a boy like anybody, I don't care if he was colored.' "

Nordan pauses. His quiet voice softens. "And that changed my life so abruptly, so profoundly, that I have a hard time even telling about it. Almost no other event has had such an effect on me. Not that it transformed me into the perfect little civil rights worker overnight, but that's when I knew I would have to leave Mississippi and try to find a larger world, a world in which everybody might say, 'It's not right to talk like that about a boy, it's just not right.' "

Perhaps Nordan, 54, left the state symbolically that day, though in reality he stayed on to attend Millsaps College in Jackson and Mississippi State University, where he earned an M.A. in English. He completed his Ph.D. at Auburn University in Alabama in 1973, specializing in Shakespeare. "I wanted to be a Shakespeare scholar," he says. "But the truth is I wasn't any good at it. I didn't have the kind of analytical mind necessary to illuminate a text. And attempts to publish in the field were torture for me."

Both before and after graduate school, Nordan had a string of what he calls "book-jacket jobs," the type of work that adds color to a bio. He taught high school, sold fireworks, worked as yardman, soda jerk, lumberyard hand, hospital orderly, night watchman and book reviewer. "But it was because I couldn't get an academic job, even with a doctorate, that I became a writer," he confesses.

His first wife, Mary, was an elementary school teacher, so Nordan, unable to find regular work, stayed home and raised their three children. During those years he taught himself the craft of fiction writing. He also credits his ex-wife with invaluable help and criticism. His first book, *Welcome to the Arrow-Catcher Fair* (LSU Press), is dedicated to her, although they were divorced by the time it was published in 1983. *Wolf Whistle* is dedicated to "Li," short for Alicia, his second wife.

Friends who read Nordan's early stories in the 1970s called them cartoonish and unbelievable. "In all my years of school I had never quite understood what people meant by 'a writer's vision,' " he says. "Then one day it dawned on me what my own fictional vision is. It's a magical landscape just askew of the real, historical universe. That world, that created planet, doesn't quite square with the world I live in."

Considering that James Thurber has been a lifelong influence,

188

it's not surprising that Nordan's cockeyed story world rotates on an idiosyncratic axis. As a child growing up in Itta Bena, Miss., he was fascinated by Thurber's cartoons, though he says he couldn't figure out what they meant. "Sometime later, still just a kid, I read Thurber's *University Days*. The totally real and believable silliness of his people fascinated me. In some sense, every story I write is a retelling of his 'The Night the Bed Fell.' "

Nordan cites DC Comics as his other main influence. "I preferred the ones that mythologized a world, such as Superman with his secret identity that kept people from knowing exactly who he was." He mentions also "the rhythms of nursery rhymes and songs" as an important influence on his prose. "I hear songs, and rhythms such as jump-rope chants, before I ever get the words," he adds. "I often have to search for the right words to fit the rhythms that are already there in my mind."

Nordan's office in the 42-story, 1930 gothic Cathedral of Learning at the University of Pittsburgh, where he has taught writing since 1983, seems to be situated halfway between the real world and his "created planet." A table full of robust African violets grows under an Elvis calendar. The stately Carnegie Museum of Art can be seen through the window, and on another wall, beside a Japanese scroll, hangs a framed enlargement of the Elvis commemorative stamp.

"Oh yes," Nordan says, "Elvis was my first hero. When he became famous I thought, he's just a kid from Tupelo; anybody can do it." He is also an ardent member of the "We Remember Elvis Club" that is based in Pittsburgh.

Nordan achieved his highly visual prose style through a painstaking process that recalls the work of a draftsman—or a cartoonist. "When I was teaching myself to write fiction," he says, "I'd go through my pages and draw a red circle around every image. If I didn't have enough red circles, I considered the page incomplete, and I would go back and fill it up with images of things to see, taste, touch and smell in every paragraph."

This process, which he says has now become intuitive, is one he instills in his students. "Once we've looked at the structure of a story to determine exactly what it's about, I lead them sentence by sentence through each paragraph and ask them to reimagine every one, as I do in my own writing. I'm teaching them to paint, to draw, and also to find the right musical notes."

For Nordan, finding his style was perhaps easier than finding the right agent. His second book, *The All-Girl Football Team* (1986), was, like his first, a short-story collection. Acting as his own agent, he sold both books to LSU Press. He also handled softcover sales of the two collections; Vintage published both in 1989.

Three agents were involved in the sale of Nordan's first novel, *Music of the Swamp* (Algonquin, 1991), but because of disagreements Nordan dismissed each one. Then he met Heather Schroder of ICM, for whom he has unqualified praise. "She loves my work, and even if it doesn't make a nickel for her, she works as hard for me as for her famous writers who earn millions."

Nordan is also happy with Shannon Ravenel, his editor at Algonquin. Over the years, she had included some of his stories in the annual anthology that she edits, *New Stories From the South*. The result was that for some time Ravenel had been Nordan's editor without their actually knowing each other.

Asked if Algonquin's treatment of authors matches the handsome design of their books and jackets, Nordan answers, "Yes, emphatically yes. I've got a 20-city book tour coming up, and they've been very generous with good airline accommodations and excellent hotels." He says he is also pleased with Algonquin's advertising and promotion of his books.

Unlike such Mississippi writers as Faulkner and Eudora Welty, who spent most of their lives at home, Nordan says he feels "unable to write about the place while I'm there. I want to live in an urban setting and speak of my characters from a distance, because that way I can do it more lovingly."

Reviewers, especially some of those who work outside the South, are often nonplussed by the parade of grotesque characters in Nordan's fiction. When asked what draws him to these types, and how he's able to use them to such comic effect, Nordan says, "I think a lot of storytelling, Southern or otherwise, is about remarkable events. Death, disease and disfiguration, dwarfism and shrunken mummies, are not necessarily more common in one place than in another, but in places with a strong oral tradition these extraordinary phenomena naturally draw a lot of comment.

"My theory about the grotesque in my own work, and in storytelling generally, is that it's a way of saying, 'This is more remarkable than anything you've seen today; this is even more remarkable than your own crazy family!' " In a story called "Mr.

Nodine, Pentecost, and the Oral Tradition," which takes place in a funeral parlor, Nordan aptly writes of an elderly grandmother addicted to the gory: "The more disastrous the tale, the more it seemed to swell her fierce pride."

Normally subdued, Nordan quickens on the subject of storytelling. "Another, more arcane theory is that the South, defeated in the Civil War and occupied by outsiders, became separate and defensive. I wouldn't want to imply that slavery didn't also cause a psychological separateness, but I believe there's something inherent in being Southern that derives from the aftermath of the war. We still have the lingering attitude: 'This is how bad it was, and this is how we laugh at it.' "

Nordan grew up in a family of avid storytellers. One of his uncles would sometimes preface a tale with, "*Don't* stop me if you've heard this one," and recently, on the phone, Nordan's mother said, "I know I've told you this one, honey, but I'm gonna tell it again because I just love to hear it."

Nordan advises students to write not what they know, but rather the kinds of stories they like to hear. "Telling a story," he emphasizes, "is more than entertainment. It's a form of conversation, and also a way of remembering a certain kind of rhythm. The kind of stories I like to hear is the kind my folks told."

Stories often involve loss, and it was a sense of loss that finally freed the story of Emmett Till from the deep place where it had lodged for so many years. Just before Nordan made the surprise announcement on TV, he had lived through a family crisis which led him to re-experience "everything I had ever lost before." The result was a return to Mississippi, where he grieved anew for the death of his father, his stepfather and his own two sons.

"On the heels of all that," Nordan recalls, "with so much churning around inside me, came that moment on the TV talk show. Suddenly it was revealed to me one thing I had lost that I could get back: Emmett Till. I don't know why that's so; I can't really make sense of it. But at that moment he became part of my general loss."

Perhaps one reason for Nordan's decades-long delay in writing *Wolf Whistle* was the need to determine whom the story was about. "Only when I began to write it," he reflects, "did I realize that it is the story of the white people affected by the murder, which is surely my own story. It's not necessarily the story of those who

191

killed him, it's not the story of Emmett himself. But when I spoke his name that day on TV, I knew I had found a buried chunk of my self's permanent foundation, the granite cornerstone of something formative and durable and true."

SAM STAGGS
October 18, 1993

HOWARD NORMAN

READERS OF Howard Norman's work might well expect a meal with the author to feature salted cod washed down with five cups of coffee, which is the usual repast of the protagonist of his latest novel. This scholar of Canadiana, whose former occupation as a natural history writer/researcher took him to the Northwest Territories and Maritime Provinces, has keenly captured such rustic minutiae in two novels and a story collection. But Norman doesn't cultivate a rugged image on his home turf. To meet with an interviewer, he recommends an unassuming Thai restaurant in Washington, D.C., and arrives attired not in flannel but in jeans and a pullover, his dark brown hair slightly mussed. Soft-spoken, courteous and possessed of a down-to-earth sincerity, he seems more the writing professor than the lone traveler.

It's been seven years since Norman's National Book Award–nominated debut, a coming-of-age tale set in 1950s Manitoba titled *The Northern Lights.* Since that time, his publisher, Summit, folded and Norman signed with Farrar, Straus & Giroux for his second novel, *The Bird Artist* (Forecasts, April 25). Like his debut, *The Bird Artist* lends an exotic quality to a locale not often thought of in lyrical terms.

Set in 1911 in Witless Bay, a Newfoundland cod-fishing village, *The Bird Artist* recounts the circumstances of the murder of lighthouse keeper Botho August; the unlikely 20-year-old killer, an ordinarily passive bird-illustrator named Fabian Vas, narrates. Not only has Fabian's mother begun an affair with Botho during his father's absence, but Fabian's erstwhile lover, 24-year-old Margaret Handle, has also slept with Botho.

In some ways, Margaret is a marginal player, influencing but not ultimately controlling Fabian and the other characters. Troubled and wildly extroverted, she drinks heavily and displays an erratic temper. Although Fabian shares her bed, he considers theirs a dead-end relationship and allows his parents to arrange his marriage to a distant cousin.

Yet Norman sees Margaret as a vital presence. "I originally wrote this book because of Margaret Handle," he says. "My hope is to introduce her in such a way that one might always wonder where she is and what she's doing. She spices things up. She puppeteers many things in the book."

Margaret's promiscuity and her fondness for whiskey are never addressed in terms of morality, however. "I tried to avoid contemporary psychologizing because alcoholism wouldn't have been the term used at that time," Norman explains. "But I'll admit something to you: when I was writing this, I didn't realize how much she was drinking. It was only when it was building up toward the murder that I realized, my God, she's a mess."

That Witless Bay's denizens are completely aware of Margaret's peccadilloes reflects the insularity of the tight-knit, judgmental community. So, for that matter, does Fabian's mother's unapologetic relationship with Botho, and Fabian's desperate act—which he blames on another in a moment of fear, and then cannot live down in the knowing eyes of his motley neighbors. "In a small village, where everybody sees everything, there's really no middle ground," Norman explains, which is why his characters often follow their passions to the fullest extent.

Human deeds are not *The Bird Artist*'s only catalyst: Newfoundland itself provides a bewitching presence. "I tried to develop the landscape as a character, so it would play on people's minds," Norman says. "It's a stark, overwhelming visual place—everywhere you turn something is looming up, either weather or landscape or a sense of history. . . . It's mesmerizing and disquieting at the same time," he observes.

Newfoundland's solitary atmosphere, Norman believes, challenges "our notions of what there is to do on a day-to-day basis." Recalling his various tenures in the North, he feels that "it was never a matter of boredom, but you often see those long periods of time in isolation, the drinking, the suicide rate, the claustrophobia."

If mere mention of Newfoundland also calls to mind Annie Proulx, literary locale is not all Norman has in common with that author: He and his family spend about half their time at a farmhouse in Proulx territory—Vermont. New England is the family's retreat, while D.C. is the businesslike environment where Norman teaches writing and literature at the University of Maryland; his wife, poet Jane Shore, holds classes at George Washington University; and their daughter, Emma, attends elementary school.

This solid two-home "axis," as Norman calls it, belies the 45-year-old author's formerly peripatetic existence. Born in Toledo, Ohio, and raised in Michigan, Norman cultivated a love of the Great White North, taking jobs in Canada and receiving his M.A. in 1974 from the Folklore Institute at Indiana University. Some adolescents yearn to experience Manhattan or Prague or a tropical destination—"Canada was that for me," Norman says, with perceptible awe. "I went deep into Canada to find out if what was there was really commensurate with my imagination of it—sometimes it was, and oftentime it was much more so." He cites the country's linguistic variety as part of its appeal: "You can travel to Canada and every two or three hundred miles there's a different Indian language spoken. People think of vast open spaces—but, as isolating as times were there, it sustained me: the work, the languages, and seeing so much wildlife."

As a writer of natural history and a researcher for film companies during the '70s and early '80s, Norman toured remote locales where being multilingual "wasn't a matter of choice." Although he is not fluent, he claims some knowledge of an Inuit dialect, some Cree, and some Chippewa, and he still translates folklore and listens to tapes of these unwritten languages at least once a week. Translations including *The Wishing Bone Cycle: Narrative Poems From the Swampy Cree Indians* and the children's book *How Glooskap Outwits the Ice Giants*, as well as an anthology, *Northern Tales* (selected and edited by Norman) testify to this longtime interest.

Still roaming and discontented in 1982, Norman "picked a place on the map . . . and just went." That place was Cambridge, Mass., where Norman met his wife-to-be at a Thanksgiving dinner hosted by poet Philip Levine. Norman and Jane Shore married in 1984.

Shore encouraged Norman to write *The Northern Lights*, as did Sam Shepard, whom Norman had known since the playwright's pre-celebrity days; while Norman penned short fiction for the *Boston Globe's* Sunday magazine, he completed his first novel. The *Globe* stories would eventually be collected as *Kiss in the Hotel Joseph Conrad*.

Norman's itinerant days still weren't over—daughter Emma was born while Shore was poet-in-residence at the University of Hawaii. But in 1988, the couple finally chose their home in Vermont and their current jobs in Washington. Norman knew it was time to establish roots when he took his long-term possessions out of storage and found 11 copies of *Heart of Darkness.*

If this personal history seems convoluted, every anecdote Norman tells has similarly far-reaching implications and a complex chronology. The eerie tale of *The Bird Artist*'s origin, which is animatedly recalled by the author, characterizes his roundabout approach. "I went to Newfoundland in 1973 for a Canadian film corporation," he explains. "There was a riddle they wanted me to research. A family of eight children had all died within six weeks, and seven of them were buried next to each other, but one was buried on the opposite side of the cemetery. The sheer power of the isolation of that one little girl was overwhelming."

The residents of the town, Trepasse, were reluctant to discuss the occurrence, even though the deaths had taken place in 1838. Norman theorizes that the girl had been the first to die of an illness and was therefore punished by ostracism; his film research, however, didn't pan out. Still, the seed of another idea—in tandem with the chilling magic of the cemetery—was taking hold. "I was staying in a little Anglican church that had a back room, with a bed and a nightstand," Norman recalls, leaning forward with enthusiasm. "In that church there was a painting, a watercolor, of an ibis, a long-necked wading bird. And it was just beautiful.

"I fancied myself as loving, if not being knowledgeable about, bird artists, and maybe it was because I was isolated there with the painting—it had a sense of melancholy that [reflected] the kind of melancholy of researching this film."

The painting was dated 1911, so Norman read historical documents about the year and the artist, and talked to locals in Eastern-seaboard villages including the actual Witless Bay. "I researched it just a little bit, just enough to know who the person was—and found that he had committed a murder," says Norman. "Then I stopped. There's a point where I start to violate my sense of imagining what happened. I looked into the local trial transcripts, but only as a catalyst."

Simply knowing of the artist's crime galvanized Norman. "What I was really looking for was a sense of what the morality would have been," he says, pondering the "sheer anachronism" of a killing in a self-supporting, insular community. *The Bird Artist* reflects this fusion of remoteness and moral issues.

That so much time passed between seeing the painting and finishing the book indicates the glacial pace of Norman's novelizing. It took him seven years to finish *The Northern Lights*; another novel, whose working title is *The Museum Guard*, was in the planning stages even before *The Bird Artist* came together. But Norman is content to work this way—a methodical approach, he confidently asserts, alleviates any pressure he might feel to duplicate the success of his fiction debut. "*The Northern Lights* was published when I was 38, so I was already set in my ways," he observes. He jots dialogue and scenes in notebooks, and makes time each morning to write, even when he's teaching.

Norman's rigorous, unhurried style did influence his decision to sign with FSG for *The Bird Artist*. Other houses contacted by his agent Melanie Jackson were also interested, Norman says, but he felt most strongly about FSG's editor in chief, Jonathan Galassi. "I thought, it's a quirky book, and I thought, he really likes it. I went to New York, we talked, and next thing you know he had lots of foreign sales."

Having almost completed the research phase for his next book, Norman is ready to write. He's taken a year off from teaching, and Shore is on sabbatical, so they'll be spending time in Vermont. He has yet another project under way: a YA novel based on a boy's difficult coming of age.

Norman will also augment his volumes of folktales; he's committed to doing three children's books for Harcourt Brace, intended as "sequential volumes of 10 stories each." And Norman and director Arne Glimcher, who bought film rights to *The Bird Artist*, are collaborating on a screenplay and have scouted Newfoundland locations together. "I feel very hopeful, actually," Norman remarks, "despite a natural cynicism about the film industry that I think every writer should have." He speaks from experience; although he's done a film treatment for *The Northern Lights* and written a screenplay for his short story "Laughing and Crying," neither project has made it to celluloid.

But an aversion to conventional stardom, reflected in Fabian Vas's tireless practice of his art ("Obscurity is not necessarily failure," the character states on page 1), may keep Norman from becoming too jaded. "I abhor this '15 minutes of fame' business," he says, noting that in this aspect, *The Bird Artist* is "old-fashioned." The author seems content to let his imagination lead him through the Canadian outback. Still, celebrity can arrive in unforeseen ways: Norman's sensual treatment of frequently overlooked terrain could do for Newfoundland's tourism industry what Paul Theroux did for Oceania.

NATHALIE OP DE BEECK
July 25, 1994

EDNA O'BRIEN

"WHAT WRITING DOES IS allow us to sample each other's fate."
Edna O'Brien's low and musical voice sinks a little further than
it has to, perhaps. O'Brien is a nervous stalker of words and of
truths. She speaks with an actress's confidence in her occasion
and her prerogative, and with a verbal aristocracy that is unfail-
ingly agile. But an air of apprehensive seeking seems to convey
her, with some reasonable misgivings, to a late winter afternoon
and an interview.

It's March, and the Irish-born O'Brien has returned to New
York from her home in London for her regular annual stay, this
time to teach and watch over the last stages of production of her
new novel, *Time and Tide*. Released by Farrar, Straus & Giroux,
her 19th book has seemed to its author no easier to produce than
her first—possibly, in some respects, more demanding.

"It was very difficult to write," she concedes. "I held it in my
head for three years. The novel tears at the really visceral emotions. Although we all know about these [emotions], and they
happen to us, somehow to reimagine them and write them, you
have to go into a very concentrated and painful place. I had such
a hard, excruciating time scraping, scraping at my psyche, scraping at my heart.

"I think I write under a shadow, so to speak. I don't quite know
what that shadow is, but the shadow is en route to suffering. And
suffering is not a gratuitous ingredient in fiction; it's very central
to it. I think pain deepens people. It can make for profundity,
definitely."

Her first book, *The Country Girls* (Knopf, 1960), "was written
from a girl's point of view, and this one is from a parent's point
of view. It happens to be [that of] a mother, but I think some fathers are as congenitally attached to their children as mothers
are." O'Brien raised her two sons by herself in London after her

15-year marriage to writer Ernest Gebler ended in divorce in 1967. "I believe in this world between people who are very close, particularly blood relatives. I believe that everything is known by each party. Everything is perceived, even if never expressed."

Fulminant and fierce in her evocations of intimacy and its hazards, especially concerning women, O'Brien is not only a mother but a daughter whose "congenital attachment" to her mother has undergone great strains.

Born to a farmer's family in rural County Clare in the west of Ireland in 1936, she "was the fifth child; the child before me had died. And times weren't, to put it mildly, easy. I think my mother was exhausted, spent. She was a woman of considerable ambition, which she hadn't realized. You see, I have, although I often think I'm a bit of a disaster. I have realized some of my ambition: some of the demons and angels that roam around inside my head are given expression.

"My mother, she made rugs and things; she had an artistic bent. But I think her life was more than she could bear. What we forget as children is that our parents are children, also. The child in them has not been satisfied or met or loved, often. Not always, but very often. Oftener, actually, than is admitted.

"As a young woman, my mother had come to America. She was a very adventurous and beautiful woman. She had left this poor mountain cottage in Ireland, and it was quite a daring thing to do.

"She loved America, stayed there eight years, and then she went home and got married in Ireland. She and my father came back to America, and my brother was born in Brooklyn. *I* might have been born in Brooklyn, but I think they ran out of cash.

"They were the opposite of the archetypal Irish family, who come and make good in America, and go home and have big motor cars. They just went home. America always featured in her mythology—New York and Brooklyn and Coney Island—as being a place of wealth, of glamour, of escape. All of her life, she yearned for it."

Despite this imagination and appetite, O'Brien's mother was not sympathetic to her youngest daughter's early literary interests. In fact, very little seemed to aid or abet O'Brien when, as a child, she found her vocation.

"My mother was very adverse to the written word," she says. "She *hated* that I became a writer. When I was young and living in Dublin and would come home on holiday, she would just remove all the books. She felt that books were redolent of sin—and she had some point there." O'Brien pauses for a short, sharp laugh of ironic understanding.

Despite her mother's known antipathy for books, O'Brien dedicated *The Country Girls* to her. After her mother's death, the writer found a copy of the novel hidden away in her mother's house, with the dedication page ripped out and the rest heavily—perhaps angrily—emended in black ink.

Ireland seemed to share Mrs. O'Brien's doubts about the author. *The Country Girls* was banned (so were O'Brien's next six books); the novel's relative candor about women, sex and religion was considered shocking, and inspired a "ritual burning" of the book in O'Brien's hometown.

"I don't any longer blame my mother," she insists, "although she was very censorious." As for her other Irish readers: "Perhaps my fiction is too naked for them. They like less piercing stuff, less disturbing. That may be why they still bypass me. They've never given me a prize; I don't have a great readership in Ireland, or major reviews, or anything like that. And it hurts a bit, yes, because I like justice in life—I'd like it for you or for anyone.

"I suppose my writing was an act of rebellion," she admits, and acknowledges that this may not have been appreciated. "But I also think that you start to be a writer long before you know what rebellion is."

In O'Brien's case, writing was a calling almost before she knew what a writer was. "I was never in doubt about what I wanted to do. I'm not saying that I was certain I would succeed, but writing was always my obsession, and also, in a curious, troubling way, my *companion*. If I couldn't put words on paper, I would only feel half a person.

"I didn't go to university. I didn't grow up in a literary community. There was no library in the little village where we lived; there wasn't even a *traveling* library. At school I read passages from Shakespeare and from essayists like Addison and Leigh Hunt, and of course I read the prayer books, which are saturated with lyric language. And I read the Gospels. But there wasn't any tradition of writing or, particularly, of a woman writer. So I always thought of writing as a very secretive act, even though what one writes is delivered to the public. Always, both when I started and now, to me writing is a covert act.

"I offended my convent, my church, my priests, my family, my village with *The Country Girls*—everyone seemed to have it down on me, and it was said that the book was a smear on Irish womanhood. I had a lot of what English workingmen call aggravation—I had a lot. I was made to feel slightly ashamed. And all of this made one, if you like, *more* covert."

Yet obstacles have had their odd uses. "I don't think an academic upbringing in necessarily the best soil to become a writer," she cautions, "because so much of academia is meant to do a dissection—and creation is creation. It has to be pure and instinctive. It comes from deep within the self, from a place one doesn't know.

"So, to forge my own little way through the books that I wrote, maybe it was better that I didn't have help. It was lonelier; it was harder. But it made one more severe. I think I'm very severe about writing. I'm very severe with myself. I take writing as seriously as religion."

Certainly for a rebel she is conspicuously, if unconventionally, devout. "The words of the Gospel—the Word, so to speak, and the words—always had, and still do have, enormous attraction for me, and impose an exigence in getting them right. I'm very interested in the readings of the Catholic mystics. There have been some extraordinary writings by women mystics through the centuries, in which their love of Christ was expressed in secular terms, but it was the love of God, of Christ, of God in the person of Christ.

"It's a very baffling act, writing. Flaubert looked at the skies and spent three weeks trying to describe one. I mean, the sky exists anyhow; why should one want to put it down on paper? But it's something deeply to do with being an unfinished person—that reality, or perhaps even ecstasy, or whatever other thing we're seeking, would not exist unless it was given the form of words."

We are talking with O'Brien in an elegant suite of the Wyndham, the midtown hotel she favors, in a room where the color of everything seems to be a pale, levitating yellow, and sofas settle deeply into unrepentantly languorous curves, lit as in a gallery with startling simplicity. Her surroundings reflect her. A pot of budded tulips, their stems covered by the merest outer sheath, reveal clarity of outline, much as O'Brien's sheer sleeves do her shoulders. *Time and Tide* is dedicated to the Wyndham's proprietors, John and Suzanne Mados.

On a nearby table rest a few scattered sheets of paper—"the seeds of a new novel. I don't even dare look at it for fear of losing it," she ventures.

"The editors I've worked with have been *so* scrupulous," she declares. "So much time is given—really, a great deal of time, in a worldly world, where literature is very much a marginal thing." Pat Strachan and Jonathan Galassi, her past and present editors, call forth this comparison: "Pat makes the journey with you on foot, and Jonathan makes the journey by air. It's a very different sensibility, but both are very supportive." Galassi became the editor of O'Brien's books after Strachan left FSG; Strachan continued to edit O'Brien's short fiction at the *New Yorker* before joining Harcourt Brace Jovanovich. "And [FSG publisher] Roger Straus is amazing: he's very famous, he's very busy, he's very cosmopolitan, but he actually reads the books and rings you up himself. He has knowledge, of course, but he also has an *innocence* about it, as if this were the first book he ever got."

O'Brien's body of work includes novels, short story collections, plays, screenplays, teleplays, poetry (published privately) and nonfiction. Aside from her incunabulum on the table, too fledgling to safely discuss, she is currently working on a play about William Butler Yeats and the legendary Maud Gonne. Peter Hall will direct; the play will have its premiere next year at Dublin's Abbey Theatre.

"Some material is a play, and some material is a novel," O'Brien observes. "*Time and Tide* is a novel; it couldn't be a play. The duration of writing a play, even a three-act play, is much shorter than a novel, but you can have no longueurs in a play: it can't slide, it has to be on its feet all the time, and it has to be embattled in some form or another. A play is not the place for a lyric voice"— which happens to be one of this writer's great gifts. "But I think that all prose should be poetry, that prose should have the internal rhythm and flow and astonishment of poetry."

A previous play of O'Brien's, *Virginia*, staged at New York's Public Theater in 1985 after a London production starring Maggie Smith, had a cast of characters consisting only of Virginia Woolf, her father, her husband and Vita Sackville-West. The Yeats play is more panoramic in scope, concerning Irish politics as well as Irish letters. "It was very hard to write, because the research was immense, and to write about great public figures and keep them mythic, yet also keep them human, is not easy. I've done many, many rewrites," O'Brien says.

"I saw Maud Gonne once, in Dublin," she recalls. "She was like a black marble pillar whose head just slightly tilted forward. She was so tall, she was talking to someone and had to bend down. She wore nunlike clothes—very long black things, and black headgear. She was a very dramatic creature. I saw her, but I never spoke to her."

One might remember O'Brien in somewhat the way she remembers Maud Gonne. "You have to cast a spell upon yourself in order to cast a spell upon the reader," she has instructed us. The spell this afternoon comes from, and falls on, a tall, graceful, redheaded woman—welcoming, worried, fully commanding—turned toward something remarkably interesting that one cannot quite glimpse.

MOLLY McQUADE
May 18, 1992

MICHAEL ONDAATJE

MICHAEL ONDAATJE'S voice is striking—husky and mysterious. Its low tones betray a British education, undercut by shadings of the East from his origins in Ceylon, and moderated by the flatter sounds of Canada.

Blown across three continents, first from Sri Lanka (as Ceylon is now known), "a pendant off the ear of India," where he was born in 1943 into a boisterous colonial family, to England at age 11, he arrived in Canada in 1962 to study literature. He stayed to settle in Toronto, to become an active member of the literary community there, and to emerge as an internationally acclaimed poet and novelist. He has been back to Sri Lanka several times and he has written about it in *Running in the Family*. But in his literary landscape North America has equal prominence, notably in his dramatic prose poem *The Collected Works of Billy the Kid*; the novel *Coming Through Slaughter*, which evokes the jazz era in New Orleans; and in another novel, *In the Skin of a Lion*, set in industrial Toronto at the dawn of the century.

The English Patient, his new novel (Knopf), at first seems to be a radical departure—its setting is a ruined villa in Tuscany at the close of WW II—but in it diverse currents of time and geography and culture converge and fan out again in a surprising but inevitable rhythm. Shortlisted for this year's Booker Prize, the novel has four characters: Hanna, a young nurse; her badly burned patient, whose face is charred and whose identity is unknown; Caravaggio, a thief who has turned his skills to the service of the Allies; and Kirpal "Kip" Singh, a young Sikh from Lahore, a British-trained "sapper" engaged in the deadly work of defusing bombs. In their exhausted Eden, the world and the flickering embers of the war are shut out. Their stories and their healing are the novel's focus.

Hanna and Caravaggio were characters in *In the Skin of a Lion*, but Ondaatje didn't conceive *The English Patient* as a sequel. "I wanted to write an intimate book about a patient and his nurse," he explains. "But I missed those other characters. Gradually Hanna and Caravaggio turned up, though in many ways they are totally new characters because they were so altered by what happened in the war."

Along with Kip, they represent the dislocations that characterize the 20th century in Ondaatje's work. "All those people born in one place who live in another place have lost their source. In a new continent, the past is a shadowy area and the only way they can survive is to deal in the present," the author says, speaking from firsthand experience.

The genesis of the mysterious English patient was "a dream image of a plane crashing in the desert. I wasn't sure who [the survivor] was," Ondaatje says. Nor is the reader ever sure. Ondaatje hints that the man "who fell burning into the desert" may be the brilliant spy Almasy, a real desert explorer who worked for the Germans, and was not English at all, but Hungarian. For his stark, evocative descriptions of the desert, Ondaatje mined the archives of London's Royal Geographical Society and read the journals of 1930s explorers.

He was equally meticulous in researching Kip's harrowing job of defusing bombs, transforming the material of technical literature into something like poetry. "As a writer I find certain professions fascinating," he says.

Ondaatje's primary interest is not events, however, but emotional intimacy with his characters. "I don't like to throw characters into a plot as though it were a raging torrent where they are swept along. What interests me are the complications and nuances of character. Few of my characters are described externally; we see them from the inside out."

In *The English Patient* Ondaatje often suggests that dialogue is too flimsy to carry the depths of feeling. His habit of relying on interior monologue gives a romantic cast to his characters, ordinary people who come to seem profound and even heroic in his hands. "I'm drawn to the kind of people who behave as though there were a finite number of words," he explains.

The war penetrates their island of calm at last when Kip hears radio reports of bombings of Hiroshima and Nagasaki. While the atomic blasts form the emotional climax of the novel, Ondaatje moves toward the denouement obliquely, avoiding the standard conventions of plot and narrative voice. The epigraph for *In the Skin of a Lion*, a quote from John Berger, is significant here, too: "Never again will a single story be told as though it were the only one."

"I didn't want the reader to feel locked into one character," he says. "I love that sense that history is not just one opinion. I prefer a complicated history where an event is seen through many eyes or emotions, and the writer doesn't try to control the viewpoint. It is only when one steps back from those small things which are knitted together in the narrative that one can see, as Henry James said, 'the figure in the carpet.'"

Ondaatje, who spent a year studying film at the Canadian Center for Advanced Film Studies and has produced several movies, has tried to introduce the same flexibility in constructing a novel that he sees in film or music or art. He says he is influenced "not so much by other books as by other art forms, such as music and painting. They seem more advanced than the novel, which is stuck in a 19th-century image of what the novel should be." When he was working on *Lion*, he saw the murals by Diego Rivera in Detroit and Mexico City. Their technical scope convinced him that one could pattern and echo events or gestures by subtle means. "In one mural, Rivera shows a factory worker holding a wrench in a certain way. Across the room in a linked mural, we see a foreman holding a pencil in a certain way. [Likewise] a story can be knit together by images. This seems to me a less didactic method of building a theme."

The novel as cubist painting or mural is perhaps most apparent in *Running in the Family*, a fictionalized memoir Ondaatje wrote to recapture the world of his parents, which he knew mainly from fragments of stories he'd heard as a child. Family lore portrayed the youthful Mervyn and Doris Ondaatje as an exuberant Scott and Zelda–style pair—high-spirited, self-indulgent and doomed. Charming, brash Mervyn became an alcoholic and squandered the family inheritance. Doris divorced him and moved to England, where she worked in a hotel, leaving behind six-year-old Michael, the youngest of the four children; he joined her five years later. Mervyn remarried and had a second family, but never regained the fortune he had lost. He died when Michael was in his early 20s. Their only contact after Michael left the island had been through letters.

In England, Ondaatje attended Dulwich (the alma mater of P. G. Wodehouse, Raymond Chandler and Graham Swift) as a day student. He emigrated to Canada to study at Bishop's University, then transferred to the University of Toronto, graduating in 1965. He earned his M.A. from Queen's University in 1967.

There has always been a romantic aura surrounding his life. Before he turned 20, he met the wife of poet D. D. Jones (whom some describe as Ondaatje's mentor). An artist 13 years his senior, a mother of four, she left her husband in 1964 to marry Ondaatje; they had two children. After the marriage ended in 1979, Ondaatje met writer Linda Spalding at a conference in Hawaii. They managed to carry on a long-distance romance until she moved to Toronto to live with him in 1982. Her novel *Daughters of Captain Cook*, set in Hawaii, was published in 1988. Together they publish the small literary magazine *Brick*.

Ondaatje's reputation in the U.S. has grown gradually. His dramatic poem, *The Collected Works of Billy the Kid*, first published in Canada in 1970 by the House of Anansi Press, was picked up by editor Star Lawrence at Norton and published here in 1974. Norton also issued *Coming Through Slaughter* (1977) and *Running in the Family* (1982), with Penguin releasing paperback editions. Ondaatje is well-known in Canada as a poet; his most recent collection is *The Cinnamon Peeler: Selected Poems*, published here by Knopf in 1990.

He was first represented in America by Jill Dargeon, whom he contacted when his stage adaptation of *Billy the Kid* was in the works and someone told him he needed an agent. When she retired in 1981, Ellen Levine took over.

The first review in New York for the stage production of *Billy the Kid* was not auspicious. Ondaatje recalls with amusement the headline: "They Stop Bad Meat at the Border, Why Not This?" The play has since been performed by American theater companies without further outcry.

Perhaps the most important influence in Ondaatje's publishing career has been Knopf's Sonny Mehta. "I first met Sonny when he was working at Pan/Picador," he says. "*Running in the Family* was being published in England by Gollancz; he read an advance copy, loved it and bought paperback rights for Picador. Picador had been my ideal publisher for years. It had the atmosphere of a small press because of Sonny's interest in the writers. Sonny made you attempt difficult things, be ambitious. There was a community of writers around him from a variety of places with a great variety of writing styles. I think he and I were drawn to each other because we both have a literary taste that is very eclectic. We both like serious literature, but we read a lot of trash.

"I got to know Sonny quite well over the years. I sent him the manuscript of *In the Skin of a Lion* and he had some suggestions. It was published in England in hardcover by David Godwin at Secker & Warburg, who bought it jointly with Sonny. Before that Sonny had bought *Coming Through Slaughter*. Picador has paperback rights to all my books."

When Mehta moved from London to New York to head Knopf, he acquired *In the Skin of a Lion* for the house. He was also an important reader and editor for *The English Patient*. "Three publishers were involved in the making of the book," says Ondaatje. "There was Mehta in the States, Ellen Seligman at McClelland & Stewart in Toronto and Liz Calder at Bloomsbury in London. I received editorial notes from all three. I write a book over five or six years without showing it to anyone, and then I send it to the three or four people I trust. Sonny gave me very detailed notes. I don't think he does very much editing anymore, so it was exciting to get his close textual reaction to the book."

At 49, Ondaatje has been an active and important contributor to the Canadian literary scene for more than 25 years. His body has thickened and softened slightly and his dark hair and beard are greying, contrasting less sharply with his blue eyes. The once romantic-looking boy is slowly evolving into a patriarch of his community. A longtime, unpaid member of the editorial board of Coach House Press, he brings a few poets and writers to the house every year and edits their work. He has also edited several anthologies, including a hefty collection of Canadian stories *From Ink Lake* (Viking, 1990).

This status may affect how his work is perceived in Canada, where he has won an impressive string of major literary prizes, including the 1970 Governor General's Award for Literature. "I'm less known in the U.S., so what gets reviewed is the book. In the States, I am always reviewed by total strangers and it feels more objective. In Canada, where I'm known as an individual, and where there is a smaller literary community, the reviewer is either an enemy or a friend, and it can't help but show."

Ondaatje ended up in Toronto through a combination of circumstance, choice and chance. The same forces sent one sister back to Sri Lanka, while another sister lives in England; his mother died there in 1976. His half-sister and stepsister live in Australia. His brother is a Toronto stockbroker and financier who has homes in England, Bermuda and Nova Scotia.

Ondaatje himself is clearly a Canadian now. "Most of my friends are here. There is a writing community here. Canada and Toronto are where I learned to write. I remade myself in Toronto," he says, with the air of a man who has found his spiritual home.

BEVERLY SLOPEN
October 5, 1992

REYNOLDS PRICE

ALTHOUGH HE WRITES FRANKLY in *A Whole New Life* of the despair he felt during his four-year battle with spinal cancer, Reynolds Price in person gives the impression of being strong enough to stand up to whatever hard knocks life sends his way, not just with fortitude, but with grace.

As he wheels agilely through the kitchen, preparing coffee and matter-of-factly discussing the adjustments required to make his Durham, N.C., home livable after radiation therapy deprived him of the use of his legs, it's easy to discern the tough-mindedness that distinguishes his memoir of his illness, just out from Atheneum. In that book, while discussing what he calls "the world's most frequent and pointless question in the face of disaster—*Why? Why me?*" he writes: "I never asked it; the only answer is, of course, *Why not?*"

This answer should come as no surprise to readers of Price's nine novels, five plays and many collections of stories, poetry and essays. Since the publication of *A Long and Happy Life* in 1962, he has created a gallery of characters who live and love with a gusto tempered only by their knowledge that happiness usually comes with a price tag attached, people whose deeply Southern sense of life's essentially tragic nature is balanced by their ability to "get up each morning and *Take what comes*," as the title character puts it in *Kate Vaiden*, which won the National Book Critics Circle Award for fiction in 1986.

The 61-year-old Price cheerfully admits to sharing his characters' sense of a malevolent fate that can be stood up to but never avoided. "I think I got it partly from my father, who had this demon of anxiety—he insisted on kissing us all good-night, because who knew what might happen in the dark? His sister said that it all came from their mother, who would say, when he left for school in the morning, 'Darling, kiss me goodbye; we don't know what might happen.' "

Discussing his family, Price lays out a history plagued by alcoholism among the men and severe bouts of depression among the women—obvious sources for the tangled emotions and damaged lives he explored in novels like *The Surface of Earth* and *The Source of Light*. But he emphatically does not see his relatives as tragic figures. "My sense of them was of awfully spontaneous people, very vigorous, who had a real love of life and eagerness for what comes next."

Surrounded by family, Price was nonetheless a solitary child. (And remains a solitary man; he has never married.) "We frequently lived in areas where there were not a lot of children to play with, and I just invented my life. From the age of six I wanted to be an artist—at that point I meant a painter, but it turned out that what I really meant was I was someone who was very interested in watching the world and making copies of it."

Drawings on the walls throughout Price's home attest to his youthful ability, and to his lifelong love of theater and film; many of them are marvelously life-like portraits of the actors and actresses who were the idols of his youth. "I had this big streak of celebrity hunger in my childhood, a fascination with fame. I've never tried to figure out what relation it has to the strong, central push of wanting to be an artist, but there's obviously a connection—wanting to be somebody."

As he recounts in his 1989 memoir, *Clear Pictures*, Price reluctantly concluded that painting would never make him the kind of somebody he wanted to be. "I was a faithful copyist," he writes, "but I apparently possessed no trace of visual imagination." In his junior year of high school, the combination of an inspired English teacher and the discovery of an unlikely pair of authors turned his thoughts toward writing.

Emily Dickinson and Ernest Hemingway seem at first glance to have hardly anything in common, but each struck a chord in Price. "I came to Emily before any really serious biographies had been written; she was viewed romantically as this strangely unexplained recluse. I think the recluse in me, the little guy who knew that he was walking through a family of non-readers with a head that was making up stuff, fell in love with her. With Hemingway, I honed in as this lone and lonesome child on a similar voice in him—

rightly, I think. The best of Hemingway's work is almost like the writings of a desert hermit; it has a very ascetic tone, pulled back from the world, watching it and describing it in the most lucid, word-free prose possible."

His own prose quickly won Price professional admiration. When he was a senior at Duke University, Eudora Welty read one of his stories and was so impressed that she sent it to her agent, the legendary Diarmuid Russell. "She sent me a copy of the letter he wrote back: 'I think Mr. Price is good. Shall I circulate him?' and at the bottom wrote a little P.S., '*Good* from DR is highest praise!' And it was: Diarmuid was not ever a big praiser."

In 1961, Russell placed Price's first novel, *A Long and Happy Life*, with the fledgling house of Atheneum, which has published him ever since. The author, who has lived his entire life (except for three years at Oxford) within 60 miles of his North Carolina birthplace, likes to form lasting relationships. Russell remained Price's agent until his death in 1973; Harriet Wasserman has served in that capacity ever since. He is well aware of the irony implicit in his latest book's title: "I published a book called *A Long and Happy Life* in 1962, and in '94 I'm publishing one called *A Whole New Life* while I'm going through the death of Atheneum and the question of where I go next."

Price is familiar with the vagaries of publishing—he's had four editors during his tenure with Atheneum—but he prefers not to participate in them. "My original editor, Hiram Haydn, left Atheneum after my first book and asked me to come with him to Harcourt Brace. Diarmuid Russell said something very important to me that I think very few agents think to say or can say now. He said, 'Hiram has been at five houses in 10 years: How many moves are you prepared to make? If you plan to have a serious career, to eventually do things like collected editions, you'll be very happy if everything belongs to one publisher.' I took his advice and kept it, till today." He has completed a new novel, but doesn't yet know whether he will stay with some imprint of Paramount Publishing or move elsewhere.

This uncertainty is trying for Price, who regards his primary professional bond as being with his publisher, not a particular editor. He speaks appreciatively of Harry Ford, Tom Stewart and Lee Goerner, who succeeded Haydn as his editor, but says, "I'm someone who tends to hand in a finished draft and not to feel the need of an editor who's an incubator, who says, 'How's it coming? Have they crossed the Rockies yet?' I've never wanted that kind of relationship, which is extremely new in publishing; it only began with Max Perkins. Tolstoy and Dickens never had such editors; they just wrote a book and mailed it in, and somebody corrected the spelling mistakes and printed it.

"That's basically what I always wanted an editor to be: someone who tells me that a character's eyes change from brown to blue in the course of the book. And I want someone who is really going to fight for the book within the house, to see that the book is taken as seriously as it deserves to be by production and design and especially publicity and sales. I need a good publisher more than an editor; I've never been able to work with someone looking over my shoulder."

His work habits, however, have changed dramatically since his illness. Before, "I always wrote by hand, on legal pads, and I wrote slowly. I worked on a single page until I had it right, then I write the next page. At the end I would go through the whole thing once or twice, but basically I was a page-to-page writer. Getting cancer coincided with my learning how to use a computer, so now I compose on screen and do a lot of drafts; also, I'm constantly going back, realizing I need to add three lines to page 46. I was never able to compose on the typewriter—it was so noisy and so hard to make changes—so I went from the horse and buggy to the space shuttle! I love computers, and I think they've been one component in my writing more rapidly."

Indeed, since he was first diagnosed with cancer in 1984, Price has produced 14 books, as compared with 12 in the 22 preceding years. "Lots of people made remarks like, 'Well, he's racing the Grim Reaper,' but I never had that sense for a minute. It was really very much like a manual skill that suddenly speeded up, as though I'd been able to play simple Bach pieces and suddenly I could play Bach fugues with both hands and two feet.

"I've never known why and I've never looked at it too hard, for fear it would go away. It's slowing down a bit now: I've just finished a new novel, I would love to do more autobiography, some more Bible translations . . . I've got plans, but they don't have the kind of pressure behind them that I was feeling five or six years ago. So there may have been a natural attempt to get as much done as possible in an uncertain time, but I never felt: Will I live to finish this?"

Many critics have discerned a more open, relaxed quality in such novels as *Good Hearts, The Tongues of Angels* and *Blue Calhoun,* all written since Price's illness. The author, who freely acknowledges that he is not by nature an analytical person ("I'm a bit suspicious about poking around in the psyche's dark basement"), hesitates to suggest reasons for the change. "I've written with a greater sense of ease and a greater sense of delight in the actual process of writing; that's about the only difference I can recognize, other than the normal differences one would expect from a maturing male who went through a major crisis."

That crisis is the subject of *A Whole New Life,* which chronicles the four-year ordeal that began with the discovery of a 10-inch tumor wound around Price's spinal cord, continued through several rounds of surgery and radiation treatment and included unbearable pain that was vanquished only in the summer of 1987, when the author learned to control it through biofeedback concentration techniques. The book closes in September 1988, two years after his final operation, when two MRI scans were completely normal; annual tests continue to show no sign of the cancer's return.

"I told myself all along, as any writer would, 'This is going to eventually turn up in your work,' but I'd made no specific plans to do it," says Price. "But two years ago, when I did my first coast-to-coast book tour, for *Blue Calhoun,* the strangest thing happened. At virtually every reading, someone said to me, 'I've just had a breast removed,' or 'I've got pancreatic cancer; for God's sake, write something about your experience.' I began to think, 'This is a message,' and soon after finishing that tour I came home and wrote a first draft."

Price understood people's hunger for a book about life-threatening illness; he himself had found absolutely nothing helpful to read on the subject when he was sick. "Well-meaning friends sent me a roomful of books, which ranged in quality from the mildly sentimental to the patently useless. I tried to say, especially in the last chapter, a few things that I really wish someone had told me.

"The central theme, which obviously generates the book's title, is that in a very real sense, the moment it was discovered that I had this gigantic tumor in my spinal cord, I ceased to be Reynolds Price as he had previously been known by me and my friends and family. I had to become someone else, but everybody you know and love is desperately in collusion with you to deny that your old self is dead. They want you back, so in many ways they really become a problem for you, because they're constantly involved in the denial of this new reality."

The process of becoming a new person was painful at times, Price acknowledges, but he doesn't regret it. I really think that if you gave me two switches and said, 'You can press Switch A and go back to 1984 and not go through this experience,' I wouldn't do it," he says. "Horrendous as a lot of it was, I learned an enormous amount. I'm a writer, and it was immensely fascinating."

WENDY SMITH
May 9, 1994

RICHARD PRICE

Most publicity photographs of Richard Price show a sinister, tough, streetwise New Yorker with a two-day growth of stubble and large, lugubrious eyes—the kind of character you would not like to meet in the proverbial dark alley. Yet in person, Price is anything but sinister. And you soon realize that those doleful eyes are the perfect mask for a devastatingly dry sense of humor.

We encounter Price at the Park Avenue offices of Universal Pictures, where the novelist and screenwriter—he scripted Martin Scorsese's *The Color of Money* and his segment of *New York Stories*, as well as the Al Pacino hit *Sea of Love*—writes fiction and films alike.

When we ask about his tough-guy image, he is taken aback. "I didn't realize that was how I was coming across," Price says. "The photographers usually just line me up against a dirty wall and shoot the picture. After *Clockers* they're going to want to photograph me in a sewer," he laughs.

Clockers, Price's gritty new novel about the New Jersey drug trade, will be published by Houghton Mifflin. The novel focuses on an explosive triangle of people and events: Strike, a black ghetto-educated street-level drug dealer—a Clocker; Rocco, a burnt-out homicide cop with a good heart; and an unsolved murder that brings Strike and Rocco head to head in a most unusual morality play. *Clockers*, to say the least, takes a different view of the famed war on drugs than the one we usually see on TV.

Price writes robust, staccato, real-life prose. When asked how a nice Jewish boy from the Bronx could get into the head of a character like Strike, Price says, "When I was doing the screenplay for *Sea of Love* [for which he would be nominated for an Academy Award], I started hanging out with the cops to see how they did their job. I was also teaching at [the drug-rehab clinic] Daytop

Village in the Bronx at that time, so I got to see the other side of the coin, the street kids who were in my class. It's funny: this school was right next to Westchester Square Hospital, where I was born. Life comes full circle."

Researching *Clockers* became an obsession for Price. One night he rode around with the drug dealers; the next he stayed close to the cops. He was able to bridge the two worlds because of "one cop who didn't think I could really do a good job unless I hung out with a guy he perceived to be one of the 'all-timers,' " Price explains. "He had known the guy for 20 years, and he'd had reason to pick him up several times. He called the guy on his beeper, and the guy came into the homicide office, and we talked for a couple of hours, and then this guy said, 'Why don't you come out with me a couple of nights?' That whole world operates on the principle of the favor bank. Now I owe this cop a favor and I owe the dope guy a favor. The dope guy owes the cop a favor and vice versa. There's all this currency in favors."

Be they thugs or cops, all of Price's characters are likeable— and smart. It's obvious that Price enjoyed his subject matter. He credits both the cops and the drug dealers for their generosity in bringing him into their world. His firsthand experience of the street, Runyonesque in character, makes *Clockers* believable.

Although authenticity is a hallmark of Price's fiction, he emphasizes that this novel is definitely a work of the imagination. "I don't want this book to be known primarily as evidence that 'this guy did his homework.' It's a novel. It's all made up. No matter what I saw or what I did, I still had to go and re-imagine everything."

The way *Clockers* came to be written is a story in itself. Price hadn't tackled a novel since *The Breaks* (published in 1983), and he was determined to take a creative break after a long stint in the movie industry. "I was in Hollywood for eight years, and I was used to the way things are done there," he says. "You sit down with this 'higher-up' in the organizational chain at a studio, and you try and entice him into going for your idea. You try and pitch it as succinctly and quickly as you can, because if the verbal pitch is boring, the screenplay is dead. I was used to doing that. I wanted to get set up on this book *before* I wrote it, because it was hard enough to get away from screenplays to write a book to begin with. I needed to know who was on my team before I started writing. I wanted to pre-sell this book.

"And I didn't want to write a proposal," Price goes on. "Nor did I feel I was ready to write a sample chapter, because I knew it was going to get better as I went along. So I said to my agent [Lynn Nesbit], 'I want to sit down with potential publishers for an hour and tell them a story. Then they can talk to you, and hopefully we'll have a bidding situation.' Which is what happened. We sat down with about eight publishers and everybody made an offer. Houghton Mifflin came in with the highest one. Apparently, though, nobody ever does this. Nobody waltzes in and does a verbal pitch as if they're setting up a movie. Afterward, when I realized what I had done, my reaction was profound embarrassment. But it worked."

His problem in writing the book, it turned out, was that he couldn't stop researching it. Doing the legwork fascinated him—but, he admits, it went on too long. "I was driving John Sterling [editor-in-chief of Houghton Mifflin] crazy. Finally, he said, 'Stop hanging out. Write it.' So I sat down and pounded it out. John was the person I was most intuitively affected by in terms of his enthusiasm and aggressiveness and willingness to jump in there with me. He'd get up at 4 a.m. and work on my stuff until 6, then he'd edit the manuscript on the train going to work, meet with me, and after that he'd begin running his publishing company. We did this for 11 months in varying degrees of intensity. I was very fortunate to wind up with him."

Industry insiders first heard of *Clockers* when Universal put down $1.9 million for movie rights and a Price screenplay. This would be great news to most novelists, but to Price a red flag also went up. "I'm afraid it's going to come back and haunt me, that it's going to boomerang with reviewers," he says. "My fear is that people are going to review the $1.9 million and not review *Clockers*. People might think that if it sells for that much, how good can it really be? Or how much integrity can it have?"

Price's career began in the early 1970s, when, after graduating from Cornell and receiving a fiction fellowship at Stanford, he was working on a MFA at Columbia University. Two members of the faculty there—Daniel Halpern, publisher of the Ecco Press, and Frank MacShane, a translator and biographer—introduced him to agent Carl Brandt, to whom he showed his novel-in-progress. "Brandt looked at it and said, 'You only have a chapter, but when you're ready, I'm here.' So I had an agent, and that really helped me. It made me feel that there was something there, not just fantasy."

The book Price was writing turned out to be his highly acclaimed first novel *The Wanderers*, published by Houghton Mifflin in 1974 when Price was only 24 years old. *Bloodbrothers* (1976) and *Ladies' Man* (1978) were also issued by Houghton, while *The Breaks* (1983) was published under the editorship of Herman Gollob at Simon & Schuster.

Price has always had a pragmatic view of the world, so when he became one of the hottest screenwriters in Hollywood he took it in stride. The transition was easy, to hear him tell it. "My first two books were made into movies [although not written by him]. I think people in Hollywood saw in my writing an easy transfer to a script style. They thought I had potential as a screenwriter because my books were like screenplays already. Originally, though, I didn't want to do it.

"Carl Brandt was very good at protecting me from falling off the face of the earth and landing in Hollywood. He kept everybody at bay until I got these four books out. By then novel-writing was getting too taxing, and the compensation was too small for the finished product. I had to have more fun, make more money. I decided to stop banging my brains and take a little vacation in Hollywood—which turned into eight years."

Price's office at Universal in New York is smack in the middle of the casting area, where actors prepare for their auditions. "Most of the time the place is packed with actors, talking to themselves in character," Price says. Inside his office, the atmosphere tells a lot about the writer—a combination of familial devotion, New York grit and Hollywood magic. The walls are lined with polished wood bookshelves, on which are neatly stacked manuscript boxes and photos of his wife Judy Hudson, a painter, and his two young daughters, Annie and Gen. On one wall hang three original photographs by Weegee, the famed New York police photographer. Next to them is a photo of Price acting with Robert De Niro in the movie *Night and the City*, for which Price also wrote the screenplay.

Price keeps regular office hours: in at 10 a.m., out at 4 p.m. He claims he needs the discipline of the office. "I wouldn't trust myself to work at home," he says. Currently he's working on the screenplay for *Clockers*. He writes in longhand on yellow legal pads. When asked about the writer's loneliness and whether it leads to heavy drinking and/or drug use, Price is typically blunt: "Writers who do booze and drugs do it for one reason: they're jerks. Some say that they can get away with it because they're creative, they're in pain. That's crap. Why should a writer have any more pain than, say, a plumber?"

A lagniappe for Price has been the chance to appear in the films he scripted. "I'm in every one of my six movies," he says. "I played a doctor in *Night and the City*, a barfly in *The Color of Money*, an artist in *New York Stories*, a bowling alley hustler in *The Wanderers*. I played a dog-walker in *Sea of Love*, but that scene was cut. That was my biggest scene, too! I played a detective in *Mad Dog and Glory*." When asked if he'd ever take up acting seriously, he replies, "Nah. I can't act. It's just an Alfred Hitchcock ego thing."

1992 has shaped up as a busy year for Richard Price. Besides *Clockers*, two Price-scripted movies will be opening. "*Night and the City* is a remake of an old Jules Dassin/Richard Widmark 1950s film noir," Price explains. "That one I wrote when my wife was pregnant—and my kid is now looking at her eighth birthday. The other one is called *Mad Dog and Glory*, and that one I wrote right before I started working on *Clockers*. So now I have a book and two movies coming out, and it looks like I'm an octopus. But the fact of the matter is that one was written eight years ago, and the other one was written four years ago, and I've been doing *Clockers* ever since."

Can we expect to see *Clockers* on the big screen soon?

"It takes about three times as long as you think [to write a screenplay]," Price observes. "You sit down and write a first draft in three months. Then everybody's panicky, time's passing, they get a director, the director asks for changes, you put in the changes, the director goes off and does another movie instead, you get a new director, and the new director doesn't like what the other director wanted. This guy goes off and does another movie, and then you've got to wait six months. He gets a new script. They hire an actor. The actor says, 'I can't say this. The way I see this character is blah, blah, blah.' And it becomes like one of those lamb carcasses that the Tartars played polo with.

"Every time you start, you get naive all over again. You think, this one's going to be different. 'Hurry up and wait' is the expression that I use to describe the pressure of Hollywood."

On the other hand, writing books is hardly a pressure-free activity either, as Price acknowledges. "After the first book you cease to be a writer and become an author. The difference between a writer and an author is self-consciousness. As soon as you start a second book, you're in competition with yourself; you have anxiety you never had on the first one. And that never abates."

Given his bravado and willingness to take chances, it's a sure bet that Price will continue to handle the demands of his two-genre career with zest and aplomb.

DERMOT KAVANAGH McEVOY
May 4, 1992

FRANCINE PROSE

Francine prose finds she is casting an increasingly malevolent eye on much of life as she gets older. In her widely praised early books, she says, "I was working toward a sense of redemption. I don't see why I have to do that anymore."

It is difficult, in fact, to imagine redemption for several of the denizens of her latest novel, *Primitive People*, out from Farrar, Straus & Giroux. It is a mordantly funny, bitter and ultimately despairing look at some artsy upper-middle-class exurbanites, plunked down in the woods no more than a two-hour drive from Manhattan, shot from the viewpoint of a moderately sophisticated but basically innocent Haitian au pair girl caring for two children who are victims of their separated parents' horrendously messy lives.

"As I look at the world I find it's getting ever more brutal," Prose says. "I'm astonished at the way people who supposedly like each other talk to each other these days, and I was trying to get that tone into the book. I heard these bitter, mocking voices in my head, and couldn't turn them off at the end of the day. And I wanted to have them talk as they would in front of people who didn't matter—servants, children." Hence the distancing narrative device of Simone, the Haitian au pair, who could put the obsessive rudeness, the treachery and the occasional outbursts of bizarre violence that characterize life in Hudson Landing into a different cultural context: "I wanted to make sure that Simone could see that in its way it was as bad as Haiti."

Prose is a handsome, eager woman in her early 40s, with a long, graceful neck like a contessa in a Renaissance painting, a tangle of dark hair and an electric intensity that turns easily to either sudden affection or self-mockery. Her own life may be located geographically not far from Hudson Landing—an expanded farmhouse secluded in thick woods on a quiet road across the Ashokan

Reservoir from the art-and-literary colony of Woodstock in up-state New York; but her domestic life is profoundly dissimilar to that of Rosemary and Geoffrey Porter in *Primitive People*. She has been married for 15 years to Howard Michels, an artist and sculptor who answers only to "Howie" and is funny and deadpan and a brilliant cook, and there are two lively and affectionate boys, Bruno, 12, and Leon, eight, who show none of the wan abandonment of the Porters' pathetic offspring, George and Maisie.

In fact, says Prose, it was rather her own childhood she drew on: "I was a big reader, obsessive and morbid." Both her parents were doctors (her mother, in fact, is still practicing, at 76), "and I got used to grisly details at the dinner table." There was no early inclination to be a writer, and when she was recently asked for some of her juvenilia for an anthology, she took one look at the material and refused: "It was awful, not a shred of talent." She went to Radcliffe, where she majored in English, then on to graduate school at Harvard—"I thought I could just go on reading books and writing about them." She realized, however, that she didn't want an academic life, and when the chance came to break away ("My child-bride husband won a foundation grant to travel abroad, and I looked at a globe and India looked as far away as I could get"), she seized it.

It was in distant Bombay that she began to write in earnest. "I got a borrower's card at the Bombay Public Library, and though I had been reading mostly contemporary fiction, they didn't have anything beyond about 1900, so I began to sort of recapitulate the history of the novel." Her reading also included Martin Buber, a book on Jewish magic and superstition and the "stories within stories" of Isak Dinesen. The result of this strange brew, along with the discovery of "a narrative gift that didn't relate at all to my life," was her first novel, *Judah the Pious*, a sort of Hasidic fairy tale.

Prose wrote a first draft, then returned to the U.S. to study creative writing at Radcliffe. "I wrote it all over, then started reading it to the class as a work in progress—that was wonderful." Her teacher sent it to editor Harry Ford, then at Atheneum, who took it immediately. "I was 24, and got a $1000 advance, which made it possible to tell people I was a writer." The book's reception—it was well reviewed and also won a Jewish Book Council Award in 1973—made it possible for Prose to sell magazine stories, which, she notes wryly, certainly paid better than books: *Mademoiselle* rendered $800 for her first.

Thus began several years of bohemian existence. "Unlike some people I talk to now, I didn't have any idea of a writer's *career*. I lived on $10,000 a year, traveled as a hobo to Mexico, spent years sleeping on people's couches."

But it was not an unproductive period. In quick order Prose wrote *The Glorious Ones* (Atheneum, 1974), about a 16th-century troupe of traveling players, also with legendary qualities. She wrote the whole book in less than a year, the last 50 pages in one long night. Then she moved to editor Paige Cuddy at Putnam for two books: *Marie Laveau*, about a 19th-century New Orleans mulatto woman who has psychic powers, and *Animal Magnetism*, a medical fantasy. "I became aware, I think, that these weren't the kind of books Putnam did best with," Prose says with a grin.

She also went through a couple of agents before hitting upon the more lasting Georges Borchardt, and eventually found what seems like a permanent editorial home with Sara Bershtel. She published with Bershtel first at St. Martin's: *Household Saints* (1981), a book that interweaves legend into the everyday lives of a butcher and his strange family. When Bershtel moved to Pantheon, Prose went along; that house issued the books for which she is best known so far: *Hungry Hearts* (1983), about a star of the Yiddish theater who becomes possessed by one of her roles, *Bigfoot Dreams* (1987), about a woman reporter for a tabloid newspaper who invents a situation that comes to haunt her, and *Women and Children First*, a story collection. She followed Bershtel to FSG after the Pantheon breakup.

It's an *oeuvre* consistent in itself—imaginative, fantastical, often charming—but strikingly at odds with what most ambitious younger writers have sought to achieve. The inevitable question is asked: Why has it taken so long for Prose to get to writing about something familiar from her own life and experience? She agrees it has been a strange route. "I just seemed to want to do these wonderfully complicated narratives, at a remove from my own experience. It took me a long time to see the creative possibilities in the life around me, to notice that people close to you have wonderful stories as well, that there's no need to go so far afield."

Perhaps it is also partly the effect of Prose's frequent nonfiction writing for newspapers and magazines. Ever since she wrote one of the early "Hers" columns in the *New York Times*, she says, she is frequently called by magazines (some of which, she notes gleefully, "pay as much as $2 a word!") for profiles, "think pieces," travel essays; when we meet she has just returned from Sicily, where she went with her family to do a feature for the *Times* travel section.

This writing, she says, "gets me out of the house and interviewing the sort of people I might not otherwise know anything about. A piece I did for *House & Garden* about a decorator, for instance, helped me make Shelly [one of the more villainous characters in *Primitive People*] a decorator. And people often treat journalists so badly, so rudely, so offhandedly. You learn to live with it, but it made it much easier to write in the persona of Simone, my au pair girl in the book, and imagine her feelings."

Her mornings she saves for her fiction, then she fits the various assignments into the rest of the day. "It comes easily now, it's just like chatting to my computer." She loves working on the small screen. "I resisted it at first—I resist everything at first!—but now I find when I turn it on to begin work, that it's like a primal memory of a TV screen, which I used to watch all day."

She already is well into the second draft of a new novel, which, she says, has only women characters, 10 of them, revolving around a matriarchal cult figure. And it is clear that the anger and sorrow expressed in *Primitive People* has not diminished. "The more I write about how these women treat each other, I realize, the more politically incorrect I may be sounding. I may have to get into the federal protection program!"

Writers she particularly admires include Alice Munro, Diane Johnson, Deborah Eisenberg "and of course García Márquez." She adds: "I read a lot of poetry too, and there's a poem by Zbigniew Herbert, 'The Old Masters,' that always cheers me up when I'm down."

One of the things that gets her down is having a book come out. "I still dread that—I guess it's a just punishment for the pleasure you take in writing it. I worry about the reviews—not only that readers won't like it, but that they'll like it for the wrong reasons. In *Primitive People* a lot of what I most care about is the children, and what happens to them, but I worry that too many people will think of it mostly as a funny book." And in fact some early reviews confirmed her fears: "I was amazed how few of the re-

226

viewers seemed to see that one of the things I was writing about was child abuse—and also how difficult it seemed to be for some to realize that something can be funny and horrendous at the same time."

Prose still does a fair amount of teaching of creative writing. Unlike some teachers, who concentrate on the self-expression and let the form of it trail along behind, Prose concentrates on their—well—prose. "I do a lot of line editing, looking very closely at sentence structure. I try to get them to read themselves more carefully, to care about the phrases they use." She also sends them back constantly to the great Russians, to read them as a writer would.

As someone who lives, through husband Howie, in the art world as well as the literary one, Prose finds the latter much softer. "When I was looking for really bitchy dialogue, I found I got a lot of the right flavor at art openings," she says. "Publishing parties couldn't compare. I think authors are much more generous with each other, and about each other, than artists." Because she loves mulling over such contrasts, she finds another. "When an artist sees a reproduction of his work it's just that, secondhand. A writer gets to keep a book that looks better than the original!"

Primitive People, which sardonically bears a primitive painting of a proper Bostonian family on its cover, began, says Prose, with a striking visual image: "I saw the eyes cut out of all the family portraits in the attic, and that seemed to symbolize everything I wanted to do in the book, and I knew immediately how Haiti could come into it." Further visualization will be possible soon. *Household Saints* has been bought for the movies, and Nancy Savoca, who made the critically praised film *Dogfight* last year, has done a screenplay and will direct, starting in June.

The creative imagination is an extraordinary thing. Sitting, later, over Howie's excellent dinner, with a group of friends from the art and literary worlds, we listened in vain for the kind of grating hostility that informs the characters' conversations in Prose's latest novel. Instead—it was early spring—the talk was of the wonders of seed catalogues.

JOHN F. BAKER
April 13, 1992

227

ADRIENNE RICH

On the new york city subway, people read all kinds of things, from dimestore novels to the Koran. They also read poetry. For, hunched over a briefcase or a shopping bag, mulling or dozing, a rider will look up—and suddenly glimpse "Delta," a short poem by Adrienne Rich, mounted on the wall in a poster as part of the Transit Authority's "Poetry in Motion" project, cosponsored by the Poetry Society of America. The poem lulls and challenges for as long as the trip. It is a private voice made public, and a communal link. "If you think you can grasp me, think again," the poem tempts, urging an entry into some more expansive place. It continues, in forthright persuasion, "My story flows in more than one direction"—as does anyone's, or could.

Poetry as a common property—as common as mass transit—is a theme dear to Rich, who deplores the hard times that have imposed short hours on libraries, and the mass-market mentality that all but excludes poetry from many bookstores. She criticizes "a certain kind of by-rote presentation of poetry" as a killjoy to poems and their readers, and condemns the lopsided "distribution of culture." She believes in poetry as "a questing." The questing can be made by many people in many forms, from sonnets to rap, with consequences larger than a reader, a writer or even a book alone.

In her new prose work, *What Is Found There: Notebooks on Poetry and Politics* (Norton), Rich considers the business, for poets, of questing—and other necessary things. "The origins and nature of poetry are not just personal," she writes, convinced that poetry is innately political and an agent for change. "The question for a North American poet is how to bear witness to a reality from which the public—and maybe part of the poet—wants, or is persuaded it wants, to turn away."

Few turn away, nowadays, from Rich's public appearances.

These are usually standing-room-only affairs attended by the faithful, and her recent powerful reading at New York University was no exception for the much-laureled writer. Yet, sitting in her Manhattan hotel suite, the 64-year-old Rich, in town during her extensive author tour, seems by manner almost modest. A Southern tranquillity of syllables is surprising; her earnest affirmatives interrupt it. She smiles: small curtains seem to rise on mischievous cheeks. Dark eyes gaze, warm and shrewd. The writer is physically small, and arthritis slows her now, but tenacity and dissent have made her who she is.

Those, and also the willingness to pursue change, personal or political. "You do have to have will to persevere," Rich says. "You do have to have *will* to not give up the first time someone sends your poetry back, or the first time you stand on a streetcorner trying to hand out fliers, and people are tearing them up and stamping them into the mud. You *have* to persevere; and you also have to be willing to be alone or very few in number for a while, in order to generate anything. I'm convinced of that, even though I feel that there are so many people out there who hunger for the kinds of connection that poetry makes, and who hunger for the kinds of social connectedness that we need . . . I think it is important to possess a short-term pessimism and a long-term optimism—not to expect everything of any given 'campaign,' but to believe that, piece by piece, changes will come. It helps me to have lived through the '50s and the '40s as the young person I was—very apolitical, coming from a politically conservative background—and to understand all the pieces that went into my own politicization."

For Rich, poetry has always been "the place where I could have dialogues, where I could try ideas out," whether those ideas involved the urgencies of literature, leftism, feminism or lesbian identity, to her all matters of long concern. But ironically or not, despite her habit of challenging orthodoxies, Rich began her poetic life as a formalist. "I needed those forms when I was very young," she says. "They allowed me to touch things that I wouldn't have been able to touch bare-handed. Form allowed the exploration of rather chaotic material." And though her work abandoned a formalist bent, Rich claims not to reject formalism utterly as an idea. "At best, when you're working with a form, you're [also] working against it; that creates an excitement."

In another irony, the feminist began writing at the encouragement of her father, a "very patriarchal" doctor who nevertheless introduced Rich to the work of Mary Wollstonecraft, hoping his daughter would "realize herself, while sending mixed messages about what that would mean." Growing up as the child of an assimilated Jewish father and a Gentile mother in "a very Southern climate in Baltimore," Rich felt "split at the root, a border person, with all of my family from the South, yet not really being of that world myself."

Her father also gave her "a wonderful gift for a child"—a rhyming dictionary. "It not only had rhymes in it, but a section showing the format for the traditional poetic forms, with examples. It was only when I began to write as a grown woman out of the struggles of my own existence more candidly and less formally that he . . . 'withdrew his support' would be a mild way of putting it." Her mother, a musician, helped as well to provide "a good education for a poet."

The early education led to another at Radcliffe College. In the same year that she graduated with honors from Radcliffe, Rich's first book manuscript, *A Change of World* (Yale University Press, 1951), won a Yale Series of Younger Poets award. She acknowledges, "My first two books were much praised for their technical assurance and grace," though she calls her second, *The Diamond Cutters* (1955), "that obligatory second book that no one should have to write." Harper & Row published it, and also published *Snapshots of a Daughter-in-Law* (1963), a book in which a new question was "pressing itself to the fore: 'What does it mean to be a woman and a poet?' "

Married in 1953 to Alfred Haskell Conrad, an economist, Rich had had "three children in rapid succession" and soon found that she was "hardly reading, being tired a great deal, and writing, when I did write, only very brief poems." She explains, "I was a well–brought up and fairly protected young woman who was often torn between what I experienced as my desire and what I thought I had to do to be a 'real woman,' or acceptable. So a lot of the poems in *Snapshots* were showing the stress marks of those tensions. In those years, my quest was also to understand the world in larger terms than personal life, to get a bigger picture."

She was aided in that quest by her reading of James Baldwin, Simone de Beauvoir and Martin Luther King Jr. "De Beauvoir's

The Second Sex was a gift to me at the end of the '50s, because I saw that there was a larger context in which my struggles to understand myself in the world as a woman could be integrated ... and I could make that into poetry." Rich began "truly probing in a poem, 'Is this what *I* want to say, or is this what Poetry, with a capital 'p', has taught me is what should be said?' I think that is an important kind of interior question for young poets, and for all poets, to keep asking. Tradition is important, but the voices of tradition can, in your head, become other people's voices that you're using instead of your own."

When she broke with formalism and began writing free verse, Rich was encouraged by her discovery of poets Denise Levertov, Charles Olson and William Carlos Williams. Levertov, who became a friend, was especially influential. "A lot of the poets of my generation had been hit by this dictum of Robert Frost's that writing free verse is like playing tennis with the net down—a very disparaging dictum." Instead, Rich and others found that free verse "was as exacting an art as formalism, and it felt much more risky. Free verse was so demanding, from line to line, and from pause to pause, and from breath to breath.

"The poet Muriel Rukeyser said—and I agree with her—that we must think of a poem as a transfer of energy. Energy within the poet goes into the poem, but then must go from the poem to a reader or a listener. There has to be this transfer of energy. And how is that going to come about except through the way that the words are used in the poem, the way they are framed, the way they are poised, the torque?"

However, sometimes the transfer is intercepted or disturbed. For example, *Snapshots of a Daughter-in-Law* "was attacked," Rich calmly notes. "With that book, in which I began to break open forms and write more as a woman, I found that the critics were not so pleased with me anymore. I was told that I had become bitter and personal. The world 'political' wasn't being used then, but it would be later—as a pejorative. There was hostility out there to examination of the very issues that were most crucial to me." In addition, her tenure with Harper turned out to be a mixed blessing; "Their last poet had been Edna St. Vincent Millay, and what they basically wanted to know was: Was I going to sell like she had?"

Levertov, then advising Norton on its poetry series, recommended Rich's work, with the result that *Necessities of Life*, her next book of poetry, was published by Norton in 1966. Since then, she has remained with the house, publishing more than a dozen books of award-winning poetry and prose; her editor was for many years the late John Benedict. What accounts for such a longstanding publishing relationship?

"I remember getting a letter from John telling me how he felt about *The Will to Change* [1971]," she replies. "It was like no other letter I had gotten. The letter was full of empathy for my work and excitement about the direction it was going. It wasn't the kind of letter that said, 'Well, we really loved what you did in your last two books, and we hope you will be doing more of the same.' It wa saying, 'I can't wait to see what you do next.' We had our ups and downs, of course, but with John, there was never any sense of having to contend over what I was writing. He was there with it, though sometimes it made him very uneasy." For instance, "He scribbled questions all over the manuscript of *Of Woman Born* [1976] that betokened certain anxieties—anxieties of a man threatened and yet, in some way, attracted by changing senses of what was possible in terms of gender. But I was absolutely free to publish that book as *I* saw fit. And certainly that was always true of the poetry."

Still her ties to Norton transcend any single point of contact. "John wanted me to know everyone who was associated with my books; there are a lot of people there I greatly respect."

Unlike many poets, Rich has also written a good deal of prose on various subjects, collected in several books besides the current one. "I started writing prose because, as a poet, I was occasionally asked to write book reviews. The first published prose that I wrote was some reviews for *Poetry* magazine back in the mid-'60s. Then, as the '60s began to intensify politically, and as I became much more politically involved, living in New York and teaching on the Columbia and CCNY campuses in '68 and '69, and beginning to understand my world, both the personal and the larger, in more political terms, I also found myself in the situation of writing things like fliers and press releases and ad hoc documents. And then, as the women's movement began to crest, I began to be asked to speak, and to contribute essays to this or that publication, and I began to find that I loved writing prose, which was not something I'd ever felt I could do. One of the reasons I had not felt I could write prose was that it would have been almost appalling to me to set forth in prose the kinds of things I was trying to deal with in poetry until there was a [public] context [for it]. People seemed to take poetry much less seriously than prose. Prose would have seemed much more self-exposing."

But exposure is a part of the transfer of energy Rukeyser meant, whether brought about in sentences or stanzas, on the page or on the subway. And it seems unlikely that Rich or her readers would really regard her "exposures" as anything less than absolutely required.

MOLLY McQUADE
November 29, 1993

ANNE ROIPHE

A SOCIOLOGIST SEEKING to understand some of the cultural and religious ferment of the last four decades of the 20th century could do worse than read the eight novels and two nonfiction works of Anne Roiphe. With her thoughtful and often provocative appraisals of the zeitgeist, Roiphe has managed to offer impassioned insights into feminism, marriage, family and Jewish identity in books that draw on her personal life to explore larger social issues.

Since 1970, when her now classic second novel, *Up the Sandbox*, wittily explored emerging feminist consciousness in the context of marriage and motherhood, Roiphe has tackled subjects that a more prudent—or self-protective—woman would avoid. Outspoken and opinionated, she confronted contentious issues in American Jewish life in her nonfiction studies *Generation without Memory: A Jewish Journey in Christian America* and *Season for Healing: Reflections on the Holocaust*, and in the novels *Lovingkindness* and *The Pursuit of Happiness*, a fictionalized but candid chronicle of five generations of her own family. Now she has stepped aside, as it were, to write a slim novel that attacks no social issues but tells a heartwarming tale of middle-aged romance. *If You Knew Me* is out from Little, Brown, and its publication finds Roiphe in a reflective mood.

"After *Pursuit* I found myself wanting to write a small, old fashioned love story," Roiphe says with some bemusement. "I wanted it to have a happy ending. But to my surprise, the story that kept coming to my mind was *Ethan Frome*. Then I realized I was writing a love story that was also about guilt, and about a kind of reprieve of the sentence [that guilt brings.]"

Even a "simple" story in Roiphe's hands takes on deeper resonance. "If you're a realist, as I am, the characters cannot be movie star–beautiful and emotionally whole. There must be a smell of

234

real life about it, which automatically means nothing is perfect," she says.

So a reference to sociology might be apt, we venture, and Roiphe laughs and says, "It's funny that you should say that, because I nearly became a sociologist." Born on Christmas Day in 1935, the product of an upper-middle-class New York Jewish family and of Sarah Lawrence College, Roiphe found herself, in 1962, divorced after six years of marriage. She enrolled at NYU in sociology, but soon afterward, the novel she had written during her divorce (under the name Anne Richardson) was accepted by William Goyen at McGraw-Hill; *Digging Out* was published in 1967. "Not knowing anything, I thought, oh well, I'll just write books," she says with a self-deprecating smile. "My naïveté was appalling." But looking back, she believes that a writing career was inevitable.

"I come from a generation that thought if you examined yourself carefully you'd find some universal truth, that through the individual comes the universal," Roiphe reflects. "This is very tricky because of the fine line between where that is true and where it approaches narcissism and egotism. Occasionally I may have crossed the line, but the attempt was honorable. It was what Erica Jong was trying to do, and Philip Roth, and Harold Brodkey. The idea was not to tell every little last secret, but to observe the principle that if *I* know me and *you* know me, we will approach some truth."

That eagerness to examine her life is evident in conversation with Roiphe, who even on a wiltingly hot summer day seems charged with ideas. A tall, slim woman with a shy smile, she looks deceptively placid until she speaks; then she radiates purpose. She meets us in her bright, book-filled Riverside Drive apartment, having come into the city from her summer home in Amagansett, N.Y. Lest her sleeveless sundress and sandals bespeak a certain languor, Roiphe's energetic gray hair romps enthusiastically around her youthful face.

It was not only the post-Freudian premise about examined lives that motivated Roiphe to write. The other factor was her role as her mother's confidante and the "receiver"—from age six—of the saga of her parent's destructive marriage. "The most gripping thing in my life was the story of that marriage," she says.

The "uselessness" of her mother's life also made an abiding impression on her daughter. "The women in the upper middle class

235

of my mother's generation were cursed with having nothing to do. They were surrounded by servants. There was no corner where they could feel competent."

Digging Out was prompted by her mother's death. More than two decades later, when she returned to her family's story in *The Pursuit of Happiness* (Summit, 1991), Roiphe was able to tell a more complex tale. "I finally understood the material. I had no sense [in *Digging Out*] of being in history. Everything that I thought was wrong in my family I thought was particular to my family. By the time I wrote *Pursuit* I had a wider vision."

Between *Digging Out* and *Pursuit,* her sixth book, Roiphe ventured into controversial territory. With *Up the Sandbox,* it was accidental. "I didn't intend that book to be a feminist statement. I was not consciously a feminist," she says. Remarried in 1967 to psychoanalyst Herman Roiphe, she was then pregnant with her second child and wondering what her life would have been like had she not chosen marriage and motherhood. (Today Roiphe's family includes five daughters.) "The book came out just when a lot of other feminist books were starting to appear. Suddenly, I realized: so *that's* what it is! I had identified the problem without the political scaffolding."

Edited by Jonathan Dolger, *Up the Sandbox* made Roiphe's reputation and became a perennial seller in paperback. Dolger also edited her next novel, *Long Division* (1972); the editor for *Torch Song* (1977) was Aaron Asher at Farrar, Straus & Giroux.

By the mid-'70s Roiphe was contributing occasional pieces to the Home section of the *New York Times,* unaware of the flood of criticism she was about to incite with a feature about an assimilated Jewish family's celebration of Christmas. After defending the paradox of having a Christmas tree in a Jewish home, Roiphe was the target of furious letters excoriating her for daring to comment on *any* aspect of Judaism—given her confession that she had very little knowledge of her heritage. To a certain extent, she still doesn't understand that furor. "I thought I had described the secular Jewish experience relatively well, for which one should not have one's head chopped off," she says, with some asperity.

The *Times* piece marked a turning point in Roiphe's life. Nettled by the storm of criticism and now curious about her religion, Roiphe "went on a search" that developed into her next book, *Generation Without Memory* (1981), which brought her back to S & S and Linden Press editor Joni Evans. "I had to give myself a Jewish education, which is not the easiest thing in the world to do by yourself," Roiphe explains. She read voluminously, took classes and attended lectures as she attempted to come to terms with the ambivalence of assimilated Jews who choose not to be members of a religious community but as a result often feel guilty, "tradition-hungry" and "ritual-deprived."

The reaction from the Jewish community was "lukewarm," Roiphe admits. "The male establishment of Jewish reviewers were very hard on it. But other people who read the book found it extremely relevant." *Generation* is used in college courses and continues, independently, to reach a new audience; Roiphe says she still receives letters from people who have just discovered the book.

Obsessed with the dichotomy she had discovered, Roiphe wrote *Lovingkindness* (Summit, 1987), a novel in which a young woman from an assimilated Jewish family finds spiritual meaning in an Orthodox community in Israel, to the discomfort and bewilderment of her mother, who looks to psychiatry rather than God for answers. "That book is completely autobiographical," Roiphe says, "but—and this is essential—I am both the mother and the daughter. The spiritual, emotional and psychological relationship to Judaism that I've developed includes both the mother's and daughter's views. I am somehow able to live with being both of those people."

Roiphe was not yet finished with examining issues of Jewishness. In 1988 Summit published *A Season for Healing*, which considers the psychological effect of the Holocaust on political and emotional Jewish life. "It was a book I very much wanted to write and one I'm extremely proud of. It speaks of the ways in which we will all have to heal. I'm very grateful to Jim Silberman for having published it, although he knew it was not a popular—and maybe not even a sensible—endeavor."

Roiphe took a risk again in *Pursuit of Happiness*, her richly atmospheric novel about the Jewish immigrant experience. "The Jewish family and Jews and money are highly combustible topics, and when you're candid you run the risk of appearing to be anti-Semitic." To solve that problem, Roiphe chose to step outside the narrative and remind readers of the book's social context, a device that allowed her own voice to surface in tart, poignant asides.

Having found her ideal editor in Jim Silberman ("Every time he's wanted something cut, he's turned out to be absolutely right!"), Roiphe followed him to Little, Brown for *If You Knew Me*. She has recently shown a certain restlessness, however, by leaving her longtime agent, Carl Brandt ("a wonderful gentleman and a terrific agent"), and moving to Lisa Bankoff at ICM in order to "develop more media possibilities."

Perhaps restlessness also influenced the genesis of *If You Knew Me*, in which Roiphe displays a wry optimism about human relationships. She says her choice of setting, a quiet seaside community similar to Amagansett, parallels the village in *Ethan Frome*. The spare language—very different from what Roiphe calls her "usual flamboyance"—was also patterned deliberately on the Wharton novel. The story is quite contemporary, however, filled with humorous touches and ironic insights.

For nearly two years, the pleasure of exercising her personal views has been available to Roiphe in her biweekly *New York Observer* columns, where she vents brisk opinions ranging from a defense of journalistic freedom re the Janet Malcolm/Jeffrey Masson libel trial to a piece about her college reunion that elicited many letters because—years after the fact, and without mentioning names—she discussed unmarried pregnancy.

Clearly she has contributed her provocative intelligence to her daughter Katie Roiphe, whose own first book about date rape, *The Morning After: Sex, Fear and Feminism on Campus*, is also out from Little, Brown. A manifesto claiming that the feminist movement is unwittingly establishing a victim mentality by encouraging women to cry "rape" in response to such nonviolent incidents as "verbal coercion," the book elicited a furor of controversy when an excerpt was printed in the *New York Times Magazine*. Roiphe is forthright and ebullient in expressing her pride in Katie, and in her eldest daughter, Emily Carter, whose short story "Parachute Silk" appeared in the *New Yorker* last year.

The fact that some feminists have challenged the premise of Katie Roiphe's book does not faze her mother one bit. "I am enormously proud of her," she says, "and I think she's absolutely right. She writes so much better than I did at her age. She's much better educated than I was—and am! That's the real immigrant experience," she adds. "You want your children to be better."

But Anne Roiphe was there first. She has never taken the easy road, yet she considers herself lucky. "I've been able to write for so many years about the things that I've wanted to write about. I may not go on forever; I'm not a major commercial writer, by any means. Yet I've managed to survive and find an audience, and grow. I'm very grateful for that."

SYBIL S. STEINBERG
August 2, 1993

RICHARD RUSSO

T HE OLD PORT SECTION of Portland, Maine, where Richard Russo takes us to lunch, is not a place where the author's characters would feel at home. Although Portland suffered a postwar decline not unlike the one that befell Russo's fictional upstate New York town of Mohawk, Old Port has since been gussied up. Brick warehouses now hold craft shops and clothing stores; the quietly tasteful restaurants have nothing in common with the Mohawk Grill, that formica-countered mainstay of communal life in both *Mohawk* and *The Risk Pool*; and Sam Hall, feckless antihero of the latter novel, would look in vain for a tavern like The Elms, where he could park his son at the bar to eat peanuts while Sam ran up his tab.

North Bath, N.Y., the setting of Russo's new book, *Nobody's Fool* (Random House), aspires to gentrification, but protagonist Donald Sullivan is less interested in the restored Sans Souci hotel than in making his regular rounds between Hattie's Lunch, the local OTB parlor and the White Horse Tavern. There isn't much in Old Port that would appeal to Sully.

His creator, on the other hand, quickly finds an excellent seafood restaurant and speaks enthusiastically of the summer festival that fills Old Port's streets with musicians and crowds. Russo left Southern Illinois University in Carbondale, where he had been rapidly promoted as his first two novels were published, to take a position at Colby College in Waterville because he wanted to come back to New England. He is well aware that nowadays the alternative to gentrification too often is dying towns like the ones he portrays in his fiction.

Not that Russo is any kind of grim social realist. A short, sturdily built man of 44, he views the world and its absurdities with the same affectionate amusement he brings to bear on his characters' frequently reckless behavior. His explosive laugh erupts at

240

regular intervals, and he sees his work as having "a kind of spiritual optimism. I don't necessarily hold out any great hope that people's lives are going to change, but I think there's great dignity and the possibility of spiritual progress in struggle. I don't subscribe to the 'shit happens and then you die' school of either fiction or life."

He strongly believes, however, in the crucial impact of place on individual destinies, as can be seen in his decision to leave Mohawk and set *Nobody's Fool* in North Bath, a once-prosperous resort that hit hard times after its mineral springs ran dry in 1868 and now grinds its collective teeth enviously at the flourishing fortunes of nearby Schuyler Springs.

"I needed a different kind of environment. There wasn't any sense in Mohawk of a greater day, a kind of mythical past which the inhabitants harked back to as a Golden Age. Also, I needed a rich relative right down the road in order to make comparisons and address the book's central issues of luck and free will and fate. Demographically, Mohawk wouldn't work."

Demographics, broadly defined, are important in all of Russo's novels, which resemble Victorian fiction in their precise location of action within a particular time and place. "Place is inseparable from character. If I try to write books about people before I have a pretty good sense of the places, that's an indication that I don't know the characters as well as I need to. And it's crucial to have a sense of place as process. Sully going to Hattie's first, then the OTB, then the Horse; the rhythms of his life are inseparable from who he is and what he thinks of himself. That comes from some of the real loves of my life in terms of literature, Dickens first and foremost: how do we know Pip in *Great Expectations*, except in terms of the forge, the blacksmith's shop and the marsh? Many of the contemporary writers I like also have that feeling of the ways in which places and people interact."

Russo understands this interaction from personal experience. Dressed in jeans, a T-shirt, a dusty blue cotton jacket and a pair of olive-green Keds, he looks like a fairly typical junior faculty member, but his youth in the blue-collar town of Gloversville, N.Y., continues to shape his outlook. "Despite the fact that I have more degrees than anybody should, I've never really been able to shake my sense of being an interloper in the Colby Colleges of the world. The years when I was an undergraduate at the University of Ari-

241

zona were mightily confusing, because I would be taking classes and living the life of the mind, but every summer I would work construction with my father to earn money. In order to continue in that world of educated people, I had to go back into this other world, where my grammar would change, the actual language that I would speak wasn't the same, the way of looking at things wasn't the same.

"Most of the jobs my father had were backbreaking, brutal. The worst was a summer I spent as a grader, bent over spreading dirt along a highway and making it absolutely level. By the end of the day—talk about metaphors for the way you think of yourself and look at things!—it took forever just to straighten up. My life has become easier through education, but I know what real work is. That sense of these people and their lives trails behind me and is always a factor in my imagination. As a younger man, I equated success with putting that world behind me. In terms of my writing, in terms of my heart, it took me a long time to discover it meant more than anything else."

The first draft of *Mohawk* helped Russo find his subject matter. Always an avid reader, he was almost finished with his Ph.D. in American literature by the time he realized he wanted to create novels as well as study them. After writing some short stories and an aborted novel, he produced a 500-page manuscript about Anne Younger, who later evolved into one of many characters in *Mohawk* but in this draft was its embittered heroine, living in the Southwest.

"The novel was floundering; the only parts of it that were alive at all were the flashbacks in Mohawk, the town she had left." When a friend read the manuscript and observed that all of the interesting parts of the book were in the past, "his comments made crushing sense. Of course, it involved throwing out everything except 75 pages, admitting that I'd written a bad book and going back and writing a better one."

Nat Sobel, who had admired Russo's stories in various literary magazines, took on *Mohawk* and has been the author's agent ever since. "He continues to get most of his clients by reading literary magazines and doing the kind of work in the trenches that not many literary agents are willing to do. What I like about working with Nat is that we don't draw hard and fast lines between what he does and what I do: I trust his aesthetic judgment as well as his business judgment; he isn't always putting the dollar sign first as we think about my career."

Sobel sold *Mohawk* to Gary Fisketjon at Vintage Contemporaries, in the mid-1980s a white-hot publisher of bestselling, critically praised paperback originals. "My initial reaction was that being in paperback first diminished me, but Nat explained that I ought to be damn well thrilled, given the other authors in the series; I was going to breeze along on Raymond Carver's coattails! It couldn't have been a better thing to do. They had a 35,000 first printing; if I had gone to Random House in hardcover, I would have been lucky to get 6000, and there probably would have been no paperback."

When Fisketjon left Vintage for Atlantic Monthly Press shortly before *Mohawk* was released in 1986, Russo was faced with a difficult decision about what to do with his next novel. "Gary did an incredible job of editing *Mohawk*. It had a lot of first-novel difficulties, and he really improved it. But I tremendously liked David Rosenthal [whom Random House proposed as Russo's new editor], and there was already a group of people who were devoted to me and my work. The sales force has always been wonderful, and when they decide as they have done with me that they're really behind your work, you'd be a damn fool to think about joining another publisher."

Russo's relationship with Rosenthal, who published *The Risk Pool* in hardcover in 1988, has proved to be quite different from the one he had with Fisketjon. "David is less of a blue pencil editor than Gary was. At a couple of crucial stages in *Nobody's Fool* we've gotten together and just talked; he hasn't been sitting down with the manuscript and writing things in the margin, but rather, offering spiritual guidance and thoughts on the content. The same was true of *The Risk Pool*. As a result of what Gary did on *Mohawk*, which badly needed it, I learned so much and became so much more relentless in the revision process that *The Risk Pool* didn't require as much close sentence-to-sentence attention."

Written while his father was dying and based largely on their relationship, *The Risk Pool* is the most personal of Russo's novels, a fact reflected in the first-person narration by Sam Hall's son Ned. "It has just as wide a canvas as my other books—wider, in terms of time, because it takes place over 30 years, while *Nobody's Fool* takes place over two months—but everything was filtered through the very narrow focus of Ned's camera. *Nobody's Fool* has a wide-angle lens; we're never inside any of the characters looking out, we're always outside looking in."

That wide-angle focus is what Russo loves in 19th-century novels, which he points to as the strongest influence on his own work "because of their ambition, their wanting to see more of the world, their desire not just to look at the interior workings of a single character and situation. Kafka's *Metamorphosis* is a classic of that second kind, and the shape of literature has not been quite the same since it was written. But all writers have books they would like to have written and other books that, despite their greatness, are not ones they themselves would have wanted to write. I admire *Metamorphosis*, but if the great books were up for grabs, I would prefer to have written *Middlemarch*! Some writers want to go deeper and deeper, while others strive for breadth. Breadth is more appealing to me."

Getting that breadth in *Nobody's Fool* turned out to be an agonizing process. "*The Risk Pool* was a gift," says Russo. "Exactly what the book was about was clear to me from the beginning, and I never made any big mistakes. *Nobody's Fool* was excruciating. I started it in Sully's voice and wrote hundreds of pages before I found that his point of view was too limiting. I write a second draft as a series of narrations through various characters' eyes, then I had to throw that away when I realized this was an omniscient book; I needed to be outside all the characters with access to their thoughts."

Random House thinks highly enough of the resulting canvas to send the author on a monthlong publicity tour across the States; he'll also spend a week in England promoting the British edition. Pleased as always by his publisher's enthusiastic backing, Russo isn't looking forward to being separated from his wife and two daughters; he's also got a thorny, which-book-next? problem to solve. Some 200 pages into "an academic comedy," he feels the pull of "a darker book that may be a Mohawk book" and that might yet elbow its way onto his desk to become his current project.

One thing he tries not to worry about is the fear of repeating himself that led to some disagreements with Random House about promotional copy Russo felt overstressed similarities between *The Risk Pool* and *Nobody's Fool.* "My editor and agent have convinced me that I was overly concerned with falling into a rut, of forever writing father-son stories set in upstate New York. Like every writer, I'm afraid of being pigeonholed, but I'm trying to balance that fear with a willingness to look at my career and say that already the books I've written suggest that certain things are important to me, and I probably ought not to be all that interested in forsaking them for the sake of novelty. It took me a while," he adds with a laugh, "to realize it was okay to write books that feel like Russo novels!"

WENDY SMITH
June 7, 1993

RICHARD SELZER

"**I** OFTEN WONDERED why I was the only surgeon/writer. Now I know. What I had done by picking up a pen at the age of 40 was to make a Faustian bargain. Yes, I would be a writer, but it would cost me my beloved profession. So when the time came for me to make a choice, it had already been made for me."

Though his tone is portentous, Richard Selzer's smile bespeaks the contentment of a man whose life has seemed foreordained. The same mix of poignancy, lyricism, humor and candor distinguishes his current book, *Down from Troy* (Morrow), in which he describes his metamorphosis from practicing physician to surgeon/writer to retired doctor now making his living from his pen. The memoir deals with Selzer's childhood in Troy, N.Y., during the Depression, the secrets of his unconventional family and the factors that shaped the man he became. Conscious of the classical allusion, he has drawn a somewhat mythicized portrait of the grim, unpretty town, and perhaps mythicized himself in the process.

His adored father, a physician whose patients included the prostitutes who were among the community's main economic assets, took him on house calls and to the hospital, and groomed young Richard for the practice of medicine. His mother, an "artiste," who scorned cooking or cleaning and warbled arias at the piano, made Richard and his brother recite poetry at meals and always meant for her son to be a writer. "The Trojan war between my parents"—Selzer relishes the pun—"was won by my father's death when I was 12. It was then I gave myself to medicine the way a monk gives himself to God, because I was going to find him again through the work he did."

If there is hyperbole in that statement, one senses that it is Selzer's natural mode of expression. Deprecatingly self-described in *Down From Troy* as "shrimpish, emaciated, thin and scrawny

. . . all wrist and rib," Selzer at 64 is, rather, of average height and trim figure. Nor is he "rumpled, frayed and scuffed," but neatly dressed in the casual clothes appropriate to his new calling and to the neighborhood adjacent to the Yale campus, where he lives in a rambling old clapboard house furnished with antiques and oriental scatter-rugs—and cluttered with stuffed animals and tricycles, evidence of the Selzers' four grandchildren.

Selzer's hair is silver, and so is his tongue, which summons metaphors as fluently as it does facts. He knows now that he always had a writer's sensibility, honed and heightened by the conditions of his childhood.

"Father's office occupied the first floor of our house. From the landing of the staircase I could listen to the cries and moans of the sick people below. One doesn't grow up within earshot of human suffering the same as one would within earshot of a playground." Yet his was not a melancholy childhood, Selzer insists. "I had the feeling that I was living between parentheses. This made an observer of me; it was also isolating. These are the two essential qualities for a writer, of course."

But the writer remained hidden as Selzer pursued his medical education, a choice he says he has never regretted. Midway during his surgical residency at Yale he was drafted and sent to Japan and Korea. Then he returned to New Haven, where he practiced and taught surgery for 25 years.

"At age 40, the energy simply appeared for writing. Not knowing a thing about it, I began. I committed myself to learn the craft of writing, much as I had learned the craft of surgery." That meant reorganizing his life around an 8 p.m. bedtime. He awakened at 1 a.m. and wrote until 3, then slept another three hours to arise at 6 and go to work.

Even for a man of rigorous self-discipline, the regimen was taxing. But a look of surprise crosses Selzer's face when we comment on the sacrifices his wife and three children must have made to accommodate his schedule. After a moment of reflection, he says, "It is always difficult when one person has a passion and simply must pursue it or die. I've come to the conclusion that we are each of us responsible for our own happiness. It is the myth of the mutual dependence of the family rather than that of mutual independence which is often the cause of the family's destruction."

247

Single-minded in his sudden need to write, Selzer initially turned out horror stories. "Those were nocturnal pieces—anyone would recognize them as bats and owls. They were easy to do, no great philosophical profundities or character complexities." He was thrilled when *Ellery Queen's Mystery Magazine* published about a dozen of them, but he was soon eager to progress to other literary genres, and he realized that his destined subject was "right under my nose." His first short stories drawing on a doctor's experiences were collected in *Rituals of Surgery*, issued in 1974 by Harper's Magazine Press, "a one-man outfit" that gave him and another first-time author a "teeny publishing party, with wine in plastic cups." The other author was Annie Dillard, her book the phenomenal *Pilgrim at Tinker Creek*. "We've been friends ever since," Selzer says.

Meanwhile, *Esquire* had asked him to write essays. Over a period of three years it published the pieces later collected in *Mortal Lessons* (Simon & Schuster, 1976). "Henry Robbins had cast his benevolent eye on me," Selzer says, but the legendary editor exited S & S before the book came out, leaving Selzer in the capable hands of Nan Talese, who was the editor of title for that book and edited the next one, *Confessions of a Knife* (1979). "Then she left and I was turned over to Erwin Glikes for *Letters to a Young Doctor* (1983). When he left, I was again without an editor. I decided that was insupportable, so I left S & S.

Harvey Ginsberg beckoned at Morrow, which issued *Taking the World in for Repairs* in 1986; Becky Saletan at Random House gained the story collection *Imagine a Woman* (1990), but then she too moved on, and Selzer returned to Morrow—where now Ginsberg has retired. Selzer notes wryly that the instability afflicting the top-notch "parade of editorial talent" that has marched in and out of his life has hardly been conducive to peace of mind. On the other hand, he has been lucky with agents. John Sterling, now editor-in-chief at Houghton Mifflin, was agent for his first book; thereafter he has been represented by Georges Borchardt.

Somewhere during this time, approximately between *Letters* and *Repairs*, Selzer realized he couldn't continue to work diligently in two careers. "As a patient is anesthesized on the table, a surgeon too has to be anesthetized in order that he be at some emotional remove from the white heat of that event—which is, after all the laying open of the body—in order to do his work dispassionately and coolly. The surgeon/writer—which I had become—must not only perform the operation but must report it back in the most compelling language. What had happened over the course of those 16 years was that little by little I had stripped off my carapace, and I had begun to perceive these events with the third eye of the artist." The decision was clear. "A surgeon can unmake himself by simply stopping. A writer cannot unmake himself. Once that third eye is opened, it can never be shut."

Although Selzer had previously mined his life in many of his stories and essays, the impetus to do so again came when he read Eudora Welty's *One Writer's Beginnings*. Hoping to produce a similar book, Selzer realized almost at once that *Down from Troy* "wasn't going to be anything like her little gem. It had to be my own story. As Troy developed depth and perspective and distance and penetrability, I could look at it the way an exile looks back upon his native land, with affection and with immense pleasure."

And with an adult's understanding, Selzer was able to appreciate his father's affection for the prostitutes who comprised a large part of his practice during the years when "the very name of Troy brought a grin." While others deplored the thriving trade, Dr. Julius Selzer thought it was a good thing, according to his son, "Mother was outraged, of course." But his mother had her own peccadilloes. Referring to what he calls "her long performance as Gertrude of Troy," Selzer marvels at his mother's "decade of folly," when a succession of unsuitable husbands filed through her house. Well into her 80s, she personified gallantry to her son; "she perpetuated my childhood until the day she died."

If so, Selzer was rudely wrenched into agonizing maturity when, in 1986, he was sued for malpractice, an event he chronicles in one of the new book's most wrenching chapters. "I had already left medicine and the patient had died. It was like two ghosts being brought to the courtroom to do battle with each other." Though the case was dropped by the plaintiff before the jury could deliberate, its effect was to leave Selzer emotionally demolished. "After a lifetime of doing my best as a doctor, this one shaft was going to kill me. My only defense was to take my notebook to court every day. That was all I could do, to converse with myself."

Originally published in the *New York Times*, Selzer's account of the experience brought an "enormous response . . . letters of compassion and understanding and reassurance," especially from the medical community, and from many of his patients. Yet the effect lingers. Selzer is bitter, citing the unscrupulous lawyer and the reporter for a New Haven newspaper who admitted to distorting facts because Selzer was "HP": high profile. "When a respected and responsible journal stoops so low, one is not only tried in court but is tried before one's friends," he observes.

Yet the next year he entrusted the account of another experience—a request to facilitate the death of a man dying of AIDS—to the *Times*, where it became "a cause célèbre." Although the affair ended inconclusively—he declined to participate in the suicide attempt when he realized that his complicity could not be concealed—Selzer now regrets the entire episode. "The conservative right villified me for having been willing to engage in murder. Many gay activists villified me for being unreliable. It had an effect on me here in New Haven. I honestly never remember having an enemy till I wrote that piece."

Perhaps unaware of his ambivalence, he bursts out: "But I had to do it that way. The way I write does not permit cool distancing." Speaking slowly and emphatically, his voice steely, he intones: "*I will not have it otherwise.* If you don't want to take risks, you must throw down the pen."

Possibly it was his own brush with death that reinforced Selzer's decision to commit himself to literary risk and candor. Felled by Legionnaire's Disease last year, he spent 23 days in a coma, his chances of survival slim. Miraculously, he awoke with no recollection of having been ill; characteristically, he decided "to reinvent my illness in an imaginative, literary way." The result was a volume called *Raising the Dead*, which Whittle Communications will send to physicians through its Grand Rounds Press.

Meanwhile, Selzer is working on his next book, culled from the diaries he has assiduously compiled. Now a mass of untidy pages threatening to cascade from a bridge table on the sun porch, the book will represent the kind of paradox that Selzer enjoys: "First you tell a diary all your secrets, then you publish it!"

In his upstairs study is the scuffed desk whose stuck drawer he describes in *Down from Troy* as "the locked drawer of my dreams." Adjacent sits a typewriter; no word processor is in sight, nor will there ever be one. Selzer writes in longhand in thick notebooks, types his pages and revises and types again. His stubborn refusal to conform to modernity is a metaphor, he says, for the stages of his life. "A pen is the same size as a scalpel. When you use a scalpel blood is shed; when you use a pen, ink is spilled on the page. It is in my tissues to work this way." Like the Greek heroes he invokes, Selzer thinks in terms of fate; if, as he says, the one ambition he has left "is to be the bard of Troy," this is the way he will go about achieving it.

SYBIL S. STEINBERG
August 10, 1992

CAROL SHIELDS

W HEN HER LATEST WORK is described by the seemingly innocent phrase "a novel with an appeal to women," Carol Shields seems to shudder delicately. And yet, the appraisal is contained in an overwhelmingly favorable review of Shields's *The Stone Diaries* in a review written by none other than Anita Brookner in a recent issue of the *Spectator*. And the phrase arrives knit to the flattering qualifier, "but of an altogether superior kind." Still, a faint distress registers somewhere within the outwardly placid Shields.

"No," she says slowly and carefully, shaking her small round head with its acorn-shaped blonde bob and still wincing at what she appears to view as the "women" put-down. She does not, she believes, write for women first, last or always. The reality of her writing life is instead somewhat more complicated. Shields is willing to consider the possibilities calmly, and from more than one angle. Her voice is light and uninflected; her manner is sweetly conciliatory.

Already thriving in literary Britain and Canada, Shields is poised now to reach new American readers with the March publication by Viking of *The Stone Diaries*, her fictional life story of heroine Daisy Goodwill, as well as with the first American publication of *Happenstance*, a pair of linked novellas, in paperback by Penguin. In short, this writer shouldn't worry. The winner of major awards, from the prestigious Governor General's Award to a Booker Prize nomination for *The Stone Diaries*, Shields has drawn a devoted international following.

We are sitting in her kitchen inside a converted warehouse building near Berkeley, Calif., where her husband, Don, is a visiting scholar in the department of geotechnical engineering at the university. The old cinderblock walls have been artfully renovated; sculptural, vast and white they dominate the kitchen. *PW* and Shields sip coffee—very strong and black—and wine, decent and drinkable. Clearly Shields attends to human needs; despite her frequent absences from home in Winnipeg and annual travels to France, she knows how to make the most challenging rented space into a cozy habitat.

Kitchens come up quite a bit in *The Stone Diaries*, perhaps partly because in 1905 Daisy Goodwill is born in one—in a rural Canadian kitchen, in fact, where her mother has spent a good deal of time concocting a special pudding before Daisy makes her surprise entry into the world. The mother is fat, so much so that the pregnancy has gone unnoticed. Daisy, motherless, gradually finds a new home and family for herself, and the 20th century seems to flow softly around her slow life in a Canadian town. Then she moves south to Indiana, back again to Canada and on to motherhood of her own; at length, the novel tails the elderly Daisy to her residence in a Florida rest home. We follow her from astonished first cry to gloomily overripe old age via widowhood and breakdown. She somehow muddles through, a Canadian Candide.

Details of successive eras abound in the novel. Conveniences for keeping food cool, like ice chests, and other kitchen innovations, like Mixmasters, occupy Daisy's homes and her life, which coincides generously with the century. The novel is also replete with unexpected quasi-documentary elements, including the character's own amusing album-style "family photos," although none is provided depicting Daisy herself. Shields embellishes the story with love letters, clips, ads, botanical ramblings and diaries.

To enrich the effect of Daisy's womanly evolution, the author read old newspapers and 1902 Eaton mail-order catalogues in the library, adding a "Ladies Rhythm and Movement Club" photo from the South Manitoba Folk Museum, a photo found at a Paris postcard fair, a snap located by her London editor Christopher Potter and photos of her own children, who look disarmingly like her. "But I don't want you to think I spent a lifetime in the library," she protests, denying any scholarly ambitions and protesting that she was reared on *The Bobbsey Twins*, *The Five Little Peppers* and *Girl of the Limberlost*.

Written in a poetic manner (Shields began her writing life as a poet), the novel deals—despite some demurrals from the author—with the business of being a woman. Much of Shields's fiction does. And her women—usually in their 30s or 40s, and like their creator, mothers—take in a broad range of experience. A serious, intelligent champion of romantic love and marriage who never insults her readers—either by condoning and-they-all-lived-happily-ever-after fairy tales or by impugning testosterone—Shields believes in the possibility of happiness. Her themes are not just love, courtship and marriage, but also children and the nature of male and female sensuality, compared and contrasted. These are indeed subjects of some interest to women, though also, one guesses, to men.

"Oh, I think there's some truth in that," she concedes warily about the relevance of the "women" category to her work and her readers, when asked again. But in fact, her male characters are just as fully realized as the females. There are set pieces in both *The Republic of Love* (Viking, 1992) and *Swann* (Viking, 1989)— when deejay Tom endures memorably, hilariously bad sex in *Republic*, or when elderly reporter Cruzzi passes through a fit of rage against his wife—when Shields's kindness toward men is unfashionably apparent. Clearly she feels sympathy for them and for what she reckons as their newfound vulnerability.

"I hope men will be interested in what it's like to be a woman," she says, referring to likely readers of her work. She adds, "I mean, men *have* to be a little bit curious [about that] nowadays." She has watched some battling of the sexes from her quiet campus office at the University of Manitoba in Winnipeg, where she teaches literature, and concludes, "I mean, if men weren't curious about it all, they'd be a bit foolish. They *do* want to know what it's like [to be a woman] nowadays, don't they?"

Even if they don't, without a doubt women do. "When you think about what women read," Shields observes, "you're actually thinking about nearly all the novels that were ever written. Because over 70% of readers are women anyway. So maybe I'm fooling myself by thinking my readership is balanced." Do men attend her readings? "Sure." Her hunch: "[They are] husbands buying books for their wives." She remembers the man who once came up to her after a reading to tell her that he *would* have bought her book—if only it hadn't come out too late for his wife's birthday.

"Men *have* changed, because they've *had* to change," Shields asserts. Her male voices may ring persuasively to the ear, but she believes she is fair-handed. Like Daisy Goodwill's men in *Diaries*, one of whom falls out of a window on his honeymoon, Shields's men are sometimes confused but never utterly wicked. She attributes her mostly generous and thoughtful gallery of men—from Tom in *Republic* to Frederic in *Swann*—to a fond and loving father, brother, husband and son in her life.

Born in Oak Park, Ill., Shields left to study at Hanover College in Indiana, where she graduated in 1957, and married the same year. Five children later, she earned an M.A. in literature at the University of Ottawa. She has lived in Winnipeg for 14 years.

However, she has also spent long periods living with her family in the French Jura while her husband was at work there; hence the French interludes that appear in her short stories. "I feel I belong to all three places, in a sense," Shields says, meaning Canada, France and America. "But I find this which-country-reads-me-and-why stuff so difficult to deal with. Novels don't break down along nationalist lines." In purely personal terms, she feels considerable loyalty to Canada, having lived there since she was 22. And in her books, Shields's affection for the country is plain; she may mock it gently, yet she cherishes it, too.

How did her career as a writer begin? "My writing life was a case of very slow and late evolution," Shields modestly explains. Not until her 40th birthday in 1975 did the letter arrive from McGraw-Hill accepting *Small Ceremonies*, her first novel. Why not sooner? "I had all these kids." For years she had written poetry and stories at dawn while the children slept, and she had no agent. "In those days," Shields says, "you didn't need one in Canada."

Her habits have changed. The five younger Shieldses are now in their 20s and 30s. The parents have downsized their Winnipeg house accordingly, take plenty of sabbaticals and travel abroad as they like. When at home, she writes daily in her office, and she is currently at work on a play. Her last two stage offerings did well at home, and *Thirteen Hands*—about a women's bridge team—was performed by three professional companies in Canada. Shields's acknowledged influences include Mavis Gallant and Alice Munro, and she counts Newfoundland writer Joan Clark as her literary confidante. Since 1979, she has been represented internationally by agent Bella Pomer.

These days, she is happily computerized—and, she says, just barely edited. Her Macintosh Classic can be heard upstairs, where her husband, Don, is making pinging noises with it. But the computer entered her life with an odd result, initially: when she first changed over in the middle of writing *Republic*, she found that digital fluidity made her unbearably verbose.

"Luckily, that novel was edited by Mindy Werner at Viking in New York. It was the first time any novel I'd written was drastically cut. Mindy was wonderful; she cut two huge chunks and about a thousand smaller ones. Yes, I felt a tiny bit of pain. But at the same time, she had a kind of genius for making me think it had really been *my* idea to do the cuts." Shields attributes her growing American success to Werner's astuteness, and she's been careful not to let her keyboard run away with her again. "I get a parentheses tic easily, so *they* all get taken out now."

Happy though she is with Werner, she claims, "I have a promiscuous history with editors and went through four before *Swann*." Her first novels were published in Canada by McGraw-Hill Ryerson, "but they kind of got out of the novel business after *Happenstance* [1980], my third. So I went to Macmillan Canada for the fourth [*A Fairly Conventional Woman*, 1982]. But that didn't work out in any way—they just didn't seem to have much faith in the book."

Realizing that she'd have to move, Shields chose the Canadian house Stoddart Publishing. "I had a really good editor, Ed Carson. He worked hard with me and for me. People call him one of the best editors in Canada. So I stayed with Ed for *Swann* and *Various Miracles* [Stoddard, 1985; Penguin, 1989]. But Ed was an ambitious young man, so when he moved to Random House, I moved with him." She's still with Random in Canada, while in England she is published by the Fourth Estate imprint, also the publisher of Annie Proulx.

Like Brenda Pulaski, the housewife heroine of *Happenstance*, Shields learned she was an artist only when she reached the cusp of middle age. The discovery came slowly. Only now, in her 50s, does she feel that she has committed herself to writing. "There was a time," she concedes, "when I shrugged off my writing in embarrassment."

Her readers seem as committed to her work as she does. Many write to her, receiving postcards in reply. "That's much the best kind of review," Shields remarks of this mail. "I dash off several postcards a day. That connectedness is an important part of my life."

From three slim poetry collections, Shields has graduated in less than 20 years to a widely reviewed, highly visible presence in both Canada and the U.S. She is no longer "That Other Canadian Novelist."

ELGY GILLESPIE
February 28, 1994

CHARLIE SMITH

THE PEACOCK CAFE is one of those dark, cavernous Greenwich Village hangouts beloved by generations of New Yorkers. Tiny tables surrounded by bent-wire chairs line a long room that is decorated with dim oil paintings. Over the fireplace a gilded peacock surveys the few coffee-drinkers seated there in the post-lunch lull. A hissing espresso machine punctuates the refrain of "La donna è mobile" that is booming from speakers attached to the ceiling; throughout the afternoon, arias from Italian opera fill the air with stories of love, suffering and death.

The musical background suits a meeting with Charlie Smith. In the past 10 years, he has published three collections of poetry, a book of novellas and four novels, all notable for the author's—and his characters'—fearless willingness to plunge into extreme situations and primal emotions. The first poem in *The Palms* (Norton) caps a lyrical description of a wedding with the phrase, "it is one week/before he will find her in bed with his best friend." Smith's new novel, *Chimney Rock* (Holt), opens with a taxi driver showing protagonist Will Blake the site of the fire that killed the cabbie's mother, wife and children; it closes with another catastrophic blaze, this one at a Hollywood Hills mansion under attack during the L.A. riots.

"There's a wildness I like to put in a book," admits the author, an attractive man of 46 with curly brown hair graying at the edges and intense eyes framed by tortoise-shell glasses. His own wild days are long gone—his excesses at the moment consist of putting a horrifying amount of Sweet 'n Low in his capuccino and alternately smoking Kools and Camel Lights—but his characters would still feel right at home in an opera.

"They're people who do exactly what they want to do; they see the gloriousness of being alive and the horror of it at the same time, and they drive through those things because they want to have more life. I respect them, because they're willing to pay the price for it: they're not just sitting around saying, 'Boy, I sure would like to learn how to ski.' They're people who have long since learned how to ski and are now trying to jump trees.

"My characters richly embrace the world around them; they're like the little kid you send out into the backyard who starts immediately getting into everything, whether it's a wasps' nest or the flower bed, so he winds up getting stung and he gets to smell sweet flowers. They're looking for grace, this sense of wholeness and union with the greater side of being, which is in some way the promise in every moment, if you can get there."

As his use of the word "grace" suggests, Smith's work is suffused with metaphysical longings that traditionally find their outlet in organized religion. "I don't see myself as religious in any formal way," he comments, "but I grew up in a world of Southern preaching; that was really in a deepest way my first experience with art. A Baptist sermon starts with crisis and conflict and goes through terrible struggle and surrender to resolution. The religion itself is based on an individual's relationship to God, which is a mystical and thereby a dramatic relationship, and this is exemplified in those sermons. I loved that, I responded to the great flow of drama and eloquence these men provided."

Smith was born in Moultrie, Georgia, 30 miles from Florida and 90 from the Gulf of Mexico, into a culture that nourished his love of books and language. "I grew up in houses that had rooms set aside as libraries, and I come from people who are really good with words: my mother's the snappiest talker I ever met, and my father is an old-time Southern raconteur. Southerners tend to invest their experiences with drama, and they come from a very literary and verbal tradition, so there are lots of folks who use words in very interesting ways. That's the primal ground, but that's not what made me a writer.

"Writers become writers because they're readers. Regular folks respond to something they've seen out in the world; writers are the ones who respond to something they've seen on the page. And a writer wants to *do* that thing he's seen on the page."

As a child "in love with the world created by books," Smith was especially drawn to *David Copperfield, Green Mansions* and *Wuthering Heights*, "which I still think is probably the greatest novel in English except maybe for *Moby-Dick*; it just fills your whole heart, makes you feel everything you can feel." Tolstoy, Turgenev and especially Dostoyevsky electrified him as a teenager, but it was two American writers who had the profoundest impact.

"Faulkner is *there* for a Southerner in a way that he's there for no other group of people, simply because he was able to exemplify the way the Southern mind moves when it's talking to itself. It certainly goes beyond that: he's a great novelist and speaks to us all. But when Southerners open a book by Faulkner, there's a level of appeal and affinity that is very profound and, at least so far, inescapable.

"I'm a Southerner, and I feel unbreakable links to that tradition, that life, that history; my family got to the Carolinas in 1650, and they've been down there ever since, so that's very much a part of where I come from. But I was also educated at Exeter and spent most of my life on the road [he now lives in New York City]; my experience is not just a Southern experience. In terms of literary tradition, I feel closer to Hemingway than I do to Faulkner."

The kinship between Smith's lush prose and Hemingway's famously terse style is not immediately evident, but "if you look at Hemingway's sentences," Smith explains, "you'll notice that in their construction, each word is often unrelated to the word that comes before or after it; each stands in a discrete and clear way on its own, and the resonances in the sentences are produced by the sparks and the unacknowledged affinities between the words. That's where the originating power of Hemingway's language comes from, and this is not true of Faulkner, whose words and sentences fold towards each other.

"Since I'm a writer of poems, I tend to be acutely aware of that; in poetry, the poem comes out of the word, the word doesn't come out of the poem—it comes out of the refractoriness and resonance of life in the word itself. Hemingway is almost the only American novelist who understood that; it's the greatest center of his genius. Though I often write very long sentences, what I am after is that kind of discreteness in the words that make up the sentences, so that each carries a spark."

Smith spent many years honing that craft. His stories appeared in literary quarterlies when he was still in his teens, and he speaks warmly of his studies with Reynolds Price at Duke, but he left college to join the Peace Corps, and although he eventually got a degree in philosophy, he refers to his 20s as "my apprenticeship."

He wrote a half-dozen novels he eventually threw out, he held down a variety of jobs in a variety of places and he lived hard. "I was a wild boy; I was into all the drugs and alcohol and strange, wild living of those times."

Asked if he has had personal experiences with any of the really bizarre activities his characters get into, he smiles and replies, "I do know what it's like to go too far. And I did, I reached the end of that road. I stayed a long time at that party, but eventually I couldn't take any more—it wasn't because I didn't want to take more! I had to get straight or die, so I did." He completed the novella "Crystal River" around that time, 1977, but he didn't write any more fiction or poetry for four years.

The urge returned, however, and Smith enrolled in the writing program at the University of Iowa, where he wrote many of the poems eventually collected in *Red Roads*, as well as the novel *Canaan*. He showed the novel to Doris Grumbach, then teaching at Iowa, who promptly took it to her agent, Maxine Groffsky, who promptly sold it to Herman Gollub at Simon & Schuster. *The Paris Review* ran "Crystal River" in 1983 and gave it the Aga Khan Prize for fiction; *Canaan* was published in 1984. Smith's apprenticeship was over.

His struggles as a writer were not. Neither Gollub nor Groffsky liked his second novel, *Shine Hawk*. "*Canaan* exists on one level as a romantic family saga, and I think for certain readers and people in the industry, that was the appeal. That wasn't all there was to it—the design is extremely intricate and risky—but it does have this big Southern family thrashing around. *Shine Hawk* [a fierce novel about a triangular relationship] is not the same thing, so this same group of people didn't have the interest in it."

Fortunately, George Plimpton did. In 1987 he called Smith to say that *The Paris Review* planned to publish books in collaboration with British American Publishing; *Shine Hawk* appeared under that imprint in 1988, just one year after Dutton published Smith's National Poetry Series winner, *Red Roads*. The author settled in with Marian Young, who remains his agent today, and his literary career seemed comfortably fixed.

But British American balked at publishing the collection of novellas Smith wanted to do next, and *The Paris Review* book program foundered. Finally, Norton's Jill Bialosky took his second volume of poetry, *Indistinguishable From the Darkness*, and Young sold both the novella collection, *Crystal River,* and his next novel, *The Lives of the Dead,* to Allen Peacock, then at Simon & Schuster's Linden Press.

"Allen will go out on a limb with you, and that's the best thing I could ask for as a writer. It's just not humanly possible for anybody else to have quite the writer's sense of what a book ought to be; in some fundamental way I'm alone with it. But Allen comes closest of all the fiction editors I've had to being in that place with me in terms of his willingness to accept what I'm up to and his understanding of it. As far as I want to go, he's out there with me."

Chimney Rock, in fact, is dedicated to Peacock, whom Smith followed to Holt. "The Simon & Schuster editor [who inherited Smith when Peacock was fired] loved my work; she was a fine editor and a good person. But I knew that I needed to do some strenuous work on *Chimney Rock,* which is not the manuscript I finished in 1991. The real consequences of what had been set in motion were just too difficult and scary to face. I needed Allen so that I could say, 'This is not working out here,' then give it to him and ask, 'What do you think? Have I hammered it through enough?' I eventually threw away the second half of the book, wrote another version, then revised the first half, and Allen was very helpful in that."

Smith sees *Chimney Rock* as the culmination, after *Shine Hawk* and *The Lives of the Dead,* of "a kind of spiritual trilogy. They are books about people headed out energetically into the world, surrendering and charming their way into the hearts of things. The three books are basically steps on this journey, and with this apocalyptic breaking through for Will [at the end of *Chimney Rock*] I have a sense of completeness that I didn't have with *The Lives of the Dead.*"

So, for now, he's concentrating on his poetry, which has been appearing in the *New Yorker* as he works toward another collection. "Fiction and poetry have become more separate. I used to be able to do both at the same time, but now when I'm in a novel I pretty much have to stay there. By the time I finished *Chimney Rock,* I had a full belly of fiction and was ready to write poems."

"Poetry has its rules, and they must be followed, and they're not the same as fiction. There are things I can do in one that I can't do in the other, but that's like saying there are some things you can do with a hat that you can't do with shoes! That's true, but it's not a problem: there's a use for hats and a use for shoes. At a very early age, I tried on the hat of poetry and the shoes of fiction, and I liked them both."

WENDY SMITH
May 3, 1993

SUSAN STRAIGHT

Susan straight tells a story: "The other night I was bringing in the laundry. I usually start writing about 8 o'clock, when the kids go to bed. Dwayne'll watch a video and go to bed around 10:30 'cause he has to get up at 5:30 to work over at Juvenile Hall, and so I brought in the laundry at about midnight because I'd finished working, and I stopped out here on the porch 'cause I seen this woman who lives on our street. She's a hooker. I *think* she is, she comes out around midnight. She has a black bra top and a black miniskirt, she has long brown hair, I can't tell what color she is, it's always dark when I see her, I think she's a speed freak 'cause she talks real fast and she's real upset all the time, and she walks around the corner here and she starts pickin' the roses. I had roses all along the fence, right, this was last month, and she was like just *snappin'* roses off. So I stopped and I had the laundry in the basket on my hip and I said, 'Don't hurt yourself,' and she like jumped, and she goes, 'This is your house, huh,' and I said, 'Uh-humm,' and I said, 'I just don't want you to hurt yourself on the thorns,' you know, and she said, 'Well, I'm gonna *pick* these roses.' I said, 'Yeah, you can pick these roses, people pick roses all the time.' She goes, 'Well you know they're gonna grow back, don't you? If I pick 'em they'll grow back,' and I said, 'Yeah, they'll grow back.' And she said, 'Well, you have a awfully nice house, I hope you *know* that.' I said, 'Yeah, I know it. I mean, I *worked* for this house. I'm bringing in the laundry at midnight so I must be working hard.' She says, 'Well at least you *have* a washing machine, you don't have to take your clothes to the laundromat,' and I said, 'No, not any more, I did that.' And then she looked like she was mad at me. I say, 'You pick all that you want, it's cool with me.' She said, 'Alright, thanks,' and I said, 'And I'll see you later.' So I brought in the laundry, and I looked and she went down the fence, and she must've snapped off about 30 roses.

"There I was—midnight, I'm bringing in my laundry, and half of me goes, See, that's where you could be, and the other half of me goes, No, because I'll always work harder than that. After I folded the laundry I wasn't tired anymore. I stayed up another couple of hours, writing. In the morning, I see there's blood all *over* the sidewalk. She was picking with her bare hands."

This is straight Susan Straight: pungent, unmediated speech, the poetries only the poetries natural to the world, the street, its people; one eye wary for danger, the other sharp for what people need and what you can give them, all of it adding up to what one reviewer called the dignity and hope that Straight lends to her portraits of social despair. And the whole experience, of course, typically leads her to the typewriter.

We visit Straight in her modest two-bedroom house in Riverside, Calif., a tough, gang-plagued city of 200,000 where she lives with her husband, Dwayne Sims, and their two small girls, Gaila, age five, and Delphine, two. Her new novel, *Blacker Than a Thousand Midnights*—the story of a young black couple making its way amidst urban violence and fractured families—is just out from Hyperion, and the book will likely confirm its 33-year-old author as a writer of extraordinary gifts.

Straight is white; she is petite, blonde, and blue-eyed. Her mother is Swiss and her stepfather (she does not speak about her biological father) is from Prince Edward Island. Straight lives in the city where she was born and raised, 60 miles east of Los Angeles at the foot of the Box Springs Mountains. And though it jars some that this fair woman has written three books about black life—and very much in the voice of black Americans—it is something she hardly thinks about. She is writing about what she knows, in a voice she knows.

"I met my husband in the eighth grade," she says of Dwayne, a hulking, sheepishly handsome black man whom we later meet when he returns home from his day as a correction officer, his blue pickup spewing radiator steam. "We've been married for 11 years," says Straight. "The neighborhood I came from, everyone was Air Force. There were people that were half-German and half-black, half-Filipino and half-white. So we had friends who were half-half-half-half. But when I met Dwayne, there were people there on the [predominantly black] east side who were retired or who had been there forever, so that's where I was, I was with him.

265

So everybody sort of got to know me—it's kind of like they forgot that I was white. How I feel about it is, I don't even think about it, 'cause I'm not a writer around here. I'm Dwayne's wife, and Gaila and Delphine's mama."

How did Straight craft for herself a novelist's career? A mixture of ambition and grand doses of help from people who recognized her talent and wouldn't let her squander it.

After high school, Straight got what she calls "a full ride" to USC, which she sailed through to a B.A. in journalism in three years. A writing professor there told her to consider graduate school, so she applied to the UMass-Amherst MFA program and was accepted.

So she and Dwayne pulled up roots and drove cross-country to New England. "When I got there, I said, 'I don't know *what* the heck I'm doin' here.' I was 22, and everybody else seemed older and they knew what *they* were doing, and I went to check out Jay Neugeboren, one of the teachers, because he'd written a novel about a black guy, called *Big Man*. I looked at his picture in the library: he was a white guy, and the novel is about a black basketball player and I thought, so maybe this guy won't laugh at me, right? So I wrote my first Darnell story." Darnell, the main character in *Blacker Than a Thousand Midnights*, is featured in several of the stories in Straight's first collection, the "novel in stories" called *Aquaboogie* published by Milkweed Editions in 1990. "And he wrote on the bottom, 'This is wonderful, stop by and see me.' And it was like, if he'd laughed at me right then I'd've gone home. It woulda been over, I wouldn't even a stayed."

And there was another influence: "We lived in married student housing and James Baldwin used to come by. He said he liked our apartment 'cause it reminded him of Harlem, we had all sorts of strange neighbors. And then I took his class, my second year. You had to get chosen, there were two of us from each school, in the five-college area [UMass, Amherst College, Mount Holyoke, Smith, Hampshire]. I mean, here was my idol, you know. I'd been reading James Baldwin since I was 10. And he was totally different than Jay, 'cause he'd sit up there and he'd be real quiet. And I was always really scared, but I was glad to be in that class because there were a lot of black people in the class that didn't make fun of my language.

"And James Baldwin invited me and Dwayne back to his place

one time, and I went back there and laid out one of the stories, I think it was 'The Box,' that was in *Aquaboogie*, and he said, 'This is the heart of the story right here.' He was talking about a scene where [the main character] was at work and she was being rude to her co-workers and he said this is the heart of the story and this is what you need to think about. And I went home, and I told my husband, I don't understand what this man says? I put it away for a long time, and then about a year later I came back home and I was real discouraged and I decided to rewrite it and I got his copy out and I worked on that scene, and *TriQuarterly* bought it, the first story I ever sold, and Reginald Gibbons was the editor and wrote back that the scenes at work are what makes this story. See? That was why he was James Baldwin, and I was not."

Straight made it through the MFA in two years, and she and Dwayne, who worked "graveyard" all that time, went home. "Me and Dwayne, we're Riversiders. We came home and worked. We didn't have any money. I was pretty intimidated, I didn't try to sell anything or make any connections, and Jay again was on my case. He said, 'You know you got to send your stuff out,' but I sent it out to big magazines, and of course they weren't publishing stuff like that. Nobody was publishing anything like that. It's like now, '*Boyz N the Hood*, oh yea, we love that stuff.' But I was writing about Crips and Bloods in graduate school and nobody knew what Crips and Blood were back then. The movie *Colors* hadn't come out. I remember that story, 'Buddha,' the students said, What's with the bandanas? What, they gonna blow their noses? What's going on here? So I came home and taught ESL."

But Straight took Neugeboren's advice, and that's when Gibbons bought two stories. "Once I got that little bit of encouragement, it was just like everything changed for me. My family used to say, Well what are you staying up all night typing for, I mean c'mon. Now I hold a reason to do it, I'd say, Look, I sold this story, I made some money. I could show that check."

Straight won a grant from Poets & Writers to do two readings, in Minneapolis and New York. In Minneapolis, with her mother and four-month-old Gaila in tow, she met Emilie Buchwald of Milkweed Editions, who encouraged her to submit a story collection for the Milkweed National Fiction Prize, which carries a $3000 award and publication by the press. In New York, at Neugeboren's suggestion, she met agent Richard Parks, who took her on and helped her shape the collection that became *Aquaboogie*. The collection won the Milkweed Prize and was named one of the best books of 1990 by *PW*.

Milkweed was given first look at the manuscript of Straight's magisterial *I Been in Sorrow's Kitchen and Licked Out All the Pots*. "Emilie liked it but she wanted major changes," Straight says. "At that point, Richard'd had a bunch of calls, people that wanted to see the next book. And he asked me, do you want to make these changes, and I *thought* about it and I didn't want to write the whole book over *if* somebody else would take it the way it was. So, Richard said, 'Well, let's see if we get interest from anybody else,' and then they ended up having an auction for it—Hyperion, here I was having Delphine that week; Houghton Mifflin, is that how you say it? And Doubleday. I ended up talking to the editors from Hyperion and Doubleday. I loved them both. I didn't know what to do."

Hyperion's Pat Mulcahy won the auction with a two-book deal (Sallye Leventhal, the Doubleday bidder, then bought the floor for the paperback, now out from Doubleday/Anchor). The book—about a towering "blue-black" Gullah-speaking woman from South Carolina and the raising of her twin boys—wowed reviewers, for its elegant structure (*PW*) and its "miraculous lyrical style" (*USA Today*). The *Toronto Star* said the novel "flowers with dignity."

"I've been really happy with Pat," says Straight of her editor. "She worked on *A Thousand Midnights* as hard as I did. Three drafts we did."

Things march along for Straight, all of a piece with her life. Her next book, which Hyperion has bought, partially takes place where Dwayne's people are originally from, Oklahoma, spanning from the Tulsa riots of 1921 to the L.A. riots of 1992. Reading about America's long history of violence gives Straight, who lives amidst its present incarnation, a certain understanding. "It's like this 'haves and have-nots' sort of thing—my husband calls it the 'trickle-down effect,' the gangs and all: everybody's pissed off and now you take it out on who's closest to you. That's why men take it out on women, and no one goes and takes it out on his boss, right?"

As the interview winds down, Gaila comes into the room and wants Mommy to show her visitor the "Bear E. Bear" book. And in fact, it is the boards for a spring Hyperion children's book, by Susan Straight. The illustrations, by Marisabina Russo, perfectly capture the house we are sitting in, and the characters of Susan and Dwayne and the two little girls. It is the story of a small teddy bear who endures being lost, being found, being sent through the washing machine, before everyone is safely put to bed, like all storybook endings. Except that the reality of *this* household is that there is a light still burning, there is menace without, and Susan Straight is up writing into the night.

MICHAEL COFFEY
July 4, 1994

PAUL THEROUX

A CHARACTER IN ONE OF Paul Theroux's 16 novels says, "People don't know they're awful. They think they're nice." This statement could almost stand as an epigraph to everything Theroux has written—with the exception of the protagonist of his new novel, *Millroy the Magician* (Random House), whose eponymous hero is a present-day messiah of low-fat food and clean living. And even Theroux thinks he's nice.

Millroy, a sort of metaphysical Mr. Rogers, crosses America magically transforming, without benefit of kitchen, "big brown spuds into mashed potatoes, flour into bread, and milk into yogurt and then into fat-free ice cream," and preaching vegetarianism on TV the way certain televangelists push family values. In the past, reviewers have compared Theroux's novels to Graham Greene's; *Millroy the Magician* may remind some readers of the Frugal Gourmet.

What, we ask, lightened Theroux's dark vision, taking him from sinners in quest of redemption (as in *Chicago Loop*, 1990) to a protagonist launching a chain of diners that specialize in foods mentioned in the Bible? "It has something to do with middle age," says the author, who, like Millroy, is a vegetarian. Theroux, briefly in New York, divides his time between homes on Cape Cod and Oahu. "*Millroy the Magician* is about an obsession with food, diet and American culture. It's my own life, in a sense, writ large and embroidered upon."

Theroux, 52, is owlishly handsome. His accent combines the vowels of Massachusetts, where he grew up, with those of London, where he lived for many years. "I used to write about people who drank, smoked opium and the like," he says, sounding alternately like JFK and Cary Grant. "Then, while writing *The Mosquito Coast* [1982], I got interested in health. Allie Fox, the pro-

270

tagonist, has plenty of censorious things to say about the American diet. I gave up smoking when I finished the book."

Theroux, as well-known for his travel books as for his novels, doesn't rhapsodize over exotic foods as some travel writers do. On the contrary, he's more likely to emphasize the squeamish detail, as in this vignette from *Riding the Iron Rooster: By Train Through China* (1988): "There had been a bucket of dead eels next to the hopper in the toilet cubicle. I had glimpsed the creatures in the middle of the night. That was memorable—and a good thing, too, because the next morning I went to the dining car and asked what was on the menu, and the chef said, 'Eels!' "

This kind of bilious comedy is typical of Theroux's travel writing. Never lyrical, he has been accused of starting out in a bad mood and staying in it for the duration of a trip. "You could say the same about almost any comic writer," he counters. "In the very essence of comedy is a kind of grumpiness, where irony sounds like sarcasm and sarcasm like aggression. Sometimes my irony is taken literally by a literal-minded public.

"For example, in a crowded bus in Germany, I once said to a large man who was elbowing an old lady, 'Why don't you knock her over while you're at it?' He said indignantly, 'What! You think I'm trying to knock her over? Of course I won't.' The man thought *I* was being a brute. Germans, of course, tend not to have a sense of irony, but sometimes neither do readers—or reviewers—of my books. So, when I travel, I don't look for trouble, but I don't want to make things seem better than they are."

Jan Morris, Theroux's friend and fellow travel writer, recently said (at a dinner in Honolulu attended by Theroux and others): "None of us wants Paul to be cheerier than he is. If he's rude in writing about a place, that's why we read him." Morris, of course, recognizes the journalistic purpose behind this "rudeness."

Theroux explains, "It's amazing how prophetic you can be in travel writing if you describe a place as it is. For example, I was in China for 12 months—mid-1986 to mid-1987—for *Riding the Iron Rooster*. I saw manifestations of the student democracy movement: demonstrations, clashes with police. I wrote about this in my book, and when it was published some people cried out, 'He's too hard on the Chinese, doesn't seem to like them, great trading partner, reforms . . .' Two years later students were shot down in Tiananmen Square. If I had presented the Chinese as I wanted them to be, and not as I saw them, I would have looked like a fool."

While Theroux's fiction speaks in many voices from various points of view, the "I" of his travel writing is Theroux himself and not that of a literary persona. "I'm just reporting on the trip," he says. "A travel book is like a series of letters home."

If he wrote just a few letters from abroad to each member of his family he would have the makings of a fair-sized travel book, for Theroux is one of seven children and the father of two grown sons. Almost half the Theroux clan are writers. Besides Paul, there are older brother Alexander, a novelist, and younger brother Peter, a travel writer. Paul's son Louis is a staff writer for *Spy* magazine. (The writer Phyllis Theroux is Paul's former sister-in-law.)

Born in Medford, Mass., a Boston suburb, Theroux attended the University of Massachusetts. Shortly after graduation in 1963, he joined the Peace Corps and made his first long journey: to Malawi in East Africa, where he taught English for two years. Then, late in 1965, he was arrested for spying and convicted within hours. His sentence was relatively light: he was escorted to the airport and put on the only plane leaving Malawi that day. (Theroux tells his side of the story in an essay included in his 1985 book, *Sunrise with Seamonsters: Travels and Discoveries 1964–1984.*)

He returned to the U.S. for a brief visit, during which he was questioned by the State Department and expelled from the Peace Corps. But Theroux bears no ill will. "The Peace Corps was the best thing that ever happened to me," he says. And the unfortunate African contretemps was not entirely his fault. Though politically naïve, he was also double-crossed when articles he had written in good faith for African periodicals were discovered to have been actually commissioned by the West German equivalent of the CIA. Caught between the displeasure of his host country and that of the U.S. State Department, Theroux was a convenient scapegoat. His was an uncomfortable, untenable position: an American citizen being used as a tool of a former European colonial power on the African continent.

Immediately after his expulsion from the Peace Corps, Theroux returned to Africa, this time to Uganda, where he became a lecturer in English at Makerere University in Kampala. While there, he met and married Anne Castle, another teacher, from whom he is now divorced.

In 1968 Theroux left Africa and went to Singapore, where he again taught English (at the University of Singapore) for three years. In the meantime, he maintained a flourishing second career as novelist, having published five novels between 1967 and 1971. Deciding that he couldn't continue in both professions, Theroux resigned from his teaching job to pursue writing full-time. Since then he has averaged one book a year, as well as hundreds of stories, essays and reviews.

Theroux first gained widespread attention with *Saint Jack* (1972), a novel that director Peter Bogdanovich turned into a movie in 1979 based on a screenplay that Theroux helped write.

His next novel, *The Black House* (1974), was a gothic tale set in England, where Theroux had taken up residence. This novel has gained a certain para-literary fame in Britain as the manuscript that Theroux dropped off at the office of his publisher, Hamish Hamilton, on his way to Victoria Station to catch the train for his now-famous transcontinental journey through the Soviet Union and the Far East—in other words, *The Great Railway Bazaar: By Train Through Asia.* Theroux gives the date of manuscript delivery, and the start of his travel-writing career, as September 19, 1973.

Though travelogues are not considered hot commercial properties, *The Great Railway Bazaar* was a best-seller in the U.S. and in Britain. A typical review praised Theroux for having transformed "what was clearly a long, ultimately tedious journey by train . . . into a singularly entertaining book." Since then, a new travel book by Theroux has come to be something of an event. The biggest of these events have been *The Old Patagonian Express: By Train Through the Americas* (1979); *The Kingdom By the Sea: A Journey Around Great Britain* (1983); *Riding the Iron Rooster* (1988); and *The Happy Isles at Oceania: Paddling the Pacific* (1992).

Meanwhile, such novels as *The Family Arsenal* (1976) and *Picture Palace* (1978) had helped to turn Theroux into a literary industry, with headquarters at Houghton Mifflin. "They published my books for nearly 20 years," he says, "from *Waldo,* my first novel (1967), through the mid-1980s." Asked why he left, Theroux says, "I wanted to see what the rest of the publishing world was like. I also decided to have different publishers for fiction and nonfiction."

He decided on Putnam for nonfiction (though they initially

273

published one of his novels, the 1986 *O-Zone*), and Random House for fiction.

Theroux says that he and Houghton Mifflin parted on good terms, "at least as much as you can." When he decided to leave, he recalls emphasizing to his longtime publisher that "I have been a good and faithful employee of this firm, and I've generated a lot of revenue in which we've all shared. I haven't driven as hard a bargain as many authors." As an example, Theroux cites the "very healthy cut" that Houghton Mifflin received from his reprint sales—"up to 50%."

One of Theroux's warmest memories of his years with Houghton Mifflin is editor Joyce Hartman. "She cared about me and my career," he says, "and she also replied to letters. She wrote interesting ones and she inspired the same. I believe the best editors have been letter writers and not telephoners."

In addition to two publishers, Theroux has two agents: Andrew Wylie, who handles fiction and backlist; and for nonfiction, the author's brother Eugene Theroux, a lawyer in Washington who is an expert in Sino-American trade.

Asked to compare sales of his various books in the U.S. and Britain, Theroux says, "in Britain my hardcovers have good to modest sales, while my paperbacks—brought out there by Penguin—sell enormously. At virtually any bookseller's in the U.K., if you look on the Penguin shelf you'll find anywhere from 10 to 20 of my books, going all the way back to the 1960s. It's the same wherever English paperbacks are sold—Australia, New Zealand, Canada, South Africa. But not in the United States."

In this country, according to Theroux, "there seems to be a total lack of interest in the backlist. Several of my books are in print in hardcover, a few in paperback, but not many. In Britain, on the other hand, virtually all of my books are in print either in hardcover or in Penguin paperbacks. It seems to me that an innovative American publisher would look at my backlist and decide, 'We're not going to let these go; we'll do a uniform edition, have Theroux write new introductions, and make money from them.' The fact that publishers don't do this, with my books and those of many other writers, indicates philistinism, laziness, and lack of entrepreneurship."

In addition to novels, travel books and screenplays, Theroux has written criticism (*V. S. Naipaul: An Introduction to His Works,*

1972), plays and poetry. But some of his best work appears in his four short-story collections: *Sinning with Annie and Other Stories* (1972); *The Consul's File* (1977); *World's End and Other Stories* (1980); and *The London Embassy* (1982). Even his briefest stories represent intense emotional journeys, as he crosses the border from comedy to tragedy, from innocence to awareness to satire, with a magician's ease. It's in this form that Theroux's many fictional voices are in perfect harmony. His short stories are arias, his novels recitative.

SAM STAGGS
March 7, 1994

WILLIAM T. VOLLMANN

"I'D SAY THE BIGGEST HOPE that we have right now is the AIDS epidemic," offers William Vollmann, sipping from a glass of dark rum in his living room in a quiet section of Sacramento, Calif. "Maybe the best thing that could happen would be if it were to wipe out half or two-thirds of the people in the world. Then the ones who survived would just be so busy getting things together that they'd have to help each other, and in time maybe the world would recover ecologically, too."

Vollmann delivers this startling observation in a languid, deceptive drawl, like a pitcher with a slow, deliberate windup blazing a fastball by your eyes. You look closer to see just who this guy is, but his features recede in a haze of blandness. In person, the prolific young writer—at 32 he has published seven books of fiction and nonfiction, three of them in the last four months—is unprepossessing and somewhat odd. His bearing is distorted, or distorting: he seems wider in the hips than at the shoulders (perhaps an occupational hazard of the writing life) and looks the taller for it, narrowing toward the top; behind glasses, his right eye has a bleary cast to it, and his complexion is that of a 15-year-old. He sports a moth-eaten mustache and his sandy-colored hair looks unwashed. In conversation, he is gentle and considerate, but one gathers that his informal *uhmmms* . . . and *wells* . . . are the ways his lightning intelligence brakes for pedestrians. In blue jeans, sneakers and a madras shirt, this man who has written about everything from San Francisco's Tenderloin district to the impoverishments of Peshawar to the ravages of 17th-century Canada is an enigma dressed like a schlemiel.

Vollmann is ostensibly holding forth about his latest novel, *Fathers and Crows,* just out from Viking. But inevitably, his observations widen and address the larger historical themes of his Seven

Dream series, of which *Fathers and Crows* is the second installment. Having tracked the violent journeys of various Icelanders to Newfoundland in the first Dream, *The Ice-Shirt* (Viking, 1990), and then researched and reimagined the missionary efforts of Jesuit priests in Canada in *Fathers and Crows*, "the Young Man," as he sometimes refers to himself in his books, has seen enough of human foibles to call down the scourge of AIDS on all of mankind in hopes of setting something aright.

"The only times people really get along is if they're united against a common enemy," he calmly observes. "Perhaps that's what Sartre meant when he said, 'Two people can form a community by excluding a third.' The Huron," he says, referring to the Indian nation backed by the French in a war against the Mohawk, a conflict pitilessly described in *Fathers and Crows*, "were no better than we are. The reason they didn't have the equivalent of drive-by shootings and riots is because they had the luxury of this continuous blood feud that had gone on for as long as they could remember. So every summer they would go down and catch people who were not members of their particular nation. They'd bring 'em back and torture 'em to death and really make 'em suffer horribly, and everyone would just have the greatest time watching them die, and all the community hostility would be turned outward upon that one unfortunate person."

If Vollmann sounds a bit inured to violence, perhaps he is. He has surely made a study of it. He spent several months living among neo-Nazi "skinheads" in San Francisco, and gave a stirring account of the experience in his collection *Rainbow Stories* (Atheneum, 1988). He maintains a "professional interest" in prostitution—visiting whores and brothels in the Far East, Mexico and many ports of call in the U.S., gleaning the tales of a streetwalker's life that inform his masterful novella *Whores for Gloria*, the first of his three books published this year (from three different publishers). And, just out of college, Vollmann "made a trip to a battlefield" after convincing Afghani rebels to take him behind the lines during the early months of the Russian occupation, which ordeal he turned into *An Afghanistan Picture Show*, published last month by Farrar, Straus & Giroux.

How did this young man—the product of a stable if peripatetic American family, an honors graduate of Cornell—come to be so widely published, all without benefit of an agent? From the outlines of his life's tale, the answer seems to lie in a mixture of genius, vaunted ambition and fierce self-reliance.

Vollmann was born in Los Angeles and lived there until the age of five, when his family moved to Hanover, N.H., where his father taught business at Dartmouth. The family later moved to Rhode Island and then to Indiana, where Vollmann went to high school. Vollmann supplies these details graciously but with disinterest, as if he were talking about a person he has only reluctantly taken aboard. But a query about a personal revelation dropped into *Picture Show* (in which he prefaces a chilling tale of fording a swift and icy stream with a reference to the accidental drowning of his sister) draws a tortured response. "She drowned, yeah. Well, I was nine and she was six and she didn't know how to swim and I was supposed to be paying attention to her and I sort of forgot. The floor of the pond started out very shallow and just dropped off. . . ."

Vollmann seems almost embarrassed by the cloud of discomfort that besets the room. He gallantly moves to disperse it. "I went to college first at Deep Springs in California, in Death Valley. It's a weird, private place, sort of a whole story in itself. It was set up by the guy who pioneered alternating current, L. L. Nunn, in 1917. His idea was to create 'trustees of the nation.' He wanted to turn out this little elite leadership to go and take over the world, basically. There are a few minor twists to it—he was gay, probably, and it was an all-male school. . . ."

"It is a working cattle ranch and the students run the ranch," he continues. "There are usually 10 or 12 students. They send brochures to the boys who have SAT scores in the top one half of one percent and if you are accepted, everything is paid for. Nunn's idea was to 'develop the foundations of character' in this isolated desert valley the size of Manhattan. You're not supposed to see anyone else during the school year. Once you develop the foundations of character punching cows, then you go on to places like Telluride [Nunn set up schools within larger universities, where Deep Springers finish their schooling] at Cornell, where you play around with stocks and ballroom dancing. I liked Deep Springs; I didn't like Telluride."

Vollmann's first book, *You Bright and Risen Angels* (published by Deutsch in the U.K. and Atheneum in the U.S., and now a Penguin paperback) was about a school and master vaguely suggestive of Deep Springs and Nunn. The novel drew comparisons to the work of Pynchon and Burroughs—remarkably, considering that it had been plucked from a slush pile. "I don't believe in agents, nah. I sent *Angels* in '87 to a bunch of places. I hadn't [ever] published anything. Andre Deutsch in England was the only one interested at that time. They took it and they were just great to me and they've been great ever since. My advance for *Angels*, I think, was £12,500."

Deutsch has published all of Vollmann's work in the U.K. except *Whores for Gloria*, which Picador issued, and *Picture Show*, which has not appeared there. In fact, Deutsch has really been Vollmann's first publisher, selling American rights to Viking for *Ice-Shirt* and *Fathers and Crows*. Esther Whitby is his editor at Deutsch, "although she hated *Fathers and Crows*," Vollmann adds with a mischievous squint. "But they had to take it. I had a two-book contract. But they wised up after that. Now it's book by book."

Vollmann likes hard truths. Just as he gamely recounted his role in his sister's death, just as he understands the imperfectibility of society ("If men learned anything, sons would be smarter than their fathers," observes the narrator of *Father and Crows*), he is resignedly circumspect about his publishing future.

"I'm at a tough time in my career: I'll either make it or I'll be out of it fairly soon. On the one hand I seem to be getting better known all the time—I get fan mail all over the place. I'm getting great reviews, and that's a good sign. On the other hand, my books don't sell in huge numbers, and it seems to me that most publishers today, particularly American publishers, are more anxious to sell in large numbers than they were 10 or 20 years ago. I don't know how long they'll keep being patient."

Vollmann is not exactly pausing to see if he should continue writing. Viking has already accepted the Sixth Dream, called *Rifles*—about the ill-fated Franklin expedition to the North Pole in 1933—and will publish it next year. *Thirteen Stories*, which is in the *Whores for Gloria* vein, is being brought out in the U.S. by Fred Jordan at Pantheon (Deutsch has already published it in the U.K.). Vollmann wants John Glusman at FSG to see a "book-length essay on firearms" (Glusman, while at Atheneum, published *Angels* and *The Rainbow Stories*), and he has just finished *Butterfly Stories*, which Deutsch has bought and Pantheon is pondering.

Nor is Vollmann letting the hard truths of literary publishing dampen his hopes for *Fathers and Crows*. "In many ways I think this book is comparable to *War and Peace*. I'd like to see these books taught in history classes." Through the book's mixture of exhaustive research (the 73 volumes of *Jesuit Relations*, the writings of Ignatius Loyola and the diaries of Samuel de Champlain are just a sampling of the source material) and imaginary characters weaving in and out of the past and present, Vollmann has aimed to create a "symbolic history . . . an account of origins and metamorphoses which is often untrue based on the literal facts as we know them, but whose untruths further a deeper sense of truth" [from the end notes to *Fathers and Crows*].

Vollmann is not the first to suggest that a mingling of fact and fiction is at the heart of history and art. After all, Herodotus was no mean dissembler, and Shakespeare disfigured a king or two. But it isn't so easy to recall writers who have blended the sacred and the profane in the manner that Vollmann has in all his books. In *Fathers and Crows*, Kateri Tekakwitha, a Huron woman who converted to Catholicism after encountering the missionary Jesuits—and now a candidate for canonization as a saint by the Church—walks through the novel as if with a message to deliver. At book's end, her previously smallpox-scarred face clear and beautiful, Kateri strides through the red-light district in modern-day Montreal with a priest at her side. Seeing scantily clad women huddling in the cold, she approaches them with the call of "sisters," reaching across centuries and cultures to make a bond.

"I'm fond of prostitutes," admits Vollmann, when asked about their prevalence in his work. "I love watching them pick guys up. It's beautiful, the various ballerina-like movements that they perform on the corner. I think that we're all prostitutes. We all do things that we otherwise wouldn't choose to do, for the sake of getting somewhere else. And there is nothing wrong with being a prostitute. I like to remind myself of that by looking at prostitutes and talking to them."

Asked about the identification of the venerable and holy Kateri with Montreal's ladies of the night, Vollmann doesn't hesitate. "On the one hand Kateri has prostituted herself—to the Jesuits. She is trying to become a French girl, something she is not. On another level, prostitutes are despised people, and as an Indian she is despised also. Thirdly, most of these Catholic priests were very haughty and perhaps overly moralistic, ready to expel someone for being a fornicator, or if necessary having them executed for adultery. A true Christianity, if it existed, would insist on the equality of all the people who lived."

Soon Vollmann will be off on another research trip, this time to Mexico. It no doubt will be a refreshing break from his 16-hour days at the computer or in libraries. "I need to make $30,000 a year or so on these books, that's all. The trips I can write off, mostly. When I go away, I take my notebook, and when I come back I've got pages and pages of great stuff to put in my computer, and it's fun, it never seems like work. I'm always enjoying myself."

MICHAEL COFFEY
July 13, 1992

PAUL WATKINS

"PEOPLE MY AGE are looking back to the voices dying out—to a time when the world was on a hinge. I look to the past to see how themes echo in time. I think that we are linked not necessarily by time, but by emotion and morality," says the novelist Paul Watkins, whose latest book, *The Promise of Light* (Random House), deals almost exclusively with issues of personal legacy and responsibility.

Watkins's fourth novel in five years, *The Promise of Light* is set in the 1920s, and concerns Ben Sheridan, a first-generation Irish-American who learns that the man who raised him was not his father. When he returns to Ireland to search for his true patrimony, Ben becomes involved with the Irish Republican Army. Introduced to a world of violence and betrayal, he reevaluates his life and his Irish heritage.

An expert in creating characters burdened by their pasts, Watkins describes his protagonists as men who must confront their demons before they can move on with their lives. Typically, his heroes are driven by deep-rooted obsessions, from which Watkins creates what he calls "a sense of urgency" in his works. His characters' emotional crusades, and what *PW* hailed as his "versatility and skill for adventure writing of a high order," make his fiction convincing and compelling.

A writer of unusual maturity, Watkins at age 28 admits that his fiction is largely a product of his personal history, the distillation of a remarkable life to date. He was born in California after his father, an Olympic javelin thrower and oceanographer of Welsh heritage, came to North America in the 1950s. Watkins senior died at age 42; Paul lived with his mother in Rhode Island until he was seven, then was sent to a boarding school near Oxford that he dubs "a direct feeder into Eton."

Looking back on his days at Britain's posh "public" school, Watkins recalls being "caught up in a system that I did not believe in but was not strong enough to question." His education included mandatory training for the British military. "I was surprised not so much at being led, but at how easily I followed. I was always taught what to do, but never taught why," he says. Yet the discipline he learned was later to bear fruit in the strict habits of his craft.

At 15, he whetted his appetite for adventure by traveling through Europe unescorted. The following year, as an exchange student living with a family in Bad Godesberg, West Germany, he decided to write a novel about the battlefields of WW II, and trekked through the Ardennes Forest, where the Battle of the Bulge was fought. He wrote this fledgling piece of work in 1980, when he was 16, and revised it several times as he matured.

Meanwhile, he had returned to the U.S. to attend Yale, from which he graduated in 1986 with a B.A. in German. He then enrolled in Syracuse University's graduate writing program, where his teacher was writer Tobias Wolff. Wolff introduced his star pupil to his agent, Amanda "Binky" Urban, who became Watkin's agent too for *Night Over Day Over Night*. About Urban, Watkins says, "Whenever I heard about what an agent should do, her name came up. I never considered anyone else. She has been the greatest constant in my publishing career." Sold to Knopf, where it was edited by Elisabeth Sifton, *Night Over Day* was published in the States in 1988, when its author was all of 23; issued in England by Hutchinson the same year, the novel was shortlisted for the Booker Prize.

Only a year later, Watkins' next novel, *Calm at Sunset, Calm at Dawn*, went to Houghton Mifflin after spirited bidding. Published simultaneously in Britain by Hutchinson, it won Britain's Encore Prize for best second novel in 1989. Watkins cites "tensions with my editor" as the reason he then moved to Random House, where Jon Karp edited *In the Blue Light of African Dreams* (1990). Karp remains Watkins's editor, having also worked on *The Promise of Light*. "Jon has an instinctive understanding of my topics," Watkins observes. "I feel our sense of communication comes from our closeness in age. I enjoy working with my peers."

He has never had protests from his editors about the wordiness of his books' titles, Watkins says. Acknowledging that they are "awkward mouthfuls," he asserts that "they announce themselves. They are the most striking images in each book. I like the visual symmetry of the words on the page, not how they are pronounced."

The largely autobiographical basis for his work is for Watkins a form of coming to terms with his experiences. "I knew that if I didn't express them—and for me, that means putting them on paper—they would haunt me." *Calm at Sunset* evolved from his service aboard a fishing trawler, where he worked between semesters at Yale. "While I was at sea on the fishing boat, with my teeth knocked out [an experience he later transferred to his protagonist] at three in the morning, I saw the lights of the city and thought: 'Everyone I know and love is asleep right now!' ' Although the grueling days on the water initially discouraged him, he realized their value later on as the fictional process took shape.

For his novel *In the Blue Light of African Dreams*, Watkins spent several months in the Sahara desert and also learned to fly a biplane. Describing how he has transformed his personal experience into literature, he tells *PW*: "It's like a grain of sand in an oyster that will become a pearl. You owe more and more to the fiction, and less and less to the actual grain you started out with."

The inspiration for his latest book occurred when he heard a toast to Sinn Fein, the Irish revolutionary organization, at a dinner party. He was shocked at the speaker's temerity. "Had that man been in England, he would have left through the window," he comments.

Watkins calls his self-imposed research a period of "organized obsession," during which he concentrates almost exclusively on detail. He even selects his characters' names from gravestones in cemeteries he visits. For *The Promise of Light*, he "learned all about whiskey," he says. Displaying several bottles from a cabinet in the living room of his New Jersey home (he lives with his wife, Cathy, on the campus of a prep school where he teaches creative writing), Watkins shows us the differences in taste, smell and color, and explicates on "Highland and Lowland, Irish and Scotch. And the research wasn't always just for the book; I wanted to *know*. I am utterly fascinated with detail—past the point of it appearing useful. *That* is when it becomes most useful," he says.

With his tall, sturdy frame and firm handshake—he divides his writing into two morning sessions with an intense half hour on a Soloflex machine—it is apparent that Watkins's strength and energy require the outlet of physical adventures as well as the discipline of writing about them. In conversation, his British accent wraps itself almost indecisively around his words, as if he is revising his thoughts as he is uttering them. His ideas seem to flow in a stream of hyperconsciousness, yet he expresses himself eloquently, if only to acknowledge that he thinks too much.

"Ideas keep cropping up in my head. I wish there were three of me because I want to write all of them at the same time. I know that I can't—and in a way that's reassuring—because I know by my calculation that for the next seven years I have stuff to write. But at the same time, I'm so impatient to get all of this done, the writing becomes almost a hindrance—I can't get it out fast enough!"

Watkins claims that the novel he is working on now will be unlike his previous work, since it is set in contemporary times and concerns "environmental terrorism and a last crusade to save the planet." So far the book features several major characters and has less action and more introspection than his other stories. He is "waiting for one to emerge and take over the narrative," he says.

Aware that he has always written "boys' adventure stories," he has resolved to develop more than one character in his future work. As his novels generally stress companionship among men, Watkins is now "balancing the genders" by writing female characters.

He foresees himself writing more than novels. "In the long-range forecast, I would like to edit an anthology of writers under 30. I would like to write a book to teach from as much as read from, and a book about the art of writing itself. And, of course, I would like to write many more novels."

As a young novelist, Watkins could easily have become a member of Urban's Brat Pack, which includes Bret Easton Ellis and now Donna Tartt. His vivid prose and active life have helped him to escape that label. The *Philadelphia Inquirer* dubbed Watkins "the presumptive heir to the Hemingway/Mailer/Crane/Remarque war-chronicling Mantle of Genius." Watkins demurs: "It would be too difficult to aspire to the Mantle."

In Britain, however, he is a bestselling author who was heralded by the *Sunday Telegraph* as "the voice of his generation." And though he eschews self-promotion, Watkins admits that he feels "fortunate to be called part of the new generation.

"I am not setting out to say that this book is a book that is going to define my generation,' " he proclaims. "As soon as a generation has a name, it's effectively over. This is an age without a name. We are on the cusp of something bigger, and we have the obligation to make a mark." His characters have their own obligations and obsessions. For example, Charlie Halifax, the hero of *In the Blue Light of African Dreams,* races against time to beat Charles Lindbergh across the Atlantic.

Obviously Watkins resembles his characters in that he continually courts success. Despite his youth, he hopes "that not only in retrospect will my novels be linked thematically, but that there is a sense that each novel is pushing out against an ever-expanding barrier." He pauses for a moment, characteristically deep in thought, before continuing: "I would like for there to be a sense of timelessness [in my work] precisely so these books can endure—so that they aren't locked in to the labeling of the moment."

He is bewildered by American booksellers' need for taxonomy on the shelves, and their uncertainty about whether to classify his novels as literature or as action/adventure. Watkins suggests they be called "rite-of-passage books, as opposed to coming-of-age. They are 'voyaging' novels."

His first three novels have been issued in paperback by Avon, and the latter two on audio by Recorded Books. They have been translated into Dutch, French, Japanese and Swedish. Faber and Faber became his publisher in the U.K. with *Promise.* Watkins also completed a screenplay of *Calm at Sunset* for the independent film company Working Title Productions.

Intense and focused, Watkins is constantly exploring new avenues. "The [writing] machine is *never* off. I am never *not* working. Since I am self-employed, my use of time is important. I need time to build up my mental endurance. I like the efficiency of disciplined writing. I hate wasting time."

In fact, scavenging flea markets for research materials is how Watkins spends his leisure hours. "I like to surround myself with junk of the time sphere in which I am working," he says, offering to show *PW* the "talismans" he has collected. The walls of his study are covered with notes—"triphammers," he calls them—that he has compiled for his new novel. In one corner are the knee-high leather boots he purchased while doing research on *The Promise of Light.* There are other articles that helped him enter the milieux of his books: the German soldier's watch on his desk, and the leather flying jacket he keeps in a trunk.

Studying his personal effects, Watkins realized: "I guess I will have more adventures—whether I like it or not—and part of the reassurance of that is that I can't help but grow. As one grows, adventures come in many forms, and they aren't always as active or aggressive as the ones that have come before. There is a lot for me to learn that doesn't involve extremes of human nature."

GARY M. KRAMER
January 4, 1993

ELIE WIESEL

"Nobody will want to read something this sad," agent Georges Borchardt was told as he went from one house to the next, trying to find an American publisher for a novel already well received in France. "We don't like one-book authors," one New York savant explained. "He probably won't write anything else."

More than 30 years later, that book, *Night*, is virtually a classic, and its author, Elie Wiesel, has become a public figure, himself the subject of nearly 20 books. He has been garlanded with honorary degrees and given the most sterling of awards, including the 1986 Nobel Peace Prize. The "one-book" writer has produced some three dozen works, the newest of which, *The Forgotten*, is out from Summit.

While *Night* springs directly from Wiesel's experiences and *The Forgotten*, is, according to the author, "less autobiographical" than any of his other books, together the two novels close a circle. *Night* describes Wiesel's childhood in Sighet, Transylvania, among a devout Jewish community annihilated by the Nazis. The adolescent hero bears resolute witness to the sufferings of Auschwitz and Buchenwald; he is determined not to forget either Sighet or the camps. In *The Forgotten*, a survivor of the Holocaust named Elhanan is stricken with Alzheimer's disease. Elhanan offers up all of his memories to his grown son, Malkiel, and charges Malkiel with a mission to visit Feherfalu, the Carpathian village of his birth; he is determined that what he has seen be remembered. As in Wiesel's other works, the themes of memory and forgetting are endowed with historical and religious significance.

"It came to me one day four or five years ago," Wiesel says in a voice so soft as to demand the utmost concentration. He had been considering the range of his books—among them plays, essays, theological studies as well as novels, with topics from the Holocaust to Soviet Jewry to the Bible to mysticism. "What do they have in common? Their commitment to memory. What is the opposite of memory? Alzheimer's disease. I began to research this topic and I discovered that this is the worst disease, that every intellectual is afraid of this disease, not just because it is incurable, which is true of other diseases, too. But here the identity is being abolished. And so I do not see it as a disease, I see it as a malediction.

"I don't mention its name in the book. The word doesn't appear, simply because he doesn't want it to be mentioned. He, Elhanan. Which I understand. In Eastern Europe, they didn't pronounce the word 'cancer,' out of superstition."

Elhanan's plight is all the more desperate because he recognizes himself as a guardian of other people's memories as well as his own. As an element of the story and as an act of remembrance, Wiesel creates Elhanan's past from a relatively unknown aspect of the war, making him a member of a Jewish labor battalion in the Hungarian Army. "The Holocaust itself is so powerful that it overshadows all other subjects. It would seem the labor battalions suffered, but not *that* much. So it's less known," suggests Wiesel, adding that he also wove in "the chapter of Jewish suffering" in the Ukraine and White Russia. "There were no gas chambers there, but Jews were killed, shot. That, too, is not well known. It's an injustice. Some victims," he concludes, shifting his tone to underscore the irony, "fare better than others."

Elhanan's urgency is Wiesel's own. "What happens to things that have not been communicated?" he asks. "It is my great concern. I can write only so much, speak only so much." His faith in the primacy of commemoration is joined to his belief that only those who experienced the war are capable of writing about it with authenticity.

"It's possible for others to write about it," observes Wiesel. "But it depends how they write, if they write it with humility or with arrogance. Those who did go through that event always write with humility; those who did not, write with arrogance.

"I often think of Job and his three friends," continues the man who has been called the Job of Auschwitz. "The three friends tried to find reasons for his suffering. Job didn't want that. He wanted something else, consolation, comforting. He wanted friendship. They gave him explanation.

"This is exactly what's happening with most commentators today. They have no idea what they're writing about. I don't deny them the right. They have the right not to know. That is also a right. But it is our right, I think, to say they don't know what they're doing."

Thus the legacy for the generations born after the Holocaust is to study and not to reinvent it. "This tragedy is the most documented tragedy," says Wiesel, you can always go back to the records. I believe mainly in memoir. Memoirs are important; witness accounts, testimonies, children's songs are important—but not novels. Always with exceptions: John Hersey's *The Wall* is one. But novels, even literary criticism of the novels, are beside the point. From the literary viewpoint, they may be right, but from the viewpoint of authenticity, truth, they are wrong."

Accordingly, Wiesel urges other survivors to write, his support undaunted by the "whole wall" of manuscripts his exhortations have brought him. "Every survivor who asks me for a preface or for a review or for a letter of recommendation gets one, because I think their writing is the most important of all." He would like to see each memoir published, "even in small editions, maybe a thousand copies to distribute to other writers. [The survivors] deserve that, to know that their story has not been forgotten or ignored. If they are not bestsellers, so what? There are funds for so many silly and useless things, why not have a fund for something so important?"

There was no one to give such encouragement to Wiesel when he confronted his own wartime experiences. "I made a vow of silence, not to speak about it, not to write about it for 10 years [after liberation]," he recalls. In those 10 years Wiesel was brought to France, one of 400 children "who had nowhere to go." He learned French by reading Racine and other classic writers, and he turned his childhood love of religious texts toward philosophy, the field he studied when he entered the Sorbonne in 1948.

Wiesel began working as a journalist while at the Sorbonne. "You don't need a degree to be a foreign correspondent," he says knowingly. With the State of Israel newly created, he set about finding an Israeli paper that did not yet have a Paris correspondent. "And the only one that did not was the one that could not afford to! It [*Yediot Aharonot*] was the poorest paper imaginable. But they said, "Why not? and so I came to Paris. I made maybe

$50 a month. I suffered from hunger for many years, even after I came to New York [in 1956] as a correspondent. Then I made $200 a month, which included everything, even expenses.

For *Yediot Aharonot* Wiesel wrote in Hebrew; he also contributed to French and Yiddish newspapers, including the *Jewish Daily Forward.* When the 10 years of vowed silence had elapsed, he chose to write in Yiddish, producing an 800-page novel titled *And the World Was Silent* (published in Argentina in 1956). Cut drastically and rewritten in French, the book became *Night.*

Discussing the process of shortening *Night,* which in its Avon/Discus mass market paperback numbers 128 pages, Wiesel refers to "the marvelous example of Giacometti, the great sculptor. He always said that his dream was to do a bust so small that it could enter a matchbook, but so heavy that no one could lift it. That's what a good book should be."

French publishers were initially resistant, despite the intervention of François Mauriac. "Even Mauriac himself, the most distinguished writer in France [and recipient of the 1952 Nobel Prize for literature] couldn't find it a publisher," Wiesel remembers. "Finally he took it to Editions de Minuit, Samuel Beckett's publisher, and it was accepted." The book appeared in 1958 to a "very, very big reception," which Wiesel carefully attributes not to any specific merits but to the hand of Mauriac.

Meanwhile Georges Borchardt, the French press's agent and later Wiesel's, found his submission refused by all the major American publishers. "All of them," Wiesel repeats. Arthur Wang of Hill & Wang eventually bought the work for $100.

Two books in two years followed from Hill & Wang, *Dawn* and *The Accident.* While Editions du Seuil became Wiesel's primary publisher, a number of American houses have had the privilege. "For me it's always a personal thing," he explains. He was lured to Atheneum by Cornelia and Michael Bessie—"I was very fond of them; I still am"—and gave them *The Town Beyond the Wall* (1964). But before he signed he approached Arthur Wang. "He said, 'Look, we are too small for you. I think you will do better.' He allowed me to go," Wiesel says, his appreciation still evident.

His friend Arthur Cohen, then at Holt, Rinehart, got the next three books, and when Cohen left Holt, Wiesel went to Jim Silberman at Random House, which brought out the bestselling *A*

Beggar in Jerusalem in 1970. Ten years and half a dozen books later, Wiesel followed Silberman to Simon & Schuster and joined the Summit list.

At Summit he was to be rewarded with editor Ileene Smith, whom he unreservedly calls the best in the business. "She knows how to be with the text. Some editors—so I've heard, I've never had this experience—try to change a text. But she, never. She understands the motivation for every sentence, she hears the voice of the author. She is there to be the echo, to hear, not substitute her voice. When the book is finished, she knows what to do with it. She is unique."

Although Wiesel became an American citizen in 1963 and makes his home in New York City, he continues to write in French, the language of what he terms his "formative years," adding, "I came to France at a time when I needed a new language." His spoken English is rhythmic and polished, far better than that of most native speakers, yet he claims that his command is faulty: "I respect English too much to write in it." Accordingly, he says that his translator, not he himself, works most closely with his American editors. But his translator has most often been Marion Wiesel, to whom he has been married since 1969. (Because of Marion Wiesel's increasing obligations to the charitable foundation she and her husband started with the Nobel Prize money, however, *The Forgotten* went to Stephen Becker, who also translated *The Town Beyond the Wall*.)

Currently, Wiesel is at work on a memoir of his own—"a huge project." But never has Wiesel worked solely on one undertaking. For 20 years he's taught; currently he spends two days a week of the fall semester at Boston University, where he is a professor of philosophy and of religious studies as well as holder of the Andrew Mellon chair in the humanities. He never repeats a course, and his choices are far-ranging: the recorded deaths of great masters; hope and despair in ancient and modern literature; Kafka. His teaching assistants, however, grade the students' papers. "Not because I don't have time, although that's true. But because I couldn't give a bad grade. I couldn't hurt a student."

The demands for Wiesel's attention are great. "I say no, no, no, no until I have to say yes," he says, but he travels at least once a month to Europe for various causes and lends support to scores of institutions around the world. Many Americans remember him as the chair of the President's Commission on the Holocaust in 1979.

Since he received the Nobel Prize, pressures have intensified. He and his wife have used the prize funds to sponsor international symposia for Nobel laureates, most recently on the topic of hate, and have also established an ethics prize for university students. Currently, Marion Wiesel is creating a center for Ethiopian Jewish children in Israel.

How does he accomplish so much? "I'm a disciplined person," says Wiesel. "I write four hours every day, except Shabbat and Jewish holidays. Then I have four hours to read or research or study. In the other hours I do everything else." How? "I don't sleep much," he says with a generous smile.

ELIZABETH DEVEREAUX
April 6, 1992

STEPHEN WRIGHT

STEPHEN WRIGHT strikes an incongruous figure, a constellation of paired contradictions: rangy and imposing in leather jacket and biker boots, he nonetheless looks soft and bookish and sports a delicate nose ring. His hair, blond and graying, falls to shoulder length but is thinning on top. His mouth is a flat slash that seems expressionless until it erupts into the broken lines of some sarcastic, howling remark. The eyes, when not quick with a fresh idea, are dead as lug bolts.

A man of exacting opinions, Wright is not exactly sure how old he is ("I was born in '46, or I am 46. Or seven. Let me see, I'm ..."), and yet he knows the "voice of the age" when he hears it. "I like the *New Yorker*," he says with a kind of giddy, skidding laugh that, one soon discovers, is often prelude to a merciless assault. "But it all sounds the same, as if one editor has perfected every line. It's the voice of the age, isn't it? And you know what? This is the stuff that, as times moves on, falls into dust. It looks all hot and nice now, but that's the trick of good writing: What can you get into the words that will make them live beyond the passing moment? That's the mystery."

Talking to Wright, as we did for a couple of hours in a cafe on Greenwich Avenue in New York City, is to understand what an extreme and ineffable vocation writing can be. "There has to be a certain amount of real obsession in order to rout out your best language," he says with some weariness. "It's one of the reasons I'm so slow. The language I want to get at seems to dwell so deeply that it takes *a lot* of time and effort."

Wright seems genuinely in awe of the route that brought him to writing—from an Ohio State dropout, to reluctant intelligence officer in Vietnam, back to college, on to the Iowa Writer's Workshop and finally to a succession of New York publishers—with a peculiar inevitability, as if he had no choice in the matter. "If you have to write you will, and if you don't have to, you won't, because everything in life is going to conspire for you not to; and if you *can* live without doing it, you *should*, you really should. I don't really recommend it. To anyone."

Wright has published three novels in 11 years. And, like his first two, his latest, *Going Native* (Farrar, Straus & Giroux), is receiving glittering praise. *PW*, in a starred review, touted its "absolutely brilliant maximalist prose," and Michiko Kakutani, in a rave in the *New York Times*, called it "an uncompromising 1990's version of *On the Road* that gives us an alarming picture of a country pitched on the edge of an emotional and social abyss."

But *Going Native*, which tells the tale of one Wylie Jones, who flees a suburban life to travel cross-country on a terror-filled spree, is more than a "road novel" and more than a book about murder and mayhem. It's a writer's writer's book—not only is the language conscripted into the service of the story, but the structure itself becomes another image of the book's theme, something few authors ask of their books, and fewer and fewer readers today expect or are even familiar with. And that's what worried Wright. "For me, being true to the material is finally the governing factor in how a book is structured," he explains. "But I wasn't sure of this one. I started out with a contemporary suburban backyard barbecue scene, and I think I had a notion of the end, the West Coast and the ocean, but exactly how it was going to be put together I had no idea. So I did the first scene, and then the crucial revelation happened. I realized that each chapter *had* to begin in a new locale and with a new set of characters. And of course the second I realized this, my next thought was, well, you're fucked."

But Wright carried on. Wylie Jones, nominally the protagonist of *Going Native* (the true protagonist is arguably the mercurial American spirit), barely appears in most chapters and is never in the foreground. Instead, the book becomes eight brilliant, self-contained stories with Wylie skulking in the background.

The reason he didn't choose a more traditional narrative, says Wright, is that "the story itself is boring." Wright takes a particular delight in saying this. He laughs his distinctive laugh—a kind of George Bush snicker that then gets away from him and has to be run down with joyous breathlessness. When he returns to his point, you know what it is going to be: a larger indictment. "And why is it boring? Because we've heard it so much. The story itself is as old as the Pilgrims and before; it's the very essence of the particularly American male culture; that is, when the going gets tough, you open the door and you step out; the country is founded on this premise. It's imbedded in our psyches."

For Wright, "the sense of self that this book is portraying could only be illustrated by this kind of structure: the contemporary American self, very fluid, very mysterious, and the whole notion of causation not only under question, but abandoned."

Wright acknowledges again and again the "enormous compositional problems" that this presented, but he decided that the only way out was to make each separate chapter "go like the wind." And so far, reviewers seem to think *Going Native* flies.

Given Wright's origins, one tends to believe him when he says that writers are born, not made. Raised in Cleveland, he rather indifferently attended Ohio State, and he would have dropped out early on if it hadn't been for the Vietnam war, which put a certain premium on being a college student. When his grade-point average dipped below "acceptable levels," the school notified the draft board and Wright found himself at a preinduction center. "I presented a number of conditions," the writer says in a sickened whine meant to mimic his ruse of long ago, "but they were all denied." He was reclassified 1-A. He went to Nam.

"A part of me, a small part, was just curious. This was the event of our time. I could have high-tailed it to Canada or Sweden, where I have relatives. But it would have been intolerable to be cut out of my country."

Wright was an intelligence officer stationed not far from Hue, near the DMZ, a hot area. He served a year and emerged, he says, "relatively" unscathed. "When I came out," he says, "I was very focused. I knew exactly what was going on."

What was going on was the evolving realization that he wanted to write.

Wright re-enrolled at OSU and became an English major. He wrote steadily, and read himself through American literature. "I knew I had my hands on some extraordinary material," he says of the Vietnam experience. "War and death, the summation of an era. And I was witness to it."

Someone, Wright can't remember who, suggested he send something to the Iowa Writer's Workshop, and he did—what later became the first chapter of *Meditations in Green*—and he was accepted into the two-year writing program. There, he studied with John Cheever, John Irving and Vance Bourjaily, who was to play a pivotal role in Wright's career a few years later.

Wright narrates the moment: "I'm no longer going to school; one minimum wage job after another in Iowa City: hospital ward clerk, Prairie Lights Bookstore, where Jim Harris employed a great number of writers, Workshop people. I'm halfway through my book and I'm getting very impatient. Now, *I* obviously feel as though it ain't that bad, but I want to *hear* it from somebody. So I go out to Vance's farm one day, and I say, 'You know, I'm not done with this thing, but what do you think if I just start sending it out?' I wanted to hear what editors in New York had to say, and of course Vance said, 'Sure. People do this all the time, people do everything; all the little things you hear—don't do this, don't do that—it's all nonsense.' So Vance read it first. And he thought it was terrific."

Bourjaily gave him the names of four or five editors and permission to use his name in corresponding with them; Wright dug out another 20 from *LMP*. He sent along a letter and 50 or so pages of his work in progress.

"And, lo and behold, half of them sent notes saying let's see more; with a couple, I received actual letters, from some very interesting places: Random House—it was Malcolm Cowley's son, Robert, who's another one of those editors who got fired, I think, for doing too many good serious books that weren't making money. And then Scribner's said they wanted to keep a very close eye on this. I forget who the letter was from, but he quit. I never met the guy. His assistant was Michael Pietsch. He's the one who eventually took it."

Wright was unagented at the time, but when *Meditations in Green* was published in 1983, Scribners brought Wright to New York, and he used his free time to visit the offices of Georges Borchardt. "I'd say to Michael [Pietsch], 'Well, I got to go now,' I'd walk a few blocks up to Borchardt's and say, 'Hey, do you know what they just did to me!' " He laughs wickedly.

But just as Wright's career seemed to have secured itself, it began to get rocky. Scribner's was sold to Macmillan in the next year, and Pietsch soon left in the shake-up. Wright was still under contract for his next book, but when he tried to renegotiate to get some much-needed cash, Scribner's said he could take his book elsewhere if he liked. Pietsch, who had landed at Harmony, put together "a big package, a hard/soft with Ballantine" for the book that became *M31: A Romance*—a cracked but lushly told story about a family of UFO enthusiasts. But shortly after the book was published in 1988, Crown, of which Harmony was an imprint, was bought by Random House, and Pietsch eventually departed for Little, Brown. "I don't know what happened," says Wright, obviously holding his tongue. "It's all vague." The book did not do so well, but again the critical response was heartening.

Although *Meditations*, which sold about 15,000 copies in hardcover, outsold *M31*—and Wright's file of reviews for his first book, he admits, is much thicker than for his second—the reviews for *M31* are better, in his estimation. "The high point was the front-page review in the *Washington Post Book World*. It's a better book—better constructed, tighter; it may not be as accessible, but I have no doubt it's a better book."

Wright had already started his next book by the time he took the temperature of the folks at Harmony and found they were cool to the project. "And the higher up you got, the cooler they were," says Wright triumphantly. So once again, he shopped a few chapters around.

"Georges sent it everywhere. Three chapters, I think. Immediately we started getting responses. John Glusman, who had actually interviewed me once and reviewed *Meditations* in the *Christian Science Monitor*, and who I had seen at Scribner's or Colliers during the perpetual changing of the guard at Macmillan, came through with one of those FSG offers where you have something like 24 hours to take it or not. But look, it was obvious. FSG is just the sort of house I needed, and I knew that. I didn't have to think very long. And things have been great."

Walking out onto Greenwich Avenue, Wright returns to his favorite subject—the deaf ears of culture. "It's why first-rate stuff has such a tough go; it's not in that voice of the age I was talking about. I find this endlessly fascinating, *endlessly* fascinating. Why couldn't people, the moment they opened up *Moby-Dick*, why couldn't they just *see* the power coming off every page, power such as an American has hardly ever achieved? They couldn't, and not only that—they thought it was rubbish." Wright stops in the Sixth Avenue slush, gesticulating his amazement—a Hell's Angel with a gripe. People steer clear. "With Melville, what do you have, maybe one person in the whole country, Hawthorne, who understood the work." There is a pause. "And he wasn't talking to anyone! I mean, Nathaniel Hawthorne was *not* Mr. Gregarious!" Wright is laughing again, hard. It is becoming a whoop. He has delivered a punch line that perhaps only he understands. As he heads off down 9th Street, guffawing, one finally gets a fix on it, this laugh: it is healthy with scorn.

MICHAEL COFFEY
January 24, 1994

CONTRIBUTORS

JOHN F. BAKER was editor-in-chief of *Publishers Weekly* for 12 years. He is now editorial director.

MICHELLE J. BEARDEN is a reporter for the *Tampa Tribune*.

NATHALIE OP DE BEECK is a Washington, D.C., journalist and a frequent contributor to *Publishers Weekly*.

JONATHAN BING writes for *Publishers Weekly* and other journals.

DULCY BRAINARD, is a *Publishers Weekly* editor covering mysteries, poetry and lifestyles.

WILLIAM CLARK is a freelance writer and photographer who lives in northern New Mexico.

MICHAEL COFFEY is managing editor at *Publishers Weekly*. His first book of poetry, *Elemenopy*, is being published by Sun and Moon Press.

MISSY DANIEL is a writer and editor in Boston.

ELIZABETH DEVEREAUX edits children's book reviews for *Publishers Weekly*.

PAUL ELIE, who works as a book editor in New York, has written for *Commonweal, The New Republic* and *Lingua Franca*.

ELGY GILLESPIE is a travel writer and arts journalist living in San Francisco, who writes guides for Fodor's and World View. She was formerly arts feature writer at the *Irish Times* and editor of the *San Francisco Review of Books*.

ROBERT K. J. KILHEFFER is a contributing editor of *Omni* magazine, editor of the speculative fiction magazine *Century*, author of *The Omni Book of Science Facts* and a frequent contributor to *Publishers Weekly*.

GARY M. KRAMER is a freelance writer and film critic in Philadelphia.

MARGARET LANGSTAFF is freelance writer and critic living in Tennessee.

SUZANNE MANTELL is a contributing editor of *Publishers Weekly*.

Boston-based freelancer ROBERT MCCULLOUGH has written for the *Boston Globe, Sport, Keyboard* and *New Age Journal.* He is currently working on his first nonfiction title, a music book about contemporary big bands.

DERMOT KAVANAGH MCEVOY is a freelance writer and book reviewer in New York City.

MOLLY MCQUADE is a writer and editor living in New York. Her work has appeared in *New York Newsday*, the *Chicago Tribune*, the *Women's Review of Books, Lingua Franca, The Village Voice* and elsewhere. Her first book, *An Unsentimental Education*, will be published by the University of Chicago Press in 1995.

JUDITH PIERCE ROSENBERG is a freelance journalist in Lincoln, Mass. She is currently working on a collection of interviews with women visual artists and writers who have children, which will be published by Papier-Mache Press.

LISA SEE is the West Coast correspondent for *Publishers Weekly*. She is the author of *On Gold Mountain: One Hundred Years in a Chinese-American Family*.

MARIA SIMSON is paperbacks editor of *Publishers Weekly*.

BEVERLY SLOPEN is *Publishers Weekly*'s Canadian correspondent, a literary agent in Toronto, and a columnist for the *Toronto Star*.

WENDY SMITH reviews books and interviews authors for many publications, including *The New York Times, The Washington Post* and *Newsday*. She is the author of *Real Life Drama: The Group Theatre and America, 1931–1940*.

BOB SUMMER is *Publishers Weekly*'s Southern correspondent and lives in Nashville. He has contributed essays to two anthologies: *Hometowns: Gay Men Write About Where They Belong* and *A Member of the Family: Gay Men Write About Their Families*.

SAM STAGGS, who lives in Philadelphia, is an editorial associate at *Artnews* magazine.

SYBIL S. STEINBERG is Interviews editor and Fiction Forecasts editor at *Publishers Weekly*. She is a past board member of the National Book Critics Circle and currently serves on the board of the Carolina Publishing Institute.

KATHARINE WEBER'S first novel, *Objects in Mirror Are Closer Than They Appear*, will be published by Crown this year.

BIBLIOGRAPHY

(Books currently in print by interviewed authors)

MARY CATHERINE BATESON

Composing a Life, Plume Books, paper, 1990
Our Own Metaphor, Smithsonian Books, paper, 1991
Peripheral Visions, HarperCollins, 1994
Thinking AIDS, Addison-Wesley, paper, 1989
With a Daughter's Eye, HarperCollins, paper, 1994

LOUIS BEGLEY

As Max Saw It, Knopf, 1994
The Man Who Was Late, Knopf, 1993; Fawcett Books, paper, 1994
Wartime Lies, Knopf, 1991; Ivy Books, paper, 1992

MAEVE BINCHY

Circle of Friends, Delacorte, 1991; Dell, paper, 1991
The Copper Beech, Delacorte, 1992; Dell, paper, 1993
Echoes, Dell, paper, 1989
Firefly Summer, Dell, paper, 1989
Light a Penny Candle, Dell, paper, 1989
The Lilac Bus, Delacorte, 1991; Dell, paper, 1992
Silver Wedding, Delacorte, 1989; Dell, paper, 1990

ROBERT BOSWELL

Crooked Hearts, Knopf, 1987; HarperCollins, paper, 1994
Dancing in the Movies, Univ. of Iowa Press, 1986
The Geography of Desire, HarperCollins, paper, 1994
Living to be a Hundred: Stories, Knopf, 1994
Mystery Ride, Knopf, 1993; HarperCollins, paper, 1993

ROSELLEN BROWN

The Autobiography of My Mother, Dell, paper, 1994
Banquet: Five Short Stories, Penmaen Press, paper, 1978
Before & After, Farrar, Straus & Giroux, 1992; Dell, paper, 1993
Civil Wars, Knopf, 1984; Dell, paper, 1994
Cora Fry, Unicorn Press, 1989
Cora Fry's Pillow Book (with *Cora Fry*), Farrar, Straus & Giroux, 1993
The Rosellen Brown Reader, Univ. Press of New England, 1992;
      Univ. Press of New England, paper, 1994
Street Games, Milkweed Editions, paper, 1991
Tender Mercies, Dell, paper, 1994

JAMES LEE BURKE

Black Cherry Blues, Little, Brown, 1989; Avon, paper, 1990
The Convict And Other Stories, Little, Brown, 1990
Dixie City Jam, Hyperion, 1994
Heaven's Prisoners, Pocket Books, paper, 1989
In the Electric Mist with Confederate Dead, Hyperion, 1993
The Lost Get-Back Bogie, Louisiana State Univ. Press, 1986; Owl
      Books, paper, 1987
A Morning for Flamingos, Little, Brown, 1990; Avon, paper, 1991
The Neon Rain, Pocket Books, paper, 1992
A Stained White Radiance, Hyperion, 1992; Avon, paper, 1993

ROBERT OLEN BUTLER

The Alleys of Eden, Owl Books, paper, 1994
Countrymen of Bones, Owl Books, paper, 1994
The Deuce, Owl Books, paper, 1994
A Good Scent from a Strange Mountain, Henry Holt, 1992; Pen-
      guin Books, paper, 1993
On Distant Ground, Owl Books, paper, 1994
Sun Dogs, Owl Books, paper, 1994
They Whisper, Henry Holt, 1994
Wabash, Knopf, 1987; Ballantine, paper, 1988

FRANK CONROY

Body & Soul, Houghton Mifflin, 1993
Midair, Penguin Books, paper, 1993
Stop-Time, Penguin Books, paper, 1977

DENNIS COOPER

Closer, Grove/Atlantic, paper, 1990
Discontents, Amethyst Press, paper, 1991
Frisk, Grove/Atlantic, 1991; Grove/Atlantic, paper, 1992
Try, Grove/Atlantic, 1994
Wrong, Grove/Atlantic, 1992

LEN DEIGHTON

ABC of French Food, Bantam, 1990
Berlin Game, Ballantine, paper, 1984
Blitzkreig, Ballantine, paper, 1982
Blood, Tears and Folly, HarperCollins, 1993
Catch a Falling Spy, Ballantine, paper, 1986
City of Gold, HarperCollins, 1992; HarperCollins, paper, 1993
Close-Up, HarperCollins, paper, 1992
Game, Set & Match, Knopf, 1989
Goodbye, Mickey Mouse, Ballantine, paper, 1983
The Ipcress File, Ballantine, paper, 1985
London Match, Ballantine, paper, 1986
MAMista, HarperCollins, 1991; HarperCollins, paper, 1992
Mexico Set, Knopf, 1985; Ballantine, paper, 1985
Only When I Laugh, Warner Books, paper, 1987
Spy Hook, Ballantine, paper, 1989
Spy Line, Knopf, 1989; Ballantine, paper, 1991
Spy Sinker, HarperCollins, 1989; HarperCollins, paper, 1991
Spy Story, Ballantine, paper, 1985
Violent Ward, HarperCollins, 1993
XPD, Ballantine, paper, 1983

E(DGAR) L(AURENCE) DOCTOROW

Billy Bathgate, Random House, 1989; HarperCollins, paper, 1990
The Book of Daniel, Random House, 1971; Fawcett Books, paper,
    1987; Vintage Books, paper, 1991
Drinks Before Dinner, Random House, 1979
Lives of the Poets, Random House, 1984; Avon Books, paper, 1986
Loon Lake. Fawcett Books, paper, 1988; Vintage Books, paper, 1992
Ragtime, Random House, 1975; Bantam Books, paper, 1984; Vin-
    tage Books, paper, 1992

The Waterworks, Random House, 1994
Welcome to Hard Times, Fawcett Books, paper, 1988; Vintage
      Books, paper, 1992
World's Fair, Fawcett Books, paper, 1986; Vintage Books, paper,
      1992

HARRIET DOERR

Consider This, Harcourt Brace, 1993
Stones for Ibarra, Penguin Books, paper, 1988

ERNEST J. GAINES

The Autobiography of Miss Jane Pittman, Bantam, paper, 1982
Bloodline, Norton, paper, 1976
Catherine Carmier, Vintage Books, paper, 1993
A Gathering of Old Men, Vintage Books, paper, 1984
A Lesson Before Dying, Knopf, 1993; Vintage, paper, 1994
Of Love and Dust, Vintage Books, paper, 1994

WILLIAM GIBSON

Burning Chrome, Ace Books, paper, 1987
Count Zero, Ace Books, paper, 1987
Mona Lisa Overdrive, Bantam, 1988; Bantam, paper, 1989
Neuromancer, Ace Books, paper, 1984
Virtual Light, Bantam, 1993
—with BRUCE STERLING:
The Difference Engine, Bantam, 1991; Bantam, paper, 1992

ELLEN GILCHRIST

The Anna Papers, Little, Brown, paper, 1989
The Annunciation, Little, Brown, paper, 1985
Drunk with Love, Little, Brown, paper, 1987
Falling Through Space, Little, Brown, paper, 1988
I Cannot Get You Close Enough, Little, Brown 1990; Little, Brown,
      paper, 1991
In the Land of Dreamy Dreams, Little, Brown, paper, 1985
Light Can Be Both Wave and Particle, Little, Brown, 1989; Little,
      Brown, paper, 1990

Net of Jewels, Little, Brown, 1992; Little, Brown, paper, 1993
Starcarbon, Little, Brown, 1994
Victory Over Japan: Stories, Little, Brown, paper, 1985

JOHN GRISHAM

The Chamber, Doubleday, 1994
The Client, Doubleday, 1993; Dell, paper, 1994
The Firm, Doubleday, 1991; Dell, paper, 1992
The Pelican Brief, Doubleday, 1992; Dell, paper, 1993
A Time to Kill, Wynwood Press, 1991; Doubleday, 1993; Dell, paper, 1992

PETE HAMILL

The Drinking Life, Little, Brown, 1994
Loving Women, Windsor Publishing, paper, 1990
Tokyo Sketches, Kodansha, 1993

CARL HIAASEN

Double Whammy, Warner Books, paper, 1989
Native Tongue, Knopf, 1991; Fawcett, paper, 1992
Strip Tease, Knopf, 1993; Warner, paper, 1994
Tourist Season, Warner Books, paper, 1987

JANETTE TURNER HOSPITAL

Charades, Bantam, 1989; Bantam, paper, 1990
Dislocations, Louisiana State Univ. Press, 1988
Isobars, Louisiana State Univ. Press, 1991
The Last Magician, Henry Holt, 1992; Ivy Books, paper, 1993
—writing as ALEX JUNIPER:
A Very Proper Death, Scribner's, 1991

ROBERT D. KAPLAN

The Arabists, Free Press, 1993
Balkan Ghosts, St. Martin's, 1993; Vintage Books, paper, 1994
Surrender or Starve, Westview Press, 1988

RHODA LERMAN

Animal Acts, Henry Holt, 1994
The Book of the Night, Holt, Rinehart & Winston, 1984
Call Me Ishtar, Doubleday, 1973
Eleanor, Holt, Rinehart & Winston, 1979
The Girl That He Marries, Holt, Rinehart & Winston, 1976
God's Ear, Henry Holt, 1992

DAVID McCULLOUGH

Brave Companions, Touchstone Books, paper, 1992
The Great Bridge, Touchstone Books, paper, 1983
The Johnstown Flood, Touchstone Books, paper, 1987
Mornings on Horseback, Touchstone Books, paper, 1982
The Path Between the Seas, Touchstone Books, paper, 1978
Truman, Simon Schuster, 1992; Touchstone Books, paper, 1993

ALICE McDERMOTT

At Weddings and Wakes, Farrar, Straus & Giroux, 1992; Dell, paper, 1993
A Bigamist's Daughter, HarperCollins, paper, 1988
That Night, HarperCollins, paper, 1992

TERRY McMILLAN

Disappearing Acts, Viking Penguin, 1989; Washington Square Press, paper, 1990; Pocket Books, paper, 1993
Mama, Washington Square Press, paper, 1991; Pocket Books, paper, 1994
Waiting to Exhale, Viking Penguin, 1992; Pocket Books, paper, 1993

PAUL MONETTE

Afterlife, Crown, 1990; Avon Books, paper, 1991
Becoming a Man, HarperCollins, paper, 1993
Borrowed Time, Harcourt Brace, 1988; Avon Books, paper, 1990
The Gold Diggers, Alyson Publications, paper, 1988
Halfway House, Crown, 1991; Avon Books, paper, 1992
Last Watch of the Night, Harcourt Brace, 1994
Love Alone, St. Martin's, paper, 1988

The Politics of Silence, Library of Congress, 1994
Taking Care of Mrs. Carroll, St. Martin's, paper, 1988

MARY MORRIS

The Bus of Dreams, Penguin Books, paper, 1986
Crossroads, Houghton Mifflin, 1983
A Mother's Love, Doubleday, 1993; Delta Books, paper, 1994
Nothing to Declare, Penguin Books, paper, 1989
Vanishing Animals, and Other Stories, Penguin Books, paper, 1991
The Waiting Room, Doubleday, 1989; Penguin Books, paper, 1990
Wall to Wall, Doubleday, 1991; Penguin Books, paper, 1992

WALTER MOSLEY

Black Betty, Norton, 1994
Devil in a Blue Dress, Norton, 1990; Pocket Books, paper, 1991
Red Death, Norton, 1991; Pocket Books, paper, 1992
White Butterfly, Norton, 1992; Pocket Books, paper, 1993

MARCIA MULLER

Edwin of the Iron Shoes, Warner Books, paper, 1993
Eye of the Storm, Warner Books, paper, 1993
Pennies on a Dead Woman's Eyes, Mysterious Press, 1993; Warner
    Books, paper, 1993
The Shape of Dread, Mysterious Press, 1989; Warner Books, paper,
    1993
There's Something in a Sunday, Mysterious Press, 1989; Warner
    Books, paper, 1993
Till the Butchers Cut Him Down, Mysterious Press, 1994
Trophies and Dead Things, Mysterious Press, 1990; Warner Books,
    paper, 1991
Where Echoes Live, Mysterious Press, 1991; Warner Books, paper,
    1992
Wolf in the Shadows, Mysterious Press, 1993; Warner Books, pa-
    per, 1994

V. S. NAIPAUL

Among the Believers, Vintage Books, paper, 1982
An Area of Darkness, Penguin Books, paper, 1992

A Bend in the River, Vintage Books, paper, 1989
The Enigma of Arrival, Vintage Books, paper, 1988
A Flag on the Island, Penguin Books, paper, 1993
Guerrillas, Vintage Books, paper, 1990
A House for Mr. Biswas, Penguin Books, paper, 1993
In a Free State, Vintage Books, paper, 1984
India: A Million Mutinies Now, Penguin Books, paper, 1992
India: A Wounded Civilization, Vintage Books, paper, 1977
Miguel Street, Penguin Books, paper, 1994
The Mimic Men, Penguin Books, paper, 1976
Mr. Stone and the Knights Companion, Penguin Books, paper, 1994
The Mystic Masseur, Penguin Books, paper, 1977
The Overcrowded Barracoon, Vintage Books, paper, 1984
The Suffrage of Elvira, Penguin Books, paper, 1976
Three Novels, Knopf, 1982
A Turn in the South, Knopf, 1989; Vintage Books, paper, 1990
Way in the World, Knopf, 1994

LAWRENCE NAUMOFF

The Night of Weeping Women, Ivy Books, paper, 1989
Rootie Kazootie, Ivy Books, paper, 1991
Silk Hope, NC, Harcourt Brace, 1994
Taller Women, Harcourt Brace Jovanovich, 1992; Harvest Books,
    paper, 1994

JOHN NICHOLS

Conjugal Bliss, Henry Holt, 1994
An Elegy for September, Henry Holt, 1992; Ballantine, paper, 1993
A Ghost in the Music, Norton, paper, 1987
Keep It Simple, Norton, 1992; Norton, paper, 1993
The Milagro Beanfield War, anniversary ed., Henry Holt, 1994
The Sky's the Limit, Norton, 1990
The Sterile Cuckoo, Norton, paper, 1987
The Wizard of Loneliness, Norton, paper, 1987

LEWIS NORDAN

The All-Girl Football Team, Vintage Books, paper, 1989
Music of the Swamp, Algonquin Books, 1991; Algonquin Books,

paper, 1992
Welcome to the Arrow-Catcher Fair, Louisana Sate Univ. Press, 1983;
    Vintage Books, paper, 1989
Wolf Whistle, Algonquin Books, 1993

HOWARD NORMAN

The Bird Artist, Farrar, Straus & Giroux, 1994; Picador, paper, 1995
How Glooskap Outwits the Ice Giants, Little, Brown, 1989
Kiss in the Hotel Joseph Conrad and Other Stories, Penguin Books,
    paper, 1990
The Northern Lights, Washington Square Press, paper, 1988
Northern Tales, Pantheon, 1990; Pantheon, paper, 1994
The Wishing-Bone Cycle, Ross-Erikson, paper, 1982

EDNA O'BRIEN

The Country Girls Trilogy and Epilogue, Farrar, Straus & Giroux,
    1986; Plume Books, paper, 1987
An Edna O'Brien Reader, Warner Books, paper, 1994
A Fanatic Heart, Farrar, Straus & Giroux, 1984; Plume Books, pa-
    per, 1985
The High Road, Farrar, Straus & Giroux, 1988; Plume Books,
    1989
House of Splendid Isolation, Farrar, Straus & Giroux, 1994
Lantern Slides, Farrar, Straus & Giroux, 1990; Plume Books, pa-
    per, 1991
Night, Farrar, Straus & Giroux, 1987
A Pagan Place, Graywolf, 1984
Time and Tide, Farrar, Straus & Giroux, 1992; Warner Books, pa-
    per, 1993
Virginia: A Play, Harcourt Brace Jovanovich, 1981; Harvest
    Books, paper, 1985

MICHAEL ONDAATJE

The Cinnamon Peeler, Knopf, paper, 1992
The Collected Works of Billy the Kid, Penguin Books, paper, 1984
Coming Through Slaughter, Penguin Books, paper, 1984
The English Patient, Knopf 1992; Vintage Books, paper, 1993
In the Skin of a Lion, Penguin Books, paper, 1988

Running in the Family, Vintage Books, paper, 1993

REYNOLDS PRICE

August Snow, Dramatists Play Service, 1990
Blue Calhoun, Atheneum, 1992; Ballantine, paper, 1994
Clear Pictures, Atheneum, 1989; Ballantine, paper, 1990
The Collected Stories of Reynolds Price, Atheneum, 1993; Plume
    Books, paper, 1994
A Common Room, Atheneum, 1987; Atheneum, paper, 1989
The Foreseeable Future, Atheneum, 1991; Ballantine, paper, 1992
Good Hearts, Ballantine, paper, 1989
Kate Vaiden, Ballantine, paper, 1987
The Laws of Ice, Atheneum, paper, 1986
A Long and Happy Life, Atheneum, 1987
Love and Work, Atheneum, 1975; Ballantine, paper, 1987
Mustian, Ballantine, paper, 1987
The Names and Faces of Heroes, Ballantine, paper, 1989
Permanent Errors, Ballantine, paper, 1990
The Source of Light, Ballantine, paper, 1988
The Surface of Earth, Ballantine, paper, 1989
The Tongues of Angels, Atheneum, 1990
The Use of Fire, Atheneum, 1990
A Whole New Life, Atheneum, 1994

RICHARD PRICE

Bloodbrothers, Penguin Books, paper, 1985; Avon Books, paper,
    1993
The Breaks, Penguin Books, paper, 1984
Clockers, Houghton Mifflin, 1992; Avon, paper, 1993
Ladies' Man, Penguin Books, paper, 1985; Avon, paper, 1993
*Three Screenplays: The Color of Money, Sea of Love, Night and the
    City*, Houghton Mifflin, 1993
The Wanderers, Penguin Books, paper, 1985; Avon Books, paper,
    1993

FRANCINE PROSE

Household Saints, Ivy Books, paper, 1993

A Peaceable Kingdom, Farrar, Straus & Giroux, 1993
Primitive People, Farrar, Straus & Giroux, 1992; Ivy Books, paper, 1993
Women and Children First, Ivy Books, paper, 1989

ADRIENNE RICH

Adrienne Rich's Poetry and Prose, Norton, paper, 1993
An Atlas of the Difficult World, Norton, paper, 1991
Blood, Bread and Poetry, Norton, paper, 1986
Collected Early Poems, Norton, 1993
Diving Into the Wreck, Norton, paper, 1973
The Dream of a Common Language, Norton, paper, 1993
The Fact of a Doorframe, Norton, paper, 1993
Of Woman Born, Norton, paper, 1986
On Lies, Secrets and Silence, Norton, paper, 1980
Time's Power, Norton, paper, 1989
What Is Found There, Norton, 1993
A Wild Patience Has Taken Me This Far, Norton, 1981; Norton, paper, 1993
The Will to Change, Norton, paper, 1971
Your Native Land, Your Life, Norton, paper, 1993

ANNE ROIPHE

If You Knew Me, Little, Brown, 1993
Lovingkindness, Warner Books, paper, 1989
The Pursuit of Happiness, Summit Books, 1991; Warner Books, paper, 1992

RICHARD RUSSO

Mohawk, Vintage Books, paper, 1989
Nobody's Fool, Random House, 1993; Vintage Books, paper, 1994
The Risk Pool, Vintage Books, paper, 1989

RICHARD SELZER

Confessions of a Knife, Quill Books, paper, 1987
Down from Troy, Morrow, 1992; Little, Brown, paper, 1993
Imagine a Woman and Other Tales, Random House, 1990

Letters to a Young Doctor, Touchstone Books, paper, 1983
Mortal Lessons, Touchstone Books, paper, 1987
Raising the Dead, Viking Penguin, 1994
Rituals of Surgery, Quill Books, paper, 1987

CAROL SHIELDS

Happenstance, Penguin Books, paper, 1994
The Orange Fish, Penguin Books, paper, 1992
The Republic of Love, Viking Penguin, 1992; Penguin Books, paper, 1993
The Stone Diaries, Viking Penguin, 1994
Swann, Penguin Books, paper, 1990
Various Miracles, Penguin Books, paper, 1989

CHARLIE SMITH

Chimney Rock, Henry Holt, 1993
Indistinguishable from the Darkness, Norton, paper, 1991
The Palms, Norton, paper, 1993
Red Roads, Dutton, 1987
Shine Hawk, British American Publishing, 1988

SUSAN STRAIGHT

Aquaboogie, Milkweed Editions, paper, 1990
Blacker Than a Thousand Midnights, Hyperion, 1994
I Been in Sorrow's Kitchen and Licked Out All the Pots, Hyperion, 1992; Anchor Press, paper, 1993

PAUL THEROUX

Chicago Loop, Random House, 1991; Ivy Books, paper, 1994
The Great Railway Bazaar, Ballantine, paper, 1981
The Happy Isles at Oceania, Putnam, 1992; Fawcett, paper, 1993
The Kingdom by the Sea, Houghton Mifflin, 1983
Millroy the Magician, Random House, 1994
The Mosquito Coast, Houghton Mifflin, 1982; Avon, paper, 1983
My Secret History, Ivy Books, paper, 1990
O-Zone, Ivy Books, paper, 1987
The Old Patagonian Express, Washington Square Press, paper, 1989

Riding the Iron Rooster, Ivy Books, paper, 1989
Sailing through China, Houghton Mifflin, 1984
Sinning with Annie and Other Stories, Ivy Books, paper, 1990
Sunrise with Seamonsters, Houghton Mifflin, 1986
To the Ends of the Earth, Random House, 1991; Ivy Books, paper, 1994
Waldo, Ivy Books, paper, 1989

WILLIAM T. VOLLMANN

An Afghanistan Picture Show: Or How I Saved the World, Farrar, Straus & Giroux, 1992
Butterfly Stories, Grove/Atlantic, 1993
Fathers and Crows, Viking Penguin, 1992; Penguin Books, paper, 1993
The Ice-Shirt, Viking Penguin, 1990; Penguin Books, paper, 1993
The Rainbow Stories, Penguin Books, paper, 1992
The Rifles, Viking Penguin, 1994
Thirteen Stories and Thirteen Epitaphs, Pantheon, 1993; Grove/Atlantic, paper, 1994
You Bright and Risen Angels, Penguin Books, paper, 1988
Whores for Gloria, Pantheon, 1991; Penguin Books, paper, 1994

PAUL WATKINS

Calm at Sunset, Calm at Dawn, Avon Books, paper, 1991
In the Blue Light of African Dreams, Avon Books, paper, 1992
Night Over Day Over Night, Avon Books, paper, 1990
The Promise of Light, Random House, 1993
Stand Before Your God, Random House, 1994

ELIE WIESEL

The Accident, Noonday Books, paper, 1991
A Beggar in Jerusalem, Schocken Books, paper, 1989
Dawn, Bantam, paper, 1982
The Fifth Son, Warner Books, paper, 1991
Five Biblical Portraits, Univ. of Notre Dame Press, paper, 1983
The Forgotten, Shocken Books, paper, 1995
Four Hasidic Masters and Their Struggle Against Melancholy, Univ. of Notre Dame Press, paper, 1978

From the Kingdom of Memory, Shocken Books, paper, 1995
The Gates of the Forest, Schocken Books, paper, 1989
A Jew Today, Vintage Books, paper, 1979
Legends of Our Time, Schocken Books, paper, 1982
Messengers of God, Touchstone Books, paper, 1985
Night, Bantam, paper, 1982
The Night Trilogy: Night, Dawn, The Accident, Noonday Books, paper, 1987
A Passover Haggadah, Simon & Schuster, 1993
Sages and Dreamers, Touchstone Books, paper, 1993
Somewhere A Master, Summit Books, paper, 1984
Souls on Fire, Summit Books, paper, 1982
The Testament, Bantam, paper, 1982
The Town Beyond the Wall, Schocken Books, paper, 1982
The Trial of Bod, Schocken Books, paper, 1986
Twilight, Warner Books, paper, 1989
Zalmen on the Madness of God, Random House, 1975

STEPHEN WRIGHT

Going Native, Farrar, Straus & Giroux, 1994
M31: A Romance, Harmony Books, 1988; Ballantine, paper, 1989